Indigenous, Traditional, and Non-State Transitional Justice in Southern Africa

Indigenous, Traditional, and Non-State Transitional Justice in Southern Africa

Zimbabwe and Namibia

Edited by
Everisto Benyera

LEXINGTON BOOKS
Lanham • Boulder • New York • London

Published by Lexington Books
An imprint of The Rowman & Littlefield Publishing Group, Inc.
4501 Forbes Boulevard, Suite 200, Lanham, Maryland 20706
www.rowman.com

6 Tinworth Street, London SE11 5AL, United Kingdom

Copyright © 2019 The Rowman & Littlefield Publishing Group, Inc.

All rights reserved. No part of this book may be reproduced in any form or by any electronic or mechanical means, including information storage and retrieval systems, without written permission from the publisher, except by a reviewer who may quote passages in a review.

British Library Cataloguing in Publication Information Available

The hardback edition of this book was previously catalogued by the Library of Congress as follows:

Library of Congress Cataloging-in-Publication Data Available

ISBN 978-1-4985-9282-6 (cloth)
ISBN 978-1-4985-9284-0 (pbk.)
ISBN 978-1-4985-9283-3 (electronic)

This book is dedicated in loving memory to my mother, Violet Chipo Benyera (nee Murwira). She taught me to believe in myself and always to excel in everything I do. This work also goes out to the ladies in my life, Sheilla my wife, my daughters Rukudzo Claire Chipo (RCCB) and Runako Chiratidzo (RCB), my sister Netsai and my niece Shanice Alexandra Mudzingwa. These ladies surrounded me with love which made this work worthwhile and at times even enjoyable. My father Leonard Chirango Benyera, who kept asking when I would complete my studies, this book project is dedicated to you. Lastly, my dedication is to my paternal grandmother, Juliet Wanisai Benyera (nee Chigumira) aka vaMagirazi. She was a fountain of wisdom and was responsible for igniting my interest in traditional transitional justice mechanisms.

In loving memory of William Willard Manyengavana 1965–2019.

Contents

1 Transitology, Transitional Justice, and Transformative Justice: A Theoretical Overview   1
  Everisto Benyera

2 A Dozen Transitional Justice Realities and Some Preliminary Problematizations   17
  Everisto Benyera

3 The Case for Indigenous, Traditional, and Non-State Transitional Justice   33
  Everisto Benyera

4 Construing Transitology in the Context(s) of Democratization, Transitional Justice, and Decolonization in Africa: A Legal Anthropology Perspective   49
  Tapiwa Victor Warikandwa and Artwell Nhemachena

5 *Operation Murambatsvina*, Transitional Justice, and Discursive Representation in Zimbabwe   71
  Umali Saidi

6 "Healing the Dead" in Matabeleland, Zimbabwe: Combining Tradition with Science to Restore Personhood after Massacres   107
  Shari Eppel

7 The Aftermath of Gukurahundi: Dealing with Wounds of the Genocide through Non-State Justice Processes in Bubi (Inyathi) and Nkayi Districts, Matabeleland, North Province, Zimbabwe   123
  Ruth Murambadoro and Chenai Matshaka

8	Grassroots Mechanisms for Justice, Peace-building, and Social Cohesion in Zimbabwe's "New" Farm Communities *Tom Tom and Clement Chipenda*	141
9	Young Women in Peace-building and Development in Zimbabwe: The Case of Zimbabwe Young Women's Network for Peace-building in Mutoko *Patience Thauzeni and Torque Mude*	163
10	Stains on the Wall: Struggle to Survive Post-Genocide Violence by Nama-Herero Communities in Namibia *Tafirenyika Madziyauswa*	177
11	Uncharted Waters: Reparations through Indigenous Forms of Transitional Justice for Namibian Victims of a Colonial Genocide *Christian Harris*	205

Index	219
About the Contributors	227

Chapter 1

Transitology, Transitional Justice, and Transformative Justice

A Theoretical Overview

Everisto Benyera

INTRODUCTION

Transitology is that sub-discipline which deals with the communities in transition usually from dictatorships genocides and war. There are three basic components of transitology as a study discipline. First, there should be a violent abusive past where mass human rights abuses were committed usually by those in authority. Secondly, there must be survivors of that violent conflict(s) constituted by a mixture of perpetrators and victims. Thirdly, and finally there is an envisaged future which is peaceful and devoid of human rights abuses. Our contributions in this book center mainly on the last two aspects of transitology. Transitology is eficacious in framing trastional justice. The issue of transitional justice both as a field of study and as a practice by communities seeking historical accountability is problematic at various levels. The main problem is the marriage of transitional justice to Western liberal notions such as the rule of law, liberal democracy, and development as argued by Gready and Robins,

> The liberal peace in which transitional justice is embedded emerges from two dominant strands of contemporary globalization. The first strand privileges liberal paradigms of civil and political rights through an emphasis on elections, procedural democracy, constitutionalism and the rule of law, and various backward-looking truth and justice measures. (Gready and Robins 2014, 341)

The problems with these western origins of transitional justice are that they tend to crowd out other non-Western transitional justice mechanisms. Gready and Robins continue to expose this problematic twinning of transitional justice and development aid by asserting that,

> transitional justice has become part of a hegemonic discourse that links development and peace-building to a liberal state-building project that sees liberal democracy as its endpoint. . . . two foundational limitations, the liberal peace and top-down, state-based processes, (are worth noting) *emphasis mine*. (ibid)

The second strand is market-driven, neoliberal economics with interventions linked to the Washington Consensus. The fate of these Western imposed transitional justice programs is similar to the criticisms faced by liberal peace-centered programs. Chief among the shortcomings of Western imposed mechanisms is their obsession with the creation of institutions. This was criticized by Gready and Robins thus,

> The liberal peace has been widely criticized in fragile transitional contexts for prioritizing the creation of institutions over a contextualized engagement with the welfare of the population, creating "empty" institutions paralyzed by a lack of capacity rather than responding to the everyday needs of the new state's citizens. (ibid)

I allege the weaponization of Western imposed and sponsored transitional justice in the same way in which democracy and human rights have been exposed to be weapons of Euro North American foreign policies. In a way, I agree with the Tshepo Madlingozi's ascertion that unknown to most post-conflict communities in Africa, Western-sponsored and Western-dominated transitional justice has become another form of coloniality (Madlingozi 2015, 2007, 2010). My argument here is that Western-dominated transitional justice covers up the crimes committed by Western governments and their multinational corporations in Africa by predominantly diverting the attention of these communities toward human rights abuses committed by non-Westerners. This is the reason why generally, most of these Western-sponsored non governmental organizations rarely work on the crimes committed during slavery and colonialism. The politicization and weaponization of the International Criminal Court (ICC) (Benyera 2018) clearly demonstrates that transitional justice is for weak countries, weak economies and weak armies. Self-reliant countries such as the United States of America and Israel do not need both the ICC and transitional justice. I therefore allege that transitional justice is mourn of the weak. A question maybe asked: What then if transitional justice is this polluted and hijacked? This issue is addressed in this book in sections where we support the movement away from transitional justice and more toward transformative justice.

OF THE PERFECT PRODUCTS OF IMPERIALISM AND THE ABSENT PERPETRATOR

Human rights abuses addressed in this book have one characteristic: the denial of the victims of their humanity by the pepetrators. Having been denied their humanity, they then become legitimate targets of all forms of violence as they would have been classified as subhumans or nonhumans. In other words, the dispensable other. Nelson Maldonado-Torres termed this phenomenon Imperial Manichean Misanthropic Skepticism (Maldonado-Torres 2007, 245). This is the act of doubting and then denying the humanity of the colonized people. This is done through acts as such as colonialism, slavery, and genocides. The sum of these negative experiences has to be reversed so that the survivors can exorcise the curse of generational traumas, stigmatization and infiriorization. Here I am making a deliberate and loose causal link and presenting the totality of the negative experiences which African and other parts of the (formerly) colonized people experience. To focus on the Gukurahundi and Herero Nama genocides alone would be to address part of the problem. The end result of the processes of slavery, colonialism, imperialism, neo-imperialism, Euro North American modernity, and genocides is the production of what can termed the perfect products of imperialism. These perfect products were robbed of their humanity and agency. Indigenous, traditional, and non-state transitional justice mechanisms aim to reverse these processes by rehumanizing these perfect products of imperialism. A key tenet of indigenous, traditional, and non-state transitional justice mechanisms is that they achieve healing and closure, in some cases finding truth in the absence of the perpetrator. The presence of the perpetrator is key for transitional justice because they hold a key ingredient, the truth. This is why the deaths of apartheid protagonists such as Roelof Fredrik (Pik) Botha were regrettable because they went to their graves with the secrets of apartheid such as what happened to Mozambican president Samora Machel. Machel's death, in the absence of traditional and non-state transitional justice mechanisms will go unresolved and the Machel family would never find both the truth and closure.

In order for transitional justice mechanisms such as the Truth and Reconciliation Commission model to be effective, a perpetrator must be present. This makes it difficult for this model of transitional justice to occur in cases where the perpetrator is either absent or unwilling to participate in these processes. Traditional transitional justice mechanisms such as *ngozi* in Zimbabwe and Mozambique are capable of inflicting certain harms to the perpetrator(s) as a way of forcing them to come and participate in the reconciliation, fact finding, and peace-building initiatives.

This book therefore addresses the problem which was faced by the South African Truth and Reconciliation Commission where there were victims but without perpetrators. The question that was not asked is: How can there be victims without perpetrators? The mechanisms discussed in this book are capable of two things: either to force the perpetrator(s) to come and participate in the reconcilition and peace-building processes or to proceed with the processes without the perpetrators.

Coming to the aspect of transformative justice, it must be noted that transformative justice is not contradictory to transitional justice but is complimentary to it and builds on the work done by the former. Transformative justice is not preemptive, presumptuous, or prescriptive. It allows communities to map their desired outcomes and how these can be achieved using whatever local resources are at their disposal and when these should be achieved. Transformative justice returns and recognizes the agency of survivors (victims + perpetrators = survivors) and in this regard is compatible with decoloniality.

TRANSITIONAL JUSTICE: A THEORETICAL MAPPING OF THE FIELD OF STUDY

Transitional justice is a theory, a practice, and a discipline which has been going through multiple transitions. Since its post–World War II inception headlined by the Nuremberg Trials, transitional justice has ever since been in simultaneous developmental and transitional phases. It transitioned from its World War II conceivement where it was viewed as transition from eastern communism toward western liberal capitalism. At another level, it also implied transition from the "tyrannical" eastern communist ideologies and practices toward western democratic liberalism. This conceptualization of the transition and transitional states ended with the end of the Cold War. The second transition was from the post-cold war period up to the new millennium. This transition solidified the conceptualization of state transition as movement away not only from communism but also from other forms of regimes deemed by western liberal standards as undemocratic and therefore undesirable.

The current transitional phase is anchored by a movement away from states being accountable to International Law to a new regime where they are accountable to human rights and other international norms and standards and not to their citizens. Each phase has specific theories and practices that accompany it, for example, during the Nuremburg phase, transitional justice theories were around retributive and victor's justice. Post–Cold War era transitional justice was very much legalistic and emphasized tribunals, trials, and prosecutions. In Africa, another transition was occurring beginning in the 1960s with the independence of Ghana, then the Gold Coast. For newly independent and independence aspiring African countries, transition was taken to imply the movement away from colonialism to independence and self-determination.

The zenith of this phase was the formation of the International Criminal Court as the dominant institution in this phase. The fourth phase of the transition is accompanied by the principles of Responsibility to Protect and Humanitarian Intervention. Post-millennial transitional justice theories are now mostly about economic, social and cultural rights. Hence, one can actually map the theoretical trajectory of the transitions of transitional justice. The same can also be accomplished about the concomitant practices that accompanied each phase of transitional justice.

DISENTANGLING THE INDIGENOUS FROM THE TRADITIONAL

The indigenous and the traditional have been fatally conflated in both scholarship and practice. Yet, as I argue, there is a theoretical difference between the indigenous and the traditional in transitional justice, the former being tied to historical oppression, usually through but not limited to colonialism, while the latter is a product of long-standing modes of everyday life which themselves are subject to change and evolution. The indigenous is linked with a specific geographical location, that is, land and its natural resources, while the traditional is evolutionary, absorbing new trends and developments as it interacts with the world. This article locates the indigene in politicized identity constructions resulting from exogenous forces such as colonialism, imperialism, globalization, and coloniality.

While the various transitions were occurring, there was a constant which was holding in Africa, stretching from precolonial Africa to colonial Africa and into the so-called independence period. These are local African peacebuilding, reconciliation, healing, and reconciliation mechanisms. These range from Uganda's *mato oput* (Lundy and McGovern 2008), Rwanda's *gacaca* (Clark 2007; Wierzynska 2004), Mozambique and Zimbabwe's *magamba* spirit (Igreja 2003; Igreja, Dias-Lambranca, and Richters 2008; Igreja 2010, 2013; Igreja and Lambranca 2009; Muwati, Gambahaya, and Mangena 2006), *ngozi* (Benyera 2015; Mahoso 2012; Musanga 2017; Pfeiffer and Pfeiffer 2002; Mutekwa 2010; Benyera 2014) and *kuputisana fodya* (Murambadoro and Wielenga 2015; Benyera 2014). These mechanisms have been variously theorized both as indigenous and traditional, with the two concepts used interchangeably as if they mean the same thing. The purpose of this chapter is to lay some theoretical foundation for the conceptual differentiation of the indigenous from the traditional.

What distinguishes the traditional from the indigenous is that indigenousness is an identity constructed, shaped, and lived in the politicized context of contemporary (neo-)colonialism. In other words, the indigene in indigenous is derived from a product of land and colonialism. Indigenous refers to those people, cultures, institutions, and resources that occupy a geographically well-defined space which at one time was colonized or repelled colonial forces, especially Euro North American colonialism. This definition may be stretched to include Arab colonialism and intra Africa colonialism.

Although terms such as indigenous and traditional are used interchangeably in relation to dispute resolution, peace-building, and reconciliation, they do not hold precisely the same meanings. Traditional refers to norms and practices that draw on long-standing modes of operation. While traditions can be invented and are capable of change, the expectation is that traditional techniques and understandings have a lengthy historical pedigree (Mac Ginty 2011, 49). When used to refer to people, indigenous people are those that inhabited an area prior to colonization and continued to do during colonialism. In the case of Zimbabwe, the indigenous people are those who were in the land between the Zambezi and the Limpopo Rivers prior to 1890. This rules out white Zimbabweans from the ranks of the indigenous Zimbabweans.

THE CUSTOMARY AND THE TRADITIONAL: SIMILAR BUT NOT IDENTICAL

Having conceptually separated the traditional from the indigenous, it is also necessary to do the same with the customary and the traditional. This book is about customary, indigenous and traditional transitional justice mechanisms, it is therefore necessary to make a conceptual distinction especially between customary and traditional transitional justice mechanisms since the two are often used interchangeably. The difference between indigenous transitional justice mechanisms and the other two is more apparent and will not be discussed now.

By definition, a custom is a practice or a way of life that is common in a particular place or among a particular group of people. Customary transitional justice comprises of those practices that communities and families practice in order to find closure and truth in cases where gross human rights violations were committed as defined those specific communities. On the other end a tradition is the actual transmission of customs and belief systems from one generation to another. There is a chronological distinction between a custom and a tradition because while a custom can be a new practice, traditions would have been practiced in communities for years and passed down from generation to generation. Stated differently, a custom can become a tradition but not all traditions are customs as some customs fail to pass the test of time and are either altered or discontinued altogether. When passed from generation to generation, customs then constitute traditions.

It is important to note that customs are geographic specific as they constitute general behaviors that are acceptable in specific situations within specific communities. What is a custom in one area may not be a custom in another area. This characteristic of customs gives customary transitional justice mechanisms and edge over their counterparts such as prosecutions because of their embeddedness in communities.

For the Shona people where life is made up of three realms: the living unborn, the living living, and the living dead, customary justice generally is viewed as that justice corpus which settles matters among the living living, usually what can be termed minor disputes. However, when it comes to major wrongs such as the loss of human life, traditional transitional justice mechanisms are evoked primarily because of their perceived capability to address the three realms of life mentioned above.

CONCEPTUALIZING INDIGENOUS TRANSITIONAL JUSTICE MECHANISM

There are three markers that define the indigene; colonialism, time, and geography. As alluded to earlier on, the term indigenous applies to peoples within a well-defined geographical area who have lived in that area before Euro North American colonialism. In addition, there are also norms and practices that draw on local resources that buttress the indigene. The onslaught of colonialism and other negative factors, both exogenous and endogenous have resulted in indigenous communities adapting to changing circumstances and also adopting some of the technologies of the colonizers such as the colonizer's language. The result of these encounters between the indigene and the colonial was a series of processes of contestation, accommodation and social negotiation meant to ensure the survival of the indigene in a colonially hostile environment. Customs, social norms and other institutions that qualify as indigenous therefore predate colonialism, were practiced over a certain well define geographical area by a fairly homogenous group of people. These customs, norms, practices and institutions survived colonialism albeit having undergone some metamorphosis of sorts.

Indigenous transitional justice, however, unlike traditional counterparts, rely on a sense of place or ecological embeddedness and achieves cultural significance from the community's relation to a particular environment. Another way of identifying the indigenous, especially indigenous communities is the contestation between them and commercial interest especially in primary resource extraction. The extraction of local natural resources is viewed by indigenous communities not only as an intrusion into their way of life but also a theft of their birth right.

There are also contestations between the indigenous and the notion of development in its various forms. For indigenous communities, development consists of processes of deskilling and delinking them from their centuries-old relationships with nature and their peer communities. They do not understand the western notion of development as they perceive it as an unwelcome intrusion and a pollutant to their way of life.

THE ARGUMENTS OF THE BOOK

Having problematized transitional justice as a way of laying the foundation for this book, I will conclude this chapter by presenting the organization of the book. This book is organized into eleven chapters. This is the introductory chapter whose responsibility was to foreground, by way of problematization the issues raised by respective authors.

The problematic of distinguishing the indigenous from the traditional in transitional justice was addressed in chapter two. In this chapter he distinguished the indigene as one with geographic specificity and shares a special relationship with other forms of life around it such as water trees and animals and at one time, suffered the onslaught of colonialism and Euro North American modernity. On the other hand, the traditional is not necessarily geographic bound and is ever changing, rejecting some tenets while absorbing new traditions and practices. Traditional communities may not be geographically together, but they share common practices which due to their scatteredness also tend to vary in detail. This chapter responds to realities nine and ten where the survivors conceptualized as the perpetrator and victims must coexist in the same geographical area after the conflict. Secondly, that both survivors will have multiple identities, at one time they were perpetrators at the other victims. The chapter is therefore useful in charting a way forward for such complex transitologies.

Chapter 3 also addresses a very important issue of the importance of traditional indigenous and non-state transitional justice mechanisms. The argument of the chapter is that these mechanisms must not be analyzed or conceptualized as compliments but rather as the main source of transitional justice because in most resource-poor transitional communities, traditional indigenous and non-state transitional justice mechanisms are the dominant, if not the only mechanism available. This chapter continues the debate started at the beginning of this chapter. It is not the aim of this book to convince our readers that there is a difference between indigenous, customary, and traditional transitional justice mechanisms. Our objective is to expose non-state transitional justice mechanisms that are being used to achieve healing reconciliation and in some cases peace-building in Zimbabwe and Namibia.

Chapter 4 is a theoretical chapter which questions the link between western law justice and democratization processes when presented as prerequisites for transitional justice and the larger the decolonization project. The chapter responds to the prescription that indigenous, traditional and non-state transitional justice mechanisms must conform to international laws, norms and standards. The argument by Tapiwa Warikandwa and Artwell Nhemachena in this chapter is that framing transitional justice from a western-centric liberal democratic perspective is tantamount to perpetuating the problem as such initiatives form part of the Washington Consensus. In the broader subdiscipline of transitional justice and transitology, Warikandwa and Nhemachena respond to a very philosophical question; can the master's tool destroy the master's house? Transitional justice, for them is a tool of the west. This is true given the predominant role which especially the United States of America and its European allies play in transitional economies, from the conceptualization of mechanisms and to their sequencing, funding and implementation, these "benevolent others" are omnipresent. What the chapter exposes is that, masquerading as transitional justice practitioners foreign nongovernmental organizations and their donor governments will simply be perpetuating their home countries' national interests and whatever benefits accrue to post-conflict communities can best be described as an externality. The chapter warns against over celebrating transitional justice in Africa as it is part of Western constructs that are based on capitalist ideologies which in the final analysis perpetuate colonial injustices. In other words, what is termed indigenous traditional and non-state transitional justice mechanisms in this book must be presented as something other than transitional justice because to call them transitional justice mechanisms present an inherent contradiction. This is so because transitional justice is western centric and part of the neoliberal colonial project, hence it cannot be part of the indigenous which in essence seeks to resist the colonial.

The book project generally focuses on Zimbabwe and Namibia where Zimbabwe was a British Colony and Namibia was an apartheid extension of South Africa and previoosuly colonised by German. These two countries never had state centric transitional justice mechanisms. As announced by the then prime minister of Zimbabwe Robert Mugabe in 1980, independence was a time to let bygones be bygones (Benyera 2016b, 160; Marongwe 2012, 323). This form of induced blanket amnesia which also obtained in post-apartheid Namibia in 1990 left a huge gap in terms of seeking historical accountability, healing and reconciliation. Yet for Zimbabwe in the so-called post-independence dispensation a genocide was to occur two years into independence. Targeting predominantly Ndebele speakers in Matabeleland and Midlands provinces Gukurahundi genocide is a dark page in Zimbabwe's history.

Two chapters are dedicated to the Zimbabwe's Gukurahundi genocide of 1981–83. In chapter 6, Sheri Eppel discusses what she terms 'healing the dead' (Eppel 2009). This chapter is a central part of the book because it carries forward the reality that for the Ndebele as well as the Shona peoples, life consists of three interlinked sequential forms. These are the living unborn, the living living, and the living dead (Benyera 2015; Fontein 2010; Benyera 2016a; Eppel 2009). While the rest of the book is dedicated to the living living, this is the only chapter which addresses the issue of healing the dead. From a western-centric perspective, the dead have very little, if anything to do with the living, yet for the Ndebele and the Shona, the living dead play an important role in the lives of both the living living and the living unborn (Benyera 2014; Gundani 1994; Mawere 2012). Therefore, the happiness and well-being of the living dead is of paramount importance for the living living. This includes aiding the living dead in getting justice and closure so that they can concentrate on their role and responsibilities of blessing, guiding and of course at times sanctioning the punishment of transgratory, errand and delinquent family members.

Drawing on medical anthropology, the chapter highlights the work of local nongovernmental organizations that are involved in identifying Gukurahundi genocide human remains, exhuming them and then medically identifying them before reuniting these remains with their families. The proper identification of these human remains is well argued in this chapter as one which "unpauses" life for these families. Rites of passage and certain rites and rituals and ceremonies can then take place. Without the proper identification of the deceased, the lives of their families remain stagnant which include the absence of inheritances. Burying war victims in mass and secret graves is therefore a human rights abuse beyond comprehension. It affects generations of family members and the work of Ukutwala Trust and their international partners, the *Argentine Forensic Anthropology Team* (EAAF) who first came to Zimbabwe in 1998 must be commended as it ensures justice for whole communities, that is, the living unborn, the living living, and the living unborn.

The second chapter which addresses the Gukurahundi genocide is chapter 7. This is a case study of two districts in Matabeleland North Province which were among the most affected by the genocide. This is an empirical study on how the communities in Bubi (Inyathi) and Nkayi districts delve into their modes of everyday life to find healing and closure. In the chapter, Ruth Murambadoro and Chenai Matshaka remind the reader that in discussing Gukurahundi genocide accountability, it is important to note that there were two commissions of enquiry which were instituted by the state to look into the genocide, the Dumbutshena Commission of Inquiry and the Chihambakwe

Commission of Inquiry. While the commissions did their work and submitted their reports, the state never made these two reports public (Catholic Commission for Justice and Peace 1997). The official version by the state is that they were lost (Benyera 2017, 119). This information is important to foreground as one grapples with how communities are resorting to their modes of everyday life such as their traditions and customs in order to find healing and closure in a country where the government denies the occurrence of the genocide. Of course, former long-time leader Robert Mugabe under whose watch the genocide occurred once said that Gukurahundi was a moment of madness (Murambadoro and Wielenga 2015; Ngwenya 2018; Tafira and Ndlovu-Gatsheni 2017, 162). This chapter demonstrates the importance of bottom up healing mechanisms.

Besides the Gukurahundi genocide, there were other episodes of gross human rights violations in Zimbabwe. These include Operation Murambatsvina of 2005. This operation is the subject of chapter 5. The chapter explores the abuses which were committed when informal houses and businesses were demolished by the government. Relying on the report of the United Nations' Anna Kajimulo Tibaijuka, Umali Saidi argues for the reconsideration of housing as a basic human right from which families should not be evicted with no alternatives. In her report to the United Nations Secretary General, Tibaijuka noted,

> Popularly referred to as "Operation Tsunami" because of its speed and ferocity it resulted in the destruction of homes, business premises and vending sites. It is estimated that some 700,000 people in cities across the country have lost either their homes, their source of livelihood or both. Indirectly, a further 2.4 million people have been affected in varying degrees. (Tibaijuka 2005, 7)

While this argument has been around and supported by many civil society organizations, Saidi's chapter explores how the supposed remedy for Operation Murambatsvina violations turned out to be another episode of human rights abuses as Operation Garikai/Hlalani Kahle was a calculated failure, meant to symphony state resources in the name of the poor. He exposes certain hidden dimension such as how the operation was in fact cover up for a political project to expel known and suspected opposition party supporters in the name of urban clean-up operations.

The land reform program in Zimbabwe which commenced around the year 2000 witnessed a shift in communities and geographies as commercial farms which were predominantly white owned were given to black Zimbabweans. This resulted in a huge movement both in the ways of living and the actual constitution of the new farm communities as people migrated from overpopulated communal areas to their newly allocated land. The result of the land reform program was the creation of new communities, with cultural and traditional diversity. Human settlements in Zimbabwe are usually constituted by the same people, sharing the same blood line, totem, history, culture, and traditions. Of course, over time there were "outsiders" who joined in these family settlements. The case of new farm communities is different in that there are no indigenes and as with any community, there are bound to be conflicts. In these fairly new communities, where cultures traditions differ and may clash, the chapter by Tom Tom and Clement Chipenda explores how conflict over land ownership and boundaries in new farm communities were mediated. The choice of new farm communities was justified given the context of social fluidity and ethno-regional diversity in these already tension heighted communities. While the rest of the book considers traditional, indigenous and non-state transitional justice mechanisms in what can be termed old communities, this chapter focuses on newly formed and constituted communities. As these communities coalesce, create new traditions and customs, the chapter explores how the divisive and contentious issues of land ownership and land demarcation in the absence of government structures are resolved.

The last two chapters of the book cover the Herero-Nama genocide which was perpetrated by the imperial German colonizers between 1904 and 1908. This was the first and one of the most brutal genocides in the world (as if there is an *unbrutal* genocide). Meant to punish and exterminate the Herero and the Nama people, the genocide was operationalised through driving thousands of Hereros and Namas into the unforgiving Namib Desert for them to perish. Conservative estimates put the numbers of the German perpetrated genocide between 100,000 Hereros and 10,000 Namas. As discussed earlier on and as argued by Nelson Maldonado-Torres, the logic of the Herero Nama genocide was based on the denial of the victims of their humanity. Stated differently, the colonial Germans perpetrated the genocide because they convinced themselves that the Herero and the Nama were not human like them hence Maldonado-Torres' description of the logic as Imperial Manichean Misanthropic Sceptic (Maldonado-Torres 2018, 245). Using methods which were later replicated between 1933 and 1945 later by Nazi Germany to inflict a genocide on the Jews, concentration camps were used as sites of mass starvation, dehydration, exhaustion, and death by any means brutal. Tafirenyika Madziyauswa's chapter explores the work of three organizations: Genocide Reparations Technical Committee, The Nama Genocide Technical Committee, and lastly OvaHerero/Ovambanderu Genocide Technical Committee that are dedicated to commemorating the genocide, constructing a narrative of the genocide that is consistent with the perspective of the victims and also to seek justice for the atrocities. He places most of his focus on the strategies used by the descendants of the victims of the genocide to survive and cope with the genocide.

In the last chapter, Christian Harris continues the perspective used in the preceding chapter though a more empirical analysis of the traditions, customs, and practices used by the Herero and the Nama to commemorate the genocide and seek reparations through what he termed indigenous African human rights philosophy and practices. Harris explores the legacy of the genocide which he classified as; physiological, cultural, political, social, and demographic. Crucially, he links the land question to the genocide and argues that the land issue must be used as a mechanism to reparate victims of the genocide. He points to the imbalances in Namibia's land ownership wherein whites who are 6 percent of Namibia's population own 90 percent of the land while 94 percent of the population own 10 percent of Namibia's land. Stated differently, 144,000 white Namibians own 90 percent of land in the world's 34th largest country by area covered.

BRIEF METHODOLOGICAL JUSTIFICATION

The book is a case study of two countries Zimbabwe and Namibia. I will briefly justify the choice of these two case countries. Zimbabwe and Namibia experienced genocides albeit centuries apart. In Namibia, the Nama and Herero survivors of the German genocide for decades found healing closure and peace mainly using local customs, traditions, and other grassroots initiatives. Of course, there were numerous state-centric mechanisms and initiatives which unfortunately were on the side of the perpetrating German government and against the Namibian survivors of the genocide. The question that the two chapters dedicated to Namibia respond to is: how did the survivors of the German genocide in Namibia found healing, peace and closure, and by extension how these healing and other copying mechanisms can be perfected so that they apply to a larger population of the survivors?

For Zimbabwe, the Gukurahundi genocide which was perpetrated mainly in Matebeleland and the Midlands provinces targeted predominantly Ndebele speakers and was perpetrated by the Fifth Brigade of the Zimbabwe National Army. The official narrative is that they were protecting innocent civilians from deserters and renegade members of the Zimbabwe People's Liberation Army, (ZIPRA) which was the military wing of the Zimbabwe National People's Union (ZAPU) led by Joshua Nkomo.

Zimbabwe also experienced a genocide like Namibia. While the Namibian genocide was perpetrated by a colonizing government, the Zimbabwean genocide was perpetrated by an independent black government. The book therefore offers interesting perspectives on how ordinary citizens improvise and in a way of forging ahead with their lives, putting behind them both colonial and (post)-colonial atrocities which they survived.

BIBLIOGRAPHY

Benyera, Everisto. 2014. "Exploring Zimbabwe's Traditional Transitional Justice Mechanisms." *Journal of Social Science* 41 (3): 335–44.
Benyera, Everisto. 2015. "Presenting Ngozi as an Important Consideration in Pursuing Transitional Justice for Victims: The Case of Moses Chokuda." *Gender & Behaviour* 13 (2): 6760–73.
Benyera, Everisto. 2016a. "Expected yet Uncomprehendible: Unpacking Death through Nikolas Zakaria's Rufu Chitsidzo." *Gender & Behaviour* 14 (2): 7171–81.
Benyera, Everisto. 2016b. "On the Question of the Transition: Was Zimbabwe a Transitional State Between 2008 and 2013?" *Journal of Human Ecology* 55 (3): 160–72.
Benyera, Everisto. 2017. "On The Complexities of Prosecuting Robert Mugabe at The International Criminal Court." *Austral: Brazilian Journal of Strategy & International Relations* 6 (12): 104–22.
Benyera, Everisto. 2018. "Is the International Criminal Court Unfairly Targeting Africa? Lessons for Latin America and the Caribbean States." *Politeia* 37 (1): 1–30. doi: 10.25159/0256-8845/2403ISSN.
Catholic Commission for Justice and Peace. 1997. *Report on the 1980's Disturbances in Matabeleland and the Midlands*. Harare: Catholic Commission for Justice and Peace
Clark, Phil. 2007. "Hybridity, Holism, and 'Traditional' Justice: The Case of the Gacaca Courts in Post-Genocide Rwanda." *George Washington International Law Review* 1 (39): 765–837. doi: 10.1525/sp.2007.54.1.23.
Eppel, Shari. 2009. "A Tale of Three Dinner Plates: Truth and the Challenges of Human Rights Research in Zimbabwe." *Journal of Southern African Studies* 35 (4): 967–76. doi: 10.1080/03057070903314234.
Fontein, Joost. 2010. "Between Tortured Bodies and Resurfacing Bones: The Politics of the Dead in Zimbabwe." *Journal of Material Culture* 15 (4): 423–48. doi: 10.1177/1359183510383105.
Gready, Paul, and Simon Robins. 2014. "From Transitional to Transformative Justice: A New Agenda for Practice." *The International Journal of Transitional Justice* 8: 339–61. doi: 10.1093/ijtj/iju013.
Gundani, Paul. 1994. "The Roman Catholic Church and the Kurova Guva Ritual in Zimbabwe." *Zambezia* XXI (ii): 123–46. http://reference.sabinet.co.za/webx/access/journal_archive/03790622/120.pdf.
Igreja, Victor. 2003. "'Why Are There so Many Drums Playing until Dawn?' Exploring the Role of Gamba Spirits and Healers in the Post-War Recovery Period in Gorongosa, Central Mozambique." *Transcultural Psychiatry*, 4 (December): 460–87. doi: 10.1177/1363461503404001.
Igreja, Victor. 2010. "Traditional Courts and the Struggle against State Impunity for Civil Wartime Offences in Mozambique." *Journal of African Law* 54 (1): 51. doi: 10.1017/S0021855309990167.
Igreja, Victor. 2013. "Politics of Memory, Decentralisation and Recentralisation in Mozambique." *Journal of Southern African Studies* 39 (2): 313–35. doi: 10.1080/03057070.2013.795809.

Igreja, Victor, Béatrice Dias-Lambranca, and Annemiek Richters. 2008. "Gamba Spirits, Gender Relations, and Healing in Post-Civil War Gorongosa, Mozambique." *Journal of the Royal Anthropological Institute* 14 (2): 353–71. doi: 10.1111/j.1467-9655.2008.00506.x.

Igreja, Victor, and Béatrice Dias Lambranca. 2009. "The Thursdays as They Live: Christian Religious Transformation and Gender Relations in Postwar Gorongosa, Central Mozambique." *Journal of Religion in Africa* 39 (3): 262–94. doi: 10.1163/157006609X449946.

Lundy, Patricia, and Mark McGovern. 2008. "Whose Justice? Rethinking Transitional Justice from the Bottom Up." *Journal of Law and Society* 35 (2): 265–92. doi: 10.1111/j.1467-6478.2008.00438.x.

Mac Ginty, Roger. 2011. *International Peacebuilding and Local Resistance: Hybrid Forms of Peace*. Edited by Oliver P. Richmond. New York: Palgrave Macmillan.

Madlingozi, Tshepo. 2007. "Post-Aparthied South Afrca and the Quest for the Ellusive 'New' South Africa." *Journal of Law and Society* 34 (1): 77–98.

Madlingozi, Tshepo. 2010. "On Transitional Justice Entrepreneurs and the Production of Victims." *Journal of Human Rights Practice* 2 (2): 208–28.

Madlingozi, Tshepo. 2015. "Transitional Justice as Epistemicide: On Steve Biko's Pluralist Coexistence 'After' Conflict." In Wits Institute for Social and Economic Research Seminar, *Wits University, Johannesburg, 27 July 2015*, 1–28. Johannesburg: Unpublished.

Mahoso, Tafataona. 2012. "African Focus, Ngozi: The Philosophical Foundation of African Living Law." *The Herals*, February 4.

Maldonado-Torres, Nelson. 2007. "On the Coloniality of Being." *Cultural Studies* 2–3 (March): 240–70. doi: 10.1080/09502380601162548.

Maldonado-Torres, Nelson. 2018. "On the Coloniality of Human Rights." *Revista Crítica de Ciências Sociais* 114 (October): 117–36. doi: 10.4000/rccs.6793.

Marongwe, Ngonidzashe. 2012. *Rural Women as the Invisible Victims of Militarised Political Violence: The Case of Shurugwi District, Zimbabwe 2000–2008*. Cape Town: Universty of the Western Cape.

Mawere, Munyaradzi. 2012. "'Buried and Forgotten But Not Dead': Reflections On 'Ubuntu' In Environmental Conservation In Southeastern Zimbabwe." *Afro Asian Journal of Social Sciences* 3 (3): 1–20.

Murambadoro, Ruth, and Cori Wielenga. 2015. "Reconciliation in Zimbabwe: The Conflict between a State-Centred and People-Centred Approach." *Strategic Review for Southern Africa* 37 (1): 31–52.

Musanga, Terrence. 2017. "'Ngozi' (Avenging Spirit), Zimbabwean Transnational Migration, and Restorative Justice in Brian Chikwava's Harare North (2009)." *Journal of Black Studies* 48 (8): 775–90. doi: 10.1177/0021934717720563.

Mutekwa, Anias. 2010. "The Avenging Spirit: Mapping an Ambivalent Spirituality in Zimbabwean Literature in English." *African Studies* 69 (1): 161–76. doi: 10.1080/00020181003647264.

Muwati, Itai, Zifikile Gambahaya, and Fainos Mangena. 2006. "Echoing Silences as a Paradigm for Restorative Justice in Post-Conflict Zimbabwe: A Philosophical Discourse." *Zambezia* 33 (1/2): 1–18.

Ngwenya, Dumisan. 2018. *Healing the Wounds of Gukurahundi in Zimbabwe: A Participatory Action Research Project. The Anthropocene: Politik–Economics–Society–Science*. Vol. 19. Cham, Switzerland: Springer.

Pfeiffer, James, and Pfeiffer James. 2002. "African Independent Churches in Mozambique: Healing the Afflictions of Inequality." *Medical Anthropology Quarterly*. doi: 10.1525/maq.2002.16.2.176.

Tafira, Chimusoro Kenneth, and Sabelo J. Ndlovu-Gatsheni. 2017. "Beyond Coloniality of Markets-Exploring the Neglected Dimensions of the Land Question from Endogenous African Decolonial Epistemological Perspectives." *Africa Insight* 46 (4): 9–24.

Tibaijuka, Anna K. 2005. *Report of the Fact-Finding Mission to Zimbabwe to Assess the Scope and Impact of Operation Murambatsvina*. Geneva: United Nations.

Wierzynska, Aneta. 2004. "Consolidating Democracy through Transitional Justice: Rwanda's Gacaca Courts." *New York University Law Review* 79: 1934–70.

Chapter 2

A Dozen Transitional Justice Realities and Some Preliminary Problematizations

Everisto Benyera

INTRODUCTION

In discussing traditional, customary, and non-state transitional justice there are a dozen transitional justice realities which we need to acknowledge. These realities are a product of past practices and developments, both intentional and unintentional. Current developments and anticipated ones also shape the conceptualization, practice, and outcomes of transitional justice. While the majority of these dozen transitional justice realities are universal, we focus on how they shape and affect both the subdiscipline and practice of transitional justice in what are termed emerging democracies and post-conflict communities in (formerly) colonized countries. These realities are well documented, and most have been debated for some time, especially during the periods between the Rwandan genocide, South African Truth and Reconciliation Commission and the 10-year period post the operationalization of the International Criminal Court. This chapter consolidates these realities and problematizes them as they relate to and interact with indigenous, traditional, and non-state transitional justice mechanisms.

A working definition of transitional justice will be developed as a way of positioning these realities. In posing this working definition, I am cognizant of the debates contained in this book on what constitutes transitional justice. I am aware of the debates that situate transitional justice as an exiting paradigm and transformative justice as one which is now carrying over, building on the work done by its predecessor while attempting to address its shortcomings. Transitional justice refers to the "theories and research programs that explain, justify, compare and contest specific practices of moral and social repair, and to the political and social movements dealing with the past"

(Benyera 2016, 162). The main challenge leveled against transitional justice is that it comes with preconceived outcomes in the form of the five pillars. These five pillars of transitional justice include fact-finding or truth seeking, trials either domestically or international at the International Criminal Court. These trials however do not include those done at local level using traditional and customary institutions. Then there are reparations, institutional reforms and memorialization, and collective memory (Chitsike 2012, 4–6). A slight variation of the five pillars was presented by the late theologian Reverend Alex Boraine as, "accountability, truth recovery, reparations, institutional reform and reconciliation" (Boraine 2006, 19–25).

As the name suggests, transformative justice is more transformative especially of the structural causes of conflict. In conceptualizing transformative justice as the successor of transitional justice, Gready and Robins positioned transformative justice as, "change that emphasizes local agency and resources, the prioritization of process rather than preconceived outcomes and the challenging of unequal and intersecting power relationships and structures of exclusion at both the local and the global level" (Gready and Robins 2014, 340). Transformative justice is therefore not contradictory but complimentary to transitional justice as aptly captured by Gready and Robins in these words:

> While transformative justice does not seek to completely dismiss or replace transitional justice, it does seek to radically reform its politics, locus and priorities. Transformative justice entails a shift in focus from the legal to the social and political, and from the state and institutions to communities and everyday concerns. Transformative justice is not the result of a top-down imposition of external legal frameworks or institutional templates, but of a more bottom-up understanding and analysis of the lives and needs of populations. (Gready and Robins 2014, 340)

This reality is still nascent and will not be pursued beyond this point in this book. The dozen realities explored here were selected based on their close interaction with indigenous, traditional, and non-state transitional justice mechanisms. The purpose for exploring these dozen realities is to lay the foundation for other contributors in this book volume to further explore these interactions. These realities will be briefly introduced and the first one is the need for local indigenous, traditional, and non-state transitional justice mechanisms to confirm to international law, norms, standards, as well as to local traditions. This reality was laid down by the United Nations secretary general in 1992 when he elucidated what were aptly termed the Guidance Note of the Secretary General: United Nations Approach to Transitional Justice (United Nations Secretary General 2010). The effect of this guidance note was to ensure that there was no 'free reign' for indigenous, traditional, and non-state transitional justice mechanisms.

The second reality is that transitional justice has emerged as the dominant paradigm through which post-conflict, post-dictatorship, and post-authoritarian communities are reconstituted. Linked to the above is the third reality which is characterised by the development of the field of transitional justice as a distinct area of study and field of practice. Transitional justice now has a complete set of tools, best practices, experts, consultants and even specialized non-governmental organizations.

The fourth reality is the emergence of the truth commission as the *optimus prime* institution and mechanism within the dominant paradigm of transitional justice. The fifth reality is the role of outsiders in post-conflict communities. By outsiders, I mean those that were not either the perpetrators, the survivors nor the bystanders. The sixth reality is the presence of traditional, customary, and non-state transitional justice mechanisms as a reality in the transtional justice landscape which must also be accorded some space. The seventh reality is the condition in which local transitional justice mechanisms are in. Another transitional justice reality is the existence of the International Criminal Court. The ninth reality relates to the fact that members of post-conflict communities face a common challenge in that perpetrators and their victims must coexist in the same geographical space. Reality number 10 is concerned with that perpetratorship and offendership are not mutually exclusive as today's perpetrators could be tomorrow's victims and vice-versa.

Reality number 11 is traced from the time of the Nuremberg trials to the Rwandan Tribunal and the concomitant *Gacaca* court to the famed South African Truth and Reconciliation Commission, wherein along the way, transitional justice has amassed many responsibilities and power which goes far beyond establishing what happened in the past and who was culpable. It is presented here that transitional justice has amassed a lot of institutional power which is both a challenge and resource. The final reality is the tying of transitional justice to developmental donor requirements. These realities will be explained and problematized as a way of setting the scene for the chapters which will follow.

ONE: THE NEED FOR LOCAL JUSTICE TO CONFORM TO INTERNATIONAL LAW

The first reality is that traditional, customary, and non-state transitional justice mechanisms, generally referred to as local transitional justice must be in conformity with both international standards and local traditions. This reality is derived from the work of the United Nations in its attempt to shape transitional justice. While this perspective is acknowledged, a challenge arises when the two are not in tandem. For example, there are other forms of local justice which are inconsistent with certain international legal norms.

Appeasing avenging spirits with the girl child among the Shona people of Zimbabwe is still wrongly prevalent, yet inconsistent with various gender, women and human rights norms, international treaties, conventions, and laws.

It is a fact of transitional justice practice in the global south that the transitional justice agenda is one set predominantly in the global north. As externally driven processes, transitional justice in the global south is predominantly state-centric (Benyera 2015), privileges the perspectives of those who fund these programs and in the process beholding post conflict communities to the liberal peace paradigm on which transitional justice is bed rocked. Under these circumstances goals of transitional justice become predominantly those of the elites, either in Washington or in African capitals.

To mitigate against these challenges the aim of this book is to profile transitional justice programs that have "gone against the grain" and somehow laid the foundation for transformative justice in Africa. The mechanisms discussed in this book privilege what Chantal Mouffe termed *the political* over what she termed *politics* (Mouffe 2005). In her words; "by 'the political' I mean the dimension of antagonism which I take to be constitutive of human societies, while by 'politics' I mean the set of practices and institutions though which an order is created, organizing human coexistence in the context of conflictuality provided by the political (Mouffe 2005, 9).

Borrowing from Mouffe, this book privileges the political over politics. This is done by exploring non-state transitional justice mechanisms from wider traditional and indigenous practices, process, and modes of everyday life informed by what imbedded local phenomenon. The challenge is that these local transitional justice mechanisms have to be in tandem with international law otherwise, according to the predominant transitional justice paradigm, such practices and mechanisms will be illegal under international law and those presiding over them and their counterparts sanctioning them will be guilty of committing crimes in the process of attempting of right historical wrongs. The question is: Can international law and local transitional justice "find each other" for the benefit of victims of human rights abuses especially those in fragile post-conflict economically poor countries?

TWO: TRANSITIONAL JUSTICE AS THE DOMINANT POST-CONFLICT PARADIGM

The second reality is that transitional justice has emerged as the dominant paradigm through which post-conflict, post-dictatorship, and post-authoritarian communities are reconstituted. The implication of the dominance of transitional justice is that other forms of post-conflict healing, reconciliation, and peace-building either have to fit into the transitional justice paradigm or have to play a complementary role to transitional justice. This then amounts to transitional justice becoming a neo-imperial form of justice which either swallows, displaces, or subordinates the local. The preoccupation of the International Criminal Court (ICC) with crimes committed predominantly by Africans in a world awash with other possible cases which the Court can pursue is an often-cited case of western forms of justice being used to recolonize Africa. Under these circumstances, the ICC is also perceived as displacing local judiciaries, most of which will be in need of reform before they could play their role as impartial dispensers of justice. The incapacities of post conflict local judiciaries notwithstanding, the argument is that where post-conflict judiciaries possess both the competence and willingness to prosecute, the ICC "overtakes" them and imposes itself on the cases. This was a major argument in the work of the ICC in the case of Salim Gadhafi of Libya.

The fact that transitional justice is now the major lens through which post-conflict healing and reconciliation mechanisms are conceived, funded, implemented, and evaluated is problematic at various levels. Transitional justice owes its existence to the liberal peace paradigm (Brown and Ni Aolain 2015, 135; Lundy 2011; Richmond 2015). This implies that it automatically inherits the challenges embedded in the liberal peace processes. Because the liberal peace paradigm is hegemonic and processes born out of it will also tend to exhibit hegemonic tendencies. These include having liberal democracy as an endpoint of all transitional justice processes (Huntington 1991a, 1991b). Obviously, this does not resonate with all post-conflict and conflict-ridden communities especially those in fragile states.

I take note of the obsession of transitional justice with two issues. First, it is obsessed with democratic elections as both a marker of a successful political transition and also as a demarcatory process which allows communities to put behind them the lugubrious past.

Embedded in this electoral obsession are issues of procedural democracy, constitutionalism, and the rule of law. While there is nothing wrong in communities seeking these, the challenge comes when they are put forward as a fundamental, a must exist before everything else, in the process displacing and surbodinating local priorities.

Secondly, liberal peace paradigm processes of transitional justice privilege politics over the political. There is an inherent obsession with official institutions and institutionalism emdeded in transitional justice. The two most favorite being the truth and reconciliation commission and the general commission of enquiry. While there is nothing wrong with westernized institutions being used in post-conflict Africa. The challenge is that of capacity, given that most of these nations will be fragile and will be lacking certain capacities essential for them to function normally.

THREE: THE DEVELOPMENT OF TRANSITIONAL JUSTICE AS A STUDY DISCIPLINE AND FIELD OF PRACTICE

Linked to the above is the emergence of the field of transitional justice as a distinct area of study and field of practice. Transitional justice now has a complete set of tools, best practices, experts, consultants and even specialized nongovernmental organizations. This reality creates a number of problems for both the perpetrators and the survivors such as the ownership of their agency. It also raises two important questions: Where should transitional justice mechanisms originate and who has the right to start these processes? Is it the government, international community (and who is the international community), civil society organizations, nongovernmental organizations, international organizations, multilateral organizations, the perpetrators or the survivors? Each of the abovementioned constituencies has a legitimate claim in the transitional justice processes and there is need for balance in the conceptualization, implementation, ownership, and monitoring and evaluation of transitional justice mechanisms and processes. The reality is that the elites, both within and outside the communities where transitional justice mechanisms will be implemented have tended to monopolize the conceptualization and implementation of transitional justice. Where funding is needed, the elites in charge of funding these programs usually dictate what mechanisms or in what format the community's preferred mechanisms must be implemented. Elite dominance is a reality of a capitalist world, one where those who command power deploy it to meet their needs. In cases where their needs coincide with those of the communities then the later benefit from these.

FOUR: THE TRUTH COMMISSION AS THE *OPTIMUS PRIME* INSTITUTION IN TRANSITIONAL JUSTICE

The fourth reality is the emergence of the truth commission as the *optimus prime* (best first) institution within the dominant paradigm of transitional justice. The truth commission originated from Latin America, was perfected in South Africa and then exported elsewhere including Zimbabwe. The truth commission has attained the status of the tool of choice in the transitional justice toolkit. If there are any question about the truth commission that is asked before it's adoption, it would be how to make the institution fit into the specific post-conflict communities. This has a crowding-out effect on local transitional justice mechanisms. It's adoption almost amounts to a top-down quasi one-size-fit-all *modus operandi*. The major challenge with the truth commission is its temporary status and what then happens to post-conflict communities where the truth commission was used when the commission concludes its works and submits its reports. Increasingly the truth commission has tended to crowd out other mechanisms. Its cozy relationship with liberal institutions and liberal tendencies such as the obsession with western sponsored post conflict democracy and elections as the only ways of demarcating the heinous past from a peaceful future is problematic at various levels. Besides stiffing local initiatives, the notion that democracy is a precondition for economic prosperity was belied by developments in bona fide dictator states such as Rwanda and Ethiopia (untill the election of Abiy Ahmed Ali in 2018), which despite their poor human rights records are among the world's fastest growing economies. China also fits into this category as it managed to economically develop in the absence of liberal democracy and free and fair regular elections.

It is therefore not amiss to argue that the truth commission has been hijacked if not captured by western institutions, states, and elites who work in cohorts with the local elites to perpetuate human rights abuses while pretending to be remedying the historical injustice using the truth commission. Countries where the truth commission was used, even with the most possible efficiency still lack historical accountability, healing, reconciliation and general social cohesion. South Africa is a case in point where the so-called unfinished business of the TRC remains a cardinal political challenge to its statecraft. The same argument was also advanced about the East Timor by Lambourne (2010). The abstract of Tanja Hohe's articles on East Timor captures the essence of the argument being made here and it reads,

> Typical for international state-building interventions, the United Nations Transitional Administration in East Timor relied on a fundamentally western model in its attempt to establish a rule of law. At independence, an official judiciary was transferred to Timorese control as part of the new government. However, this institution has proved to be one of the weakest minted during the transitional period, in part because it was placed on top of an entirely different, indigenous system of justice at the grassroots level. The concept of a crime, and means of redress, or a conflict and process of resolution, accepted as legitimate by the local population contradicted the type of judiciary being imported. UNTAET failed to appreciate the resilience of local structures, and therefore did not reconcile the two contrasting systems of justice. International approaches to post-conflict (re)construction of a rule of law have to be re-thought, taking account of indigenous notions of justice in the architecture of a formal judiciary. (Hohe 2003, 335)

What is clear is that the truth commission as part of the western liberal rule of law "crusade" is becoming another form of coloniality in post-conflict communities given the manner in which it is imposed from the top, conceived from outside these communities and cultures and also driven by elites from outside the communities. The manner in which the truth commission does not seek resonance, "romance" and symbiosis with indigenous and traditional transitional justice mechanisms exposes it as part of instruments in the hands of western nations and institutions. The challenge is that given its perceived success in South Africa, African states have subsequently adopted the truth commission as their transitional justice instrument of choice in addressing historical human rights abuses. This is evidenced by its use in Africa in countries such as Sierra Leone, Ghana, Democratic Republic of the Congo, Morocco 2004, Kenya, Liberia, Gambia started the process in 2017 and Zimbabwe in 2008. Zimbabwe's National Peace and Reconciliation Commission is yet to be operationalized as it grapples with nascent challenges of institutional set up in a country characterized by recurrent and reproduced political conflicts. As for Zimbabwe, the challenges with the National Peace and Reconciliation Commission are deeper as the ruling party and elites who are meant to be the prime suspects of historical human rights abuses ae the major decision makers on how the commission should be run, its mandate, funding, timeframe, and other "lifelines." This is a typical proverbial case of the hyena looking after the goats.

FIVE: THE ROLE OF "OUTSIDERS" IN POST-CONFLICT COMMUNITIES

The fifth reality is the role of "outsiders" in post-conflict communities. By "outsiders," I mean those that were not either the perpetrators, the survivors nor the bystanders and usually do not reside in the communities in question. "Outsiders" have become dominant in transitional justice through various means such as conceptualizing applicable transitional justice mechanisms, funding transitional justice processes, and providing "expert services." Most of these "experts" are specialists in their fields such as medical anthropology and trauma counseling. The challenge is that a high concentration of external stakeholders amounts to the imposition of external transitional justice solutions. Under such circumstances, local participation becomes a matter of tokenism. Embedded phenomena such as cultural interpretation of violence, justice, victimhood and perpetratorship would be diluted if not lost completely, more so, if such interpretations are at variance with international norms and standards. What then, if any is the role of "outsiders" and "experts" in transitional justice?

SIX: THE PRESENCE OF TRADITIONAL, INDIGENOUS, AND NON-STATE TRANSITIONAL JUSTICE MECHANISMS

The sixth reality is the presence of traditional, customary, and non-state transitional justice mechanisms in the broader transitional justice arena (Benyera

2014a). A sub-reality of this development is that these transitional justice mechanisms appeal to the majority of both perpetrators and survivors when compared to formal transitional justice mechanisms such as prosecutions, commissions of inquiry and truth commissions. The question that arises is: is local justice complementary to formal justice or vice-versa? Local transitional justice mechanisms gain their popularity and widespread applicability because they invoke notions of traditional, indigenous informal modes of living and they do not need any "introduction." Their perpetual presence in communities renders them omnipresent resources for historical accountability. This also makes them familiar and accessible and places them at variance with their modern counterparts such as prosecutions. Elsewhere in Zimbabwe, prosecutions as a transitional justice mechanism where criticized by survivors and communities for various reasons such as: the prominent role played by the lawyers (legal middlemen), the prominent role played by outsiders to the conflict (magistrate and public prosecutors), the lack of recognition for the survivors who are treated as (mere) state witnesses, and finally the lack of direct compensation to the survivors (Bourne 2011, 211; Brankovic 2010; Bratton 2011; du Plessis and Ford 2009, 93). What then is the role of the unofficial yet efficacious traditional, indigenous, traditional transitional justice mechanisms? Should they continue to supplement their official counterparts against the evidence that in most communities they are the main transitional justice mechanism? (Mahoso 2012; Marongwe 2012, 396; Benyera 2014b).

SEVEN: THE CONDITION OF LOCAL TRANSITIONAL JUSTICE MECHANISMS

The seventh reality is the condition in which local transitional justice mechanisms are in. After decades of colonial and western modernity-initiated onslaught, traditional, customary, and other transitional justice mechanisms exist in a condition nowhere close to their original form. Granted, culture, tradition and customs evolve with time. What is being referred to in these pages is a series of colonial adulteration, pollution, demonization, and weaponization of African customs, traditions and practices such that instead of saving the people they now serving the colonial system. An apt example is the institution of chiefdom where bona fide chiefs who refused to cooperate with the colonial administration were stripped off their chiefdoms and these chiefdoms were given to colonially compliant "chiefs" who then acted as native informers as opposed to being guardians of the people. Appealing to this type of "chief" is counterproductive to transitional justice as they are part of the problem not the solution as they, *vel prudentes vel inscii*, still serve colonial interests.

Officially, indigenous and the customary transitional justice mechanisms were put on the international spotlight in 2004 when they were included as part of the United Nations Secretary General's report. In his report the late Kofi Annan argued that there was need for due regard to be accorded to what he termed "indigenous and informal traditions for administrative justice or settling disputes" (United Nations Secretary General 2010). The challenge with this admittance was that the secretary general added a disclaimer, wherein he argued that traditional and indigenous transitional justice mechanisms must conform with both international and local tradition. Whilst conforming with local traditions is the norm, it is the conforming with international norms and standards which is problematic.

There is no way in which grassroots-based, bottom-up traditions and customs can confortably fit into international laws and regulations which are predominantly top-down. There is bound to be a gap between these local initiatives and mechanisms and international laws and regulations as the former are particularistic and the latter is generalistic and universal. If indigenous and traditional transitional justice are to be recognized as both capable on their own and complementary to their formal counterparts such as the truth commission, then there is need for them to be recognized unconditionally.

In any case, traditional and indigenous transitional justice mechanisms were going to be used whether or not they were officially recognized by the United Nations. This is not a sign of stubbornness but rather one of resilience and resourcefulness where communities resort to their modes of everyday living and community structures to find transitional justice mechanisms that resonate with their realities. This is not peculiar to Zimbabwe and Namibia which are the focus countries for this book, this practice is prevalent in many post-conflict communities such as Rwanda, Burundi, Mozambique, Sierra Leone, and Uganda. Conflict ridden Sudan and South Sudan also use a lot of traditional and indigenous transitional justice mechanisms. These local mechanisms, in conformity with the practice of democratic tendencies, deserve to be escalated first to the national, then to the regional and finally to the international arena which is the United Nations for purposes of recognition and documentation.

EIGHT: THE REALITY OF THE INTERNATIONAL CRIMINAL COURT

Another transitional justice reality is the existence of the International Criminal Court. The International Criminal Court owes part of its existence to the two predecessor International Criminal Tribunals, one for the former Yugoslavia and the other for Rwanda which set in Arusha, Tanzania. The implication of the existence of the International Criminal Court is that now there is an international legal organization with jurisdiction over the four most heinous crimes; war crimes, crimes against humanity, the crime of aggression and genocide. Despots, dictators and genocidaires can no longer hide behind the inability or the unwillingness of local judiciaries to prosecute them for international human rights crimes. That being stated, the International Criminal Court is having problems of its own. These include allegations of bias against Africa and its remoteness from the scene of most atrocities. Granted, the International Criminal Court can convene anywhere in the world. However, and thus far it has only operated from The Hague. Coupled with the reality that the court has predominantly focused on Africa and that it has demonstrated little appetite for investigating human rights violations outside Africa and especially those committed by Euro North Americans elsewhere including in the formally colonized world. The ICC's problematic relationship with the United Nations Security Council is a further source of disharmony especially for those who argue that the court is selective in its application of international criminal justice law.

Given the alleged remoteness and bias of the ICC (Benyera 2018; Branch 2017; Okafor and Ngwaba 2015; Clark 2008), local transitional justice mechanisms have a great opportunity for application in post-conflict communities. Needless to assert the need to avoid the romanticization of local transitional justice mechanisms.

NINE: THE REALITY OF POST CONFLICT SURVIVORS' CORE EXISTENCE

Members of post-conflict communities face a common challenge in that perpetrators and their victims must coexist in the same geographical space. The only instance where perpetrators and victims were geographically separated after a conflict was when the state of Israel was created in 1947. In this case, victims and survivors were relocated to Israel while the perpetrators remained mainly in Germany and Poland. Elsewhere, especially in African, post-conflict communities such as post-genocide Rwanda and Zimbabwe, perpetrators and their victims remained in the same geographical areas such as same villages. Mamdani came up with the notion of survivors' justice as a way of characterizing situations where perpetrators and victims coexisted in the post-conflict dispensation and in close geographical proximity. In respect of survivors' justice in South Africa, Mamdani argued;

> Indeed, CODESA offers us a shift of paradigm where the meaning of survivors changes to include all those who survived yesterday's catastrophe, apartheid: yesterday's victims, yesterday's perpetrators and yesterday's

beneficiaries—those described as bystanders by human rights activists. The shift of paradigm is from victims' justice to survivors' justice. (Mamdani 2010, 8)

The challenge is then how do perpetrators and their victims continue to coexist in post-conflict communities?

TEN: THE REALITY OF SURVIVORS' MULTIPLE IDENTITIES

Perpetratorship and offendership are not mutually exclusive as today's perpetrators could be tomorrow's victims and vice-versa. This was the reality in Zimbabwe's politically motivated violence of 2008 where the Movement for Democratic Change (MDC) and ZANU-PF often fluidly moved from receiving to dispensing politically motivated violence. The same arguement can be made about Zimbawe's nationalists who were abused by the white minority regime of Ian Smith, only for them to turn on their people after gaining independence in 1980 through dispensing various episodes of violence which inlude the 1982-3 Gukurahundi genocide. Addressing post-conflict injustices relies on ascribing identifiable atrocities to identifiable perpetrators. The complexities arising from today's victims being tomorrow's perpetrators besides increasing drastically the cases to be dealt with, also complicate issues such as reparations as most of the atrocities were for revenge or counter revenge for prior atrocities. Post-conflict communities therefore become trapped in trying to account for circles of violence whose origin increasingly became blurred. Reduced to its basic terms, the problematic becomes: what form of justice applies to "family members" who fought each other on opposite sides of the political divide?

ELEVEN: THE POWER OF TRANSITIONAL JUSTICE AS AN INSTITUTION

From the time of the Nuremberg trials to the Rwandan Tribunal and the concomitant *Gacaca* court to the famed South African Truth and Reconciliation Commission, along the way transitional justice has amassed many responsibilities and power which goes far beyond establishing what happened in the past and who was culpable. Transitional justice today is a huge industry complete with experts, best practices, set of tools, consultants, and Guiding Principles from the United Nations and regional bodies such as the African Union, tool kits from the United States Agency for International Development (USAID) and other western "expert" organizations (Benyera 2017, 283). The power that transitional justice as an institution has amassed includes first, the power to demarcate the heinous past from a democratic present and future. Secondly, the power to authenticate incoming regimes. Thirdly, transitional justice processes have now acquired a state building and nation building responsibility. Fourthly, transitional justice sets new norms and standards for acceptable and unacceptable behaviors. It is because of those responsibilities that metamorphized around the transitional justice program that Madlingozi argued transitional justice has become a form of constitutive power (Madlingozi 2010). This needs to be examined in a more nuanced manner especially given that the majority of transitional justice programs have been implemented in the global South.

As the institution of transitional justice grows and gains acceptability and applicability, questions have to be asked. These include: What is the role and position of the traditional, indigenous and no state mechanisms? Bearing in mind that these various traditional, indigenous, and non-state transitional justice mechanisms are not just compliments to their formal and statist counterparts, but they are in most cases the main transitional justice mechanisms available and used especially in rural parts of Africa.

TWELVE: THE TWINING OF TRANSITIONAL JUSTICE AND DEVELOPMENT AID

More worrying is the move by most western liberal institutions to tie transitional justice to developmental donor requirements. These requirements and demands are made in such a way that transitional justice becomes one of the demands that are placed on post-conflict communities as part of a post-conflict aid package which includes liberal democratization and market liberalization. Hence, I argue that transitional justice has been weaponized by the west against the global south. The unwritten rule for receiving post-conflict international and donor aid has become; if you want to receive our help; transition, democratize, liberalize, and develop.

Twinning transitional justice with liberal democracy is not an entirely positive project for the communities in transitional. The tenets used to ascertain democratization negate the nuances of human rights fundamentals such as human development. Democratization can be argued to be happening in transition countries while in actual fact, the lived experiences of certain classes and groups of citizens remain largely untransitioned and untransformed. These liberal democracy tenets include the problematic notion of economic growth. I allege that democratization as part of political transition privileges economic growth at the expense of human transformation and development. Economic growth does not have a human face as an economy can grow even in a country at war. I will use five cases where economic development occured while negating the human development of communities in transition.

There are cases of jobless growth which occurs when economic growth does not expand employment opportunities (Ajakaiye et al. 2016). Jobless growth occurred in Uganda (2006–2011) with the "GDP average yearly growth was 6.86% (1990–1999), 5.52% (2000–2005), and 7.7%" (Bbaale 2013) and Rwanda (Malunda 2013). There is also ruthless growth, which is growth which simultaneously increases inequality poverty and unemployment. This type of growth is usually accompanied by voiceless economic growth. This is growth which alienates the majority and continues to benefit the privileged minorities. Rootless growth also occurs in transitional economies and it is when growth exterminates cultures and diversity. Finally, futureless economic growth also occurs and this is growth which squanders resources with little or no regard for future generation's needs (Muchena 2009). The economic growth of Rwanda and Ethiopia discussed earlier are apt examples of the disjuncture between peace, democracy on one side, and economic growth and prosperity in the other. It's a proven fallacy that peace and democracy are a prerequisite for economic growth and prosperity.

CONCLUSION

This chapter explored a dozen phenomena in transitional justice which were termed transitional justice realities. The aim was to hint on some of the themes and addressed in this book and also to some of the problematics in the field so that others can take them up and make a contribution. These realities are evolving and *sui generis*, yet I could not escape the tendency to at times generalize which I admit was meant for emphasis. The choice of twelve realities has no significance at all and readers should not read into it. I thought through and itemized these realities and managed to find twelve which I then developed and hence the name of the chapter. I am dissuading readers from linking them to significant twelves such as the twelve apostles in the Bible.

REFERENCES

Ajakaiye, Olu, T. Afeikhena Jerome, David Nabena, and Alabi A. Olufunke. 2016. "Understanding the African Lions: Grwoth Traps and Opportunities in Six Dominant African Economies – Understanding the Relationship Between Growth and Employment in Nigeria." Washington, DC: Brookings Institution Press. www.wider.unu.edu/sites/default/files/wp2015-124.pdf.

Bbaale, Edward. 2013. "Is Uganda's Growth Profile Jobless?" *International Journal of Economics and Finance* 5 (11): 105–23. doi: 10.5539/ijef.v5n11p105.

Benyera, Everisto. 2014a. "Exploring Zimbabwe's Traditional Transitional Justice Mechanisms." *Journal of Social Science* 41 (3): 335–44.

Benyera, Everisto. 2014b. "The Contribution of Mass Graves to Healing and Closure: The Case of Chibondo in Mt Darwin, Zimbabwe." *International Journal of Humanities and Social Sciences* 4 (1): 2250–3226.

Benyera, Everisto. 2015. "Idealist or Realist Transitional Justice: Which Way for Zimbabwe?" *Journal of Social Science* 45 (3): 199–211.

Benyera, Everisto. 2016. "On the Question of the Transition: Was Zimbabwe a Transitional State Between 2008 and 2013?" *Journal of Human Ecology* 55 (3): 160–72.

Benyera, Everisto. 2017. "Joshua Nkomo on Transitional Justice in Zimbabwe." In *Joshua Mqabuko Nkomo of Zimbabwe*, edited by S. Ndovu-Gatsheni, 279–95. Cham: Palgrave-Macmillan. https://link.springer.com/chapter/10.1007/978-3-319-60555-5_12.

Benyera, Everisto. 2018. "Is the International Criminal Court Unfairly Targeting Africa? Lessons for Latin America and the Caribbean States." *Politeia* 37 (1): 1–30. doi: 10.25159/0256-8845/2403ISSN.

Boraine, Alexander. 2006. "Transitional Justice: A Holistic Interpretation." *Journal of International Affairs* 60 (1): 17–27.

Bourne, Richard. 2011. *Catastrophe: What Went Wrong in Zimbabwe?* London and New York: Zed Books. doi: 10.1007/s13398-014-0173-7.2.

Branch, Adam. 2017. "Dominic Ongwen on Trial: The ICC's African Dilemmas." *International Journal of Transitional Justice* 11 (1): ijw027. doi: 10.1093/ijtj/ijw027.

Brankovic, Jasmina. 2010. *Advocating Justice Civil Society and Transitional Justice in Africa: Civil Society and Transitional Justice in Africa.* Johannesburg: Centre for the Study of Violence and Reconciliation and the African Transitional Justice Research Network.

Bratton, Michael. 2011. "Violence, Partisanship and Transitional Justice in Zimbabwe." *The Journal of Modern African Studies* 49 (3): 353–80. doi: 10.1017/S0022278X11000243.

Brown, Kris, and Fionnuala Ni Aolain. 2015. "Through the Looking Glass: Transitional Justice Futures through the Lens of Nationalism, Feminism and Transformative Change." *International Journal of Transitional Justice* 9 (1): 127–49. doi: 10.1093/ijtj/iju027.

Chitsike, Kudakwashe. 2012. *Transitional Justice Options for Zimbabwe: A Guide to Key Concepts.* Cape Town: Institute of Justice and Reconciliation.

Clark, Phil. 2008. "Law, Politics and Pragmatism: The ICC and Case Selection in Uganda and the Democratic Republic of Congo." In *Courting Conflict: Justice: Peace and the ICC in Africa*, edited by Wadell and Clark, 37–46. London: Royal African Society.

du Plessis, Max, and Jolyon Ford. 2009. "Transitional Justice: A Future Truth Commission for Zimbabwe?" *International and Comparative Law Quarterly* 58 (1): 73. doi: 10.1017/S002058930800081X.

Gready, Paul, and Simon Robins. 2014. "From Transitional to Transformative Justice: A New Agenda for Practice." *The International Journal of Transitional Justice* 8: 339–61. doi: 10.1093/ijtj/iju013.

Hohe, Tanja. 2003. "Analysis Justice without Judiciary in East Timor." *Conflict, Security & Development* 3 (3): 335–57. doi: 10.1080/1467880032000151626.

Huntington, Samuel P. 1991a. "How Countries Democratize." *Political Science Quarterly* 106 (4): 579–616.

Huntington, Samuel P. 1991b. *The Third Wave: Democratization in the Late Twentieth Century*. Norman: University of Oklahoma Press.

Lambourne, W. 2010. "Unfinished Business: The Commission for Reception, Truth and Reconciliation and Justice and Reconciliation in East Timor." In *Development of Institutions of Human Rights*, edited by LA Barra and Stephen D. Roper, 195–207. London: Palgrave Macmillan.

Lundy, Patricia. 2011. "Paradoxes and Challenges of Transitional Justice at the 'Local' Level: Historical Enquiries in Northern Ireland." *Contemporary Social Science* 6 (1): 89–105. doi: 10.1080/17450144.2010.534495.

Madlingozi, Tshepo. 2010. "On Transitional Justice Entrepreneurs and the Production of Victims." *Journal of Human Rights Practice* 2 (2): 208–28.

Mahoso, Tafataona. 2012. "African Focus, Ngozi: The Philosophical Foundation of African Living Law." *The Herals*, February 4, 2012.

Malunda, Dickson. 2013. "Employment Intensity of Non Agricultural Growth in Rwanda: Analyzing the Links between Growth, Employment, and Productivity in Rwanda." In *IPAR 3rd Annual Research Conference, Kigali: Umubano Hotel 13–14 November 2013*, 1–37. Kigali: IPAR.

Mamdani, Mahmood. 2010. "Lessons of Nuremberg and CODESA: Where Do We Go from Here?" Bloemfontein: University of the Free State. www.ufs.ac.za/docs/librariesprovider20/centre-for-africa-studies-documents/all-documents/memorial-lectures-98-eng.pdf?sfvrsn=b434fb21_0.

Marongwe, Ngonidzashe. 2012. *Rural Women as the Invisible Victims of Militarised Political Violence: The Case of Shurugwi District, Zimbabwe 2000–2008*. Cape Town: Universty of the Western Cape.

Mouffe, Chantal. 2005. *On the Political: Thinking in Action*. Journal of Consciousness Studies. London and New York: Routledge. doi: 10.2307/2057923.

Muchena, Deprose. 2009. "The Great Nose Dive of 2008. The Global Financial Crisis and Lessons for Africa." *Open Space: A Digest of the Open Society Initiative for Southern Africa* 2 (4): 31–39.

Okafor, Obiora Chinedu, and Uchechukwu Ngwaba. 2015. "The International Criminal Court as a 'Transitional Justice' Mechanism in Africa: Some Critical Reflections." *International Journal of Transitional Justice* 9 (1): 90–108. doi: 10.1093/ijtj/iju025.

Richmond, Oliver P. 2015. "The Dilemmas of a Hybrid Peace: Negative or Positive?" *Cooperation and Conflict* 50 (1): 50–68. doi: 10.1177/0010836714537053.

United Nations Secretary General. 2010. *Guidance Note of the Secretary-General: United Nations Approach to Transitional Justice*. New York: United Nations.

Chapter 3

The Case for Indigenous, Traditional, and Non-State Transitional Justice

Everisto Benyera

INTRODUCTION

The indigenous and the traditional have been fatally conflated in both scholarship and practice. Yet there is a theoretical difference between the indigenous and the traditional in transitional justice, the former being tied to a historical, usually of foreign oppression and domination, usually mostly but not limited to colonialism, while the latter is a product of long-standing modes of everyday life which themselves are subject to change and evolution. The indigenous is linked with a specific geographical location, that is, land and its natural resources, while the traditional is evolutionary, absorbing new trends and developments as it interacts with the world. This article locates the indigene in politicized identity constructions resulting from exogenous forces such as colonialism, imperialism, globalization, and coloniality.

So, what exactly constitutes indigenous transitional justice mechanisms? In order to respond to this question, it is necessary to first define indigenous peoples. This is because of the direct link between indigenous transitional justice mechanisms and indigenous peoples. I am aware of the broad conceptualization of the indigenous peoples in Africa as every African, excluding whites. I will rely on the report of the African Commission Working Group of Experts on Indigenous Populations Communities define indigenous people thus:

> they have a special attachment to and use of their traditional land where by their ancestral land and territory has a fundamental importance for their collective physical and cultural survival is people's; on and experience of subjugation marginalization disposition exclusion or discrimination because these peoples have different cultures, ways of life or modes of production than the national economic and dominant model.

From this definition of indigenous peoples, we can draw what constitutes indigenous transitional justice mechanisms. First, there is the issue of specific territories or lands implying that such mechanisms must be linked to specific geographical areas and also that they must have been practiced by many generations. Secondly, these mechanisms must have been voluntarily perpetuated by these communities over time. Thirdly, they are linked to a specific language, religious practices, social organization, spiritual values modes of production a laws and institutions which are only peculiar to these communities. While the same transitional justice mechanism such as *ngozi* may be used across geographies, there are certain embedded markers which render it different in that community.

DEFINING TRANSITIONAL JUSTICE

What constitutes both the practice and study of transitional justice is no longer debatable. Transitional justice is a theory, a practice, and a discipline which has been going through multiple transitions. Since its post–World War II inception headlined by the Nuremberg Trials, transitional justice has ever since been in simultaneous developmental and transitional phases. It transitioned from its World War II conceivement where it was viewed as transition from eastern communism toward western capitalist. At another level, it also implied transition from the tyrannical eastern communist ideologies and practices toward western democratic liberalism. This conceptualization of the transition and transitional states ended with the end of the Cold War. The second transition was from the post-Cold War up to the new millennium. This transition solidified the conceptualization of state transition as movement away not only from communism but also from other forms of regimes deemed by western liberal standards as undemocratic.

The genesis of modern formal transitional justice is in international human rights law and the various international human rights movements which aimed to curtail especially military dictatorships, war crimes, and mass atrocities for which Latin America and Nazi Germany were the prime examples (Minow 1998; Teitel 2003; Herencia Carrasco 2010; Teitel 2015; Dancy and Wiebelhaus-Brahm 2015). By definition, "transitional justice is a short, medium and long term process that allows the introduction of political, legal or historical measures such as commissions of inquiry, trials, reparations, memorials, and more, as well as legal and constitutional reforms, with the aim of triggering and supporting regime transition and transformation" (Mihr 2017).

What constitutes transitional justice and the concomitant mechanisms used to attain this form of justice has been a subject of many academic endeavors (Chitsike 2012; Bell 2014; Benyera 2018, 2015, 2014a; Benyera, Mtapuri, and Nhemachena 2018; Benyera 2016, 2017, 2014b; de Grieff and Duthiee 2009; Emmanuel 2007; Fischer 2011; Loyle and Davenport 2016; Mutua 2015; Muvingi 2016; Szablewska 2015; Teitel 2003). The above literature addresses the conceptualization of transitional justice from various and valid perspectives. Benyera, for example, explores the use of traditional transitional justice mechanisms in Zimbabwe (Benyera 2014b). He further theories on the transition in transitional justice arguing that there are multiple possible destinations for transitional states such as the desired one which is sustainable democracy or transition into stagnation, or transitional into another authoritarian regime (Benyera 2016). De Grieff and Duthie argued that that transitional justice can be more sustainable if twined with broader social economic and political development (de Grieff and Duthiee 2009). There are even healing and reconciliation framework which were proposed (Machakanja 2010; Muwati, Gambahaya, and Mangena 2006; Ndlovu-Gatsheni and Benyera 2015). All these build on the canonical work by Teitel where she traced the genealogy of transitional justice (Teitel 2001). The role of third parties or outsiders in transitional justice both as enablers and inhibiters of transitional justice was explored by Muvingi who used the term donor-driven transitional justice to criticize how the misfortunes of post conflict communities have been turned into a huge and flourishing industry by western donor agencies and their sponsoring governments (Muvingi 2016).

The current transitional phase is anchored by a movement away from states being accountable to International Law to a new regime where they are accountable to human rights. Each phase has specific theories and practices that accompany it; for example, the new Nuremburg transitional justice theories were around retributive and victor's justice. Post–Cold War era transitional justice was very much legalistic, and it emphasized tribunals, trials, and prosecutions. In Africa, another transition was occurring beginning in the 1960s with the independence of Ghana. For newly independent and independence aspiring African countries, transition was taken to imply the movement from colonialism to independence. The zenith of this phase was the formation of the International Criminal Court was the dominant institution in this phase. The fourth phase of the transition is accompanied by the principles of Responsibility to Protect and Humanitarian Intervention. Post-millennial transitional justice theories are now mostly about economic social and cultural rights. Hence, one can actually map the theoretical trajectory for the transition of transitional justice. The same can also be accomplished about the concomitant practices that accompanied each phase of transitional justice.

While the various transitions were occurring, there was a constant which was holding in Africa, stretching from precolonial Africa to colonial Africa and into the independence period. These are local African peace-building, reconciliation, healing, and reconciliation mechanisms. These range from

"Uganda's *mato oput*, Rwanda's gacaca, Mozambique and Zimbabwe's *magamba* spirit, ngozi and *kuputisana fodya*" (Benyera 2016, 164). These mechanisms have been variously theorized as both indigenous and traditional with the two concepts used interchangeably as if they mean the same thing. The purpose of this chapter is to lay the theoretical foundation for the conceptual differentiation of the indigenous from the traditional.

What distinguishes the traditional from the indigenous is that indigenousness is an identity constructed, shaped, and lived in the politicized context of contemporary coloniality. In other words, the indigene in indigenous is derived from a product of land and colonialism. Indigenous refers to those people, cultures, institutions, and resources that occupy a geographically well-defined space which at one time was colonized or repelled colonially forces, especially Euro North American colonialism. This definition may be stretched to include Arab colonialism.

Although terms such as indigenous and traditional are used interchangeably in relation to dispute resolution or reconciliation, they do not hold precisely the same meanings. Traditional refers to norms and practices that draw on long-standing modes of operation. While traditions can be invented and are capable of change, the expectation is that traditional techniques and understandings have a lengthy historical pedigree (Mac Ginty 2011). Indigenous people on the other hand are those that inhabited an area prior to colonization. In the case of Zimbabwe, the indigenous people are those who were in the land between the Zambezi and the Limpopo Rivers prior to 1890. This rules out white Zimbabweans and "coloreds" from the ranks of the indigenous Zimbabweans.

While the goals of any transitional justice are *sui generic* to both the communities which suffered the atrocities and their desires and conceptualization of both (in)justice, reconciliation and peace, Chitsike and Boraine developed the five pillars of transitional justice as a universal conceptual framework for this sub discipline (Boraine 2006; Chitsike 2012). These five pillars of transitional justice include any five of the following; truth and fact finding, memorialization and collective memory, institutional reform, reparations, trials.

TRANSITIONAL JUSTICE: A DECOLONIAL PERSPECTIVE

From a decolonial perspective, the contributions of Madlingozi are key as they cast aspersions on the motive of "experts" in transitional justice whom he labels as transitional justice entrepreneurs and alleges were involved in what he termed the production of victims (Madlingozi 2010). Most importantly, Madlingozi challenges why most transitional justice programs are conceived from the global north, funded from there and predominantly implemented in the global south. According to his argument, transitional justice was weaponized into performing the tasks of disciplining communities in the global south (Madlingozi 2015).

As argued by Madlingozi the global transitional justice program has evolved into become a mechanism for the covert and overt imposition of Western epistemologies and their inferiorization of non-western epistemologies and ways of being (Madlingozi 2015). This is mainly because of the Western dominance in the transitional justice field as the majority of transitional justice programs are conceived in Euro-North America. Most of the "experts," "think tanks," and the funders of transitional justice programs are from the global north and this places a huge influence on the way transitional justice programs are implemented in the global south, most of them resutantly lacking situatedness.

We do not intend to contest the legitimacy of these imported programs, "experts" and donors. Rather it is our aim to position traditional, indigenous, and non-state transitional justice mechanisms as concomitants that must also have a role to play in the new agenda of transitional justice in the global south. Traditional, indigenous, and non-state transitional justice mechanisms must play a part in post-conflict state-building, nation-building, and government authentication processes. This is in contrast to their current position as "nice to have" artifacts in the armory of western transitional justice mainly aimed at appeasing local communities by using these mechanisms as a front for inclusiveness. We are convinced that the starting point is to demonstrate the efficacy of these transitional justice mechanisms. Hence, our choice of two case countries Zimbabwe and Namibia, that had little or no formal transitional justice programs. Most importantly, both these countries experienced genocides. The Herero of Namibia and the Shona and Ndebele of Matabeleland and the Midlands provinces in Zimbabwe present classic examples of non-state, customary, and indigenous transitional mechanisms at work.

USES OF TRANSITIONAL JUSTICE

Transitional justice is efficacious is condemning the heinous past and authenticating the demarcating future. It delegitimizes previous authoritarian regime and their practices while legitimizing future administrations with the writing or amending of the constitution being the prime tool for achieving this demarcation. Transitional justice lays the foundation for the new dispensation and this usually happen in the short term (up to five years). After a successful transitional period, the medium- and long-term deliverables will be to alter the structures of power relations which gave birth to the past atrocities. This constitutes what can be termed transformational justice and includes altering economic relations, changing and discarding toxic political cultures, instituting institutional realignment and reform, and setting new norms and standards favorable for the respect of human rights. This period takes up to a generation.

Transitional justice exists to shepherd post-conflict societies from gross human rights abuses to the rule of law. Admittedly, the rule of law is a very evasive and amorphous concept. Basically understood, the rule of law states that law must govern society as opposed to the arbitrary decisions of persons, especially those in power (Hutchinson 2011, 61). The rule of law is therefore a hedge against tyranny, dictatorships, authoritarianism and general heavy-handed governance. It also ensures that a government functions in a more predictable way usually by consistently applying laws of the land thereby curtailing impunity. The more there is governance unpredictability, high-handed governance and tyranny, dictatorship, authoritarianism, and juntaisms, then the more a government moves away from the *rule of law* towards *rule by law*, and in the process descending into gross human rights abuses, atrocities, and or state failure. The effectiveness of transitional justice can therefore be assessed on these three broad rule of law parameters; (1) is there governance predictability? (2) are laws not being made and arbitrarily deployed to benefit a few, usually the elites? This is rule by law as opposed to rule by law. (3) Finally, is the government not being heavy handed especially in dealing with political dissent, minority issues, and the observations of the various rights as prescribed in the bill of rights?

Given that formal transitional justice lasts at most five years, what institutional mechanisms and frameworks sustain this momentum in the absence of the disbanded formal mechanisms such as truth commissions. Herein lies the efficacy of the traditional, customary, and non-state transitional justice mechanisms which ordinarily use the agency of the local communities to find healing, closure, and reconciliation. These traditional, customary, and non-state transitional justice mechanisms have been used for decades to heal and reconcile communities and families, mostly in non-political feuds and their malleability landed them favorably as capable compliments to their formal counterparts. As was with the *Gacaca* courts of Rwanda, the modernization of these mechanisms can also be a source of some problems as they were not designed with complex political issues involving layers of stakeholders and additionally being required to be in conformity with international legal standards and obligations (United Nations Secretary General 2010, 2).

CONCEPTUALIZING INDIGENOUS, TRADITIONAL, AND NON-STATE TRANSITIONAL JUSTICE MECHANISMS

The overarching theme of the book is to expose the invisiblization of African traditional, customary and non-state transitional justice mechanisms. Many factors contributed to this invisibilization and these include the domination of the transitional justice field by the following western institutions; funding organizations, academic researchers consulting firms, think tanks. These western-based institutions have a crowding out effect on traditional, indigenous, and non-state transitional justice mechanisms. This dominance by western institutions in the transitional justice field in Africa perpetuates not only the subjugation of Africa but also of its institutions. The result is the application of imported transitional justice mechanisms at the direct expense of their local counterparts which at worse become extinct and dysfunctional, forgotten institutions.

The resultant transitional justice mechanisms have been referred to as imported transitional justice mechanisms. They are imported because they were conceived elsewhere and then brought into the post-conflict communities for "panel beating" and implementation. A good case is the famed South African TRC model. This model is considered as an imported institution because the office bearers such as the commissioners in most cases would not have been part of the conflict and the mechanisms itself will be alien to the community where it is brought and enacted.

Our argument is that transitional justice is no longer a mere process of "reckoning with the past" (Crocker 1999; Hayner 1994, 1996) and in a way establishing historical accountability (Benyera 2014c, 53; du Plessis 2010). Transitional justice has evolved to become a very powerful institution whose power goes far beyond assisting communities reckon with the past and establish historical accountability.

We are motivated by the realization that the global transitional justice program is fast becoming a coloniality project, one that ensures the perpetual subordination and subjugation of the global south by the Euro-North America. How is transitional justice becoming part of the transition problem? Precisely because of the constitutive power which it has amassed over the years and from across geography, which is so much power and in the absence of the local, transitional justice is in a trajectory to become another form of coloniality for Africa.

This is a deserved and necessary intervention which is part of the decolonial movement to position traditional indigenous and non-state transitional justice mechanisms as deserving a place at the proverbial table for state-building, nation-building, and state authentication. More worrying is the move by most Western liberal institutions to tie transitional justice to development and donor requirements (de Grieff and Duthiee 2009; Dixon 2017; Hellsten 2012; Muvingi 2016; Selim and Murithi 2011). Raditional, customary and non-state transitional justice mechanisms can therefore be as a 'checks and balances' against their more formal counterparts.

DISENTANGLING INDIGENOUS, CUSTOMARY, AND TRADITIONAL TRANSITIONAL JUSTICE

There has been a general academic tendency to conflate indigenous, customary, and traditional transitional justice, in the process presenting the three as if they are synonymic. In this section, I demonstrate the differences between the three forms of transitional justice. The indigenous, customary and the traditional interact and are not mutually exclusive. The three constantly interact, lend each other some attributes and this leads not to competition but complementarity. Before attempting the entanglement of the indigenous, customary and the traditional, it is necessary to make a cursory distinction between formal and informal transitional justice mechanisms.

> Informal [transitional justice] mechanisms is . . . less structured and more adaptive to society's needs. Yearly commemorations . . . memorials, films, photography, memoirs, and other actions that serve to inform future generations, to foster remembering, to promote reconciliation, . . . will be classified as informal. (Wolfe 2015, 52–53)

Their opposite are formal transitional justice mechanisms such as domestic trails, vetting, lustrations, institutional reforms, truth commissions, commissions of inquiry, and indictments at the International Criminal Court.

The most used of these three transitional justice forms is indigenous. There are three markers that define the indigene; colonialism, time, and geography. The term indigenous applies to peoples within a well-defined geographical area who have lived in that area before Euro-North American colonialism. In addition, there are norms and practices which draw on local resources that buttress the indigene. The onslaught of colonialism and other factors, both exogenous and endogenous resulted in indigenous communities adapting to changing circumstances and also adopting some of the technologies of the colonizers. The result of these encounters between the indigene and the colonial was a series of processes of contestation, accommodation and social negotiation meant to ensure the survival of the indigene in a colonially hostile environment. Customs, social norms and other institutions that qualify as indigenous therefore predate colonialism, were practiced over a certain well define geographical area by a fairly homogenous group of people who spoke a similar language. These customs, norms, practices and institutions survived colonialism albeit having undergone some metamorphosis of sorts. The Shona people are therefore indigenous to Zimbabwe and Mozambique as the Herero and the Nama are indigenous to Namibia. Indigenous transitional justice is therefore an imbedded phenomenon.

In this conceptual distinction of the indigenous from the traditional, I will rely on the definition of the indigenous as postulated by the International Labor Organization in its definition of indigenous and tribal peoples. Of course, I have serious reservations about classifying people as tribal as the term suggests barbarism and lack of both civic and political order which obviously is not the case. The International Labor Organization define indigenous peoples thus:

> indigenous peoples are people in independent countries who are regarded as indigenous on account of their descent from populations which inhabited the country, or a geographical region to which people in the country belongs, it a time or conquest or colonization or the establishment of present state boundaries and who, irrespective of their legal status, retain some or all of their own social economic cultural and political institutions. (Alan 1997, 2)

There are four markers of indignity in the above definition. These are: time, geographical space, resilience, and continuous territorial occupation. Transposing the International Labor Organization definition of the indigenous to transitional justice gives the following as a conceptual definition of indigenous transitional justice. Indigenous transitional justice consists of precolonial mechanisms that were used to pursue and attain justice after human rights violations as understood by those communities. Both the understanding and seeking of justice by these communities applied to certain geographical spaces. Hence in most cases the notion of (in)justice varied from one kingdom to another. Indigenous transitional justice mechanisms also displayed a great resilience against the onslaught of both colonialism and modernity. While these mechanisms did not remain the same, they however managed to retain their major characteristics such as the communal understanding of both victimhood and perpetratorship. Indigenous transitional justice mechanisms are practiced within specific territorial boundaries hence they usually do not appeal and are not applicable to outsiders, are mostly unwritten and derive from customs, beliefs, rituals, and practices.

Conceptually, the traditional is not the indigenous yet the indigenous is traditional. The traditional is much broader hence my argument that the indigenous sits in the traditional. According to John Mugabe, "the traditional is the totality of all knowledge and practices, whether explicit or implicit, used in the management of social economic and ecological facets of life" (Mugabe, 1998). Traditional transitional justice is based on and built-upon past societal experiences of (in)justice. It is a communal property which evolved and was developed shaped and sharpened over time, each experience contributing to the corpus of what can be termed traditional transitional jurisprudence. Characteristically, traditional transitional justice is malleable elastic, dynamic, absorptive, and always evolving. It is against its validity from what Mugabe termed being deeply entrenched in people's lives. These people need not share the same geographical or jurisdiction spaces. Hence, traditional transitional justice cut across geographies and jurisdiction. It is applicable to those in the diaspora is it is applicable to those at "home." The majority of non-state transitional justice mechanisms used in Southern Africa are traditional and not indigenous.

The main distinction between the transitional and the indigenous is that the traditional does not rely on a sense of place or ecological embeddedness (Whiteman and Cooper 2000) and achieves cultural significance from the community's relation to a particular environment. Traditional transitional justice is therefore much broader than indigenous transitional justice as it transcends the ecological notion which is so central to the indigenous. In other words, traditional transitional justice can be practiced by geographically dispersed peoples such as those in diaspora who invoke healing and reconciliation mechanisms used in the communities of their origin.

Traditional knowledge is, on the other hand, that which is held by members of a distinct culture and/or sometimes acquired "by means of inquiry peculiar to that culture and concerning the culture itself or the local environment in which it exists" (Mugabe 1998, 3). Indigenous knowledge fits neatly in the traditional knowledge category but traditional knowledge is not necessarily indigenous. That is to say, indigenous knowledge is traditional knowledge, but traditional knowledge is not necessarily indigenous (Mugabe 1998, 3).

Another way of identifying the indigenous, especially indigenous communities is the contestation between them and commercial interest especially in primary resource extraction. The extraction of local natural resources is viewed by indigenous communities not only as an intrusion into their way of life but also a theft of their birth right. There are also contestations between the indigenous and the notion of development in its various forms. For indigenous communities, development consists of processes of de-skilling and delinking them from their centuries-old relationships with nature and their peer communities. They do not understand development as they perceive it as an unwelcome intrusion and a pollutant to their way of life.

In relation to healing, peace building, reconciliation, and reparation, otherwise what is referred to in transitional justice literature as the five pillars (Chitsike 2012), indigenous refers to those modes of everyday life that have been practiced by peoples before colonialism and have mostly remained in practiced today tough in different versions and forms.

The Commission on International Humanitarian Affairs' definition of indigenous peoples has the following four attribute; a preexistence (i.e., prior to colonization or the current political dispensation), non-dominance of their political environment, cultural difference from other groups, and self-identification as indigenous (Mac Ginty 2011).

The 1982 United Nations Working Group on Indigenous Populations also has four principles which it used in defining indigenous peoples. These are; first, priority in time, with respect to the occupation and use of a specific territory. Secondly, voluntary perpetuation of cultural distinctiveness. Thirdly, self-identification, as well as recognition by other groups and state authorities, as a distinct collectivity. Lastly, an experience of subjugation, marginalization, dispossession, exclusion, or discrimination (African Commission on Human and Peoples' Rights 2012; Nettheim 1993; Mugabe 1998).

CONCLUSION

I conclude this chapter by restating the motivation of this book project, which is to respond to pertinent question such as what is the role and position of the traditional and indigenous transitional justice mechanisms in Southern Africa and in Zimbabwe and Namibia in specific. Bearing in mind that these various non-state transitional justice mechanisms are not just compliments to their formal and statist counterparts, but they are in most cases the main transitional justice mechanisms available and used especially in rural parts of Africa such as Shurugwi in Zimbabwe, Acholiland in Uganda, and Gorongosa in Mozambique (Igreja, Dais-Lambranca, and Richters 2008; Iliff 2012; Marongwe 2012; Quinn 2007a, 2007b; Huyse 2008; Igreja 2007). In order for post-conflict communities to get heling, closure and in some cases reconciliation, there is need for these aspects to be conceptualized from the bottom up so that they do not only get traction but also efficacy. In the same way in which most causes of conflicts are local, so should be the responses.

REFERENCES

African Commission on Human and Peoples' Rights. 2012. *Report of the African Commission's Working Group of Experts on Indigenous*. African Union: Copenhagen and Banjul.

Alan, R. Emery, and Associates. 1997. *Guidelines for Environmental Assessments with Indigenous People: A Report from the Centre for Traditional Knowledge*

World Council of Indigenous People. Ottawa: Centre for Traditional Knowledge of the World Council of Indigenous People.

Bell, Christine. 2014. "Dealing with the Past in Northern Ireland." *Fordham International Law Journal* 26 (1095): 1095–2003. doi: 10.1525/sp.2007.54.1.23.

Benyera, Everisto. 2014a. *Debating the Efficacy of Transitional Justice Mechanisms: The Case of National Healing in Zimbabwe, 1980–2011*. Unpublished PhD Thesis, Pretoria: The University of South Africa.

Benyera, Everisto. 2014b. "Exploring Zimbabwe's Traditional Transitional Justice Mechanisms." *Journal of Social Science* 41 (3): 335–44.

Benyera, Everisto. 2014c. "The Contribution of Mass Graves to Healing and Closure: The Case of Chibondo in Mt Darwin, Zimbabwe." *International Journal of Humanities and Social Sciences* 4 (1): 2250–3226.

Benyera, Everisto. 2015. "Rebuking Impunity through Music: The Case of Thomas Mapfumo's Masoja Nemapurisa." *Journal of Communication* 6 (2): 260–69.

Benyera, Everisto. 2016. "On the Question of the Transition: Was Zimbabwe a Transitional State Between 2008 and 2013?" *Journal of Human Ecology* 55 (3): 160–72.

Benyera, Everisto. 2017. "Joshua Nkomo on Transitional Justice in Zimbabwe." In *Joshua Mqabuko Nkomo of Zimbabwe*, edited by S Ndovu-Gatsheni, 279–95. Cham: Palgrave-Macmillan. https://link.springer.com/chapter/10.1007/978-3-319-60555-5_12.

Benyera, Everisto. 2018. "Is the International Criminal Court Unfairly Targeting Africa? Lessons for Latin America and the Caribbean States." *Politeia* 37 (1): 1–30. doi: 10.25159/0256-8845/2403ISSN.

Benyera, Everisto, Oliver Mtapuri, and Artwell Nhemachena. 2018. "The Man, Human Rights, Transitional Justice and African Jurisprudence in the Twenty-First Century." In *Social and Legal Theory in the Age of Decoloniality: (Re-)Envisioning African Jurisprudence in the 21st Century*, edited by A. Nhemachena, T.V. Warikandwa, and S.K. Amoo, 187–218. Bamenda, Cameroon: Langaa.

Boraine, Alexander. 2006. "Transitional Justice: A Holistic Interpretation." *Journal of International Affairs* 60 (1): 17–27.

Chitsike, Kudakwashe. 2012. *Transitional Justice Options for Zimbabwe: A Guide to Key Concepts*. Cape Town: Institute of Justice and Reconciliation.

Crocker, David A. 1999. "Reckoning with Past Wrongs: A Normative Framework." *Ethics & International Affairs* 13 (1): 43–64. doi: 10.1111/j.1747-7093.1999.tb00326.x.

Dancy, Geoff, and Eric Wiebelhaus-Brahm. 2015. "Timing, Sequencing, and Transitional Justice Impact: A Qualitative Comparative Analysis of Latin America." *Human Rights Review* 16 (4): 321–42. doi: 10.1007/s12142-015-0374-2.

de Grieff, Pablo, and Roger Duthiee. 2009. *Transitional Justice and Development: Making Connections. Advanced Materials Research*. New York: Social Science Research Council. doi: 10.4028/www.scientific.net/AMR.816-817.124.

Dixon, Peter J. 2017. "Transitional Justice and Development." In *Research Handbook on Transitional Justice*, edited by D. Lawther, C., Moffett, L., and Jacobs, Research H, 159–82. Cheltenham, UK and Northampton, MA: Edward Elgar Publishing.

du Plessis, Max. 2010. *Truth and Reconciliation: Lessons for Zimbabwe?* Johannesburg: South African Institute of International Affairs.

Emmanuel, Kisiangani. 2007. *Between Principle and Pragmatism in Transitional Justice South Africa's TRC and Peace Building*. Pretoria: Institute for Security Studies.

Fischer, Martina. 2011. "Transitional Justice and Reconciliation: Theory and Practice." In *Advancing Conflict Transformation. The Berghof Handbook II*, edited by Beatrix Austin, Martina Fischer and Hans. J. Giessmann, 405–430. Opladen/Farmington Hills: Barbara Budrich.

Hayner, Priscilla. 1996. "Commissioning the Questions Truth : Further Research Questions." *Third World Quarterly* 17 (1): 19–29. doi: 10.1080/01436599650035752.

Hayner, Priscilla B. 1994. "Fifteen Truth Commissions – 1974 to 1994: A Comparative Study." *Human Rights Quarterly* 16 (4): 597–655. doi: 10.2307/762562.

Hellsten, Sirkku K. 2012. "Transitional Justice and Aid." *UNU-Wider*, 1–25. www.wider.unu.edu/publication/transitional-justice-and-aid.

Herencia Carrasco, Salvador. 2010. "Implementation of War Crimes in Latin America: An Assessment of the Impact of the Rome Statute of the International Criminal Court." *International Criminal Law Review* 10 (4): 461–73. doi: 10.1163/157181210X518929.

Hutchinson, Allan C. 2011. *Is Eating People Wrong? Great Legal Cases and How They Shaped the World*. Cambridge: Cambridge University Press.

Huyse, Luc. 2008. *Tradition-Based Justice and Reconciliation After Violent Conflict: Learning From African Experiences*. Bruseels: IDEA. http://174.129.218.71/resources/analysis/upload/paper_060208_bis.pdf.

Igreja, Victor. 2007. *The Monkeys' Sworn Oath Cultures of Engagement for Reconciliation and Healing in the Aftermath of the Civil War in Mozambique*. Unpubished PhD Thesis. Leiden University Medical Center, Faculty of Medicine, and Research School CNWS, School of Asian, African, and Amerindian Studies, Leiden University. Leiden: Leiden University.

Igreja, Victor, Béatrice Dais-Lambranca, and Annemiek Richters. 2008. "Gamba Spirits, Gender Relations and Healing on Post-Civil War Gorongosa, Mozambique." *Journal of Royal Antropological Institute* 14: 350–71.

Iliff, Andrew R. 2012. "Root and Branch: Discourses of 'Tradition' in Grassroots Transitional Justice." *International Journal of Transitional Justice* 6 (2): 253–73. doi: 10.1093/ijtj/ijs001.

Loyle, Cyanne E., and Christian Davenport. 2016. "Transitional Injustice: Subverting Justice in Transition and Postconflict Societies." *Journal of Human Rights* 15 (1): 126–49. doi: 10.1080/14754835.2015.1052897.

Mac Ginty, Roger. 2011. *International Peacebuilding and Local Resistance: Hybrid Forms of Peace*. Edited by Oliver P. Richmond. New York: Palgrave Macmillan.

Machakanja, Pamela. 2010. "National Healing and Reconciliation in Zimbabwe : Challenges and Opportunities." *Leadership* 1–16.

Madlingozi, Tshepo. 2010. "On Transitional Justice Entrepreneurs and the Production of Victims." *Journal of Human Rights Practice* 2 (2): 208–28.

Madlingozi, Tshepo. 2015. "Transitional Justice as Epistemicide: On Steve Biko's Pluralist Coexistence 'After' Conflict." In *WiSER Seminar, Wits University, Johannesburg, 27 July 2015*, 1–28. Johannesburg: Unpublished.

Marongwe, Ngonidzashe. 2012. *Rural Women as the Invisible Victims of Militarised Political Violence: The Case of Shurugwi District, Zimbabwe 2000–2008*. Cape Town: Universty of the Western Cape.

Mihr, Anja. 2017. "An Introduction to Transistional Justice." In *An Introduction to Transitional Justice*, edited by Olivera Simic, 1–27. London and New York: Routledge.

Minow, Martha. 1998. *Between Vengeance and Forgiveness. Facing History after Genocide and Mass Violence*. Boston: Beacon Pre. Boston.

Mugabe, John. 1998. "Intellectual Property Protection and Traditional Knowledge: An Exploration in International Policy Discourse." In *Intellectual Property and Human Rights*, 97–122. Geneva: World Intellectual Property Organisation.

Mutua, Makau. 2015. "What Is the Future of Transitional Justice?" *International Journal of Transitional Justice* 9 (1): 1–9. doi: 10.1093/ijtj/iju032.

Muvingi, Ismael. 2016. "Donor-Driven Transitional Justice and Peacebuilding." *Journal of Peacebuilding & Development* 11 (1): 10–25. doi: 10.1080/15423166.2016.1146566.

Muwati, Itai, Zifikile Gambahaya, and Fainos Mangena. 2006. "Echoing Silences as a Paradigm for Restorative Justice in Post-Conflict Zimbabwe: A Philosophical Discourse." *Zambezia* 33 (1/2): 1–18.

Ndlovu-Gatsheni, Sabelo, and Everisto Benyera. 2015. "Towards a Framework for Resolving the Justice and Reconciliation Question in Zimbabwe." *African Journal of Conflict Resolution* 15 (2): 9–33.

Nettheim, Garth. 1993. "'The Consent of the Natives': Mabo and Indigenous Political Rights." *Sydney Law Review* 15: 223–46.

Quinn, Joanna R. 2007a. "Social Reconstruction in Uganda: The Role of Customary Mechanisms in Transitional Justice." *Human Rights Review* 8 (4): 389–407. doi: 10.1007/s12142-007-0020-8.

Quinn, Joanna R. 2007b. "Chicken and Egg? Sequencing in Transitional Justice: The Case of Uganda." *Conference Papers – International Studies Association* 14 (2): 1–23. http://ezproxy.net.ucf.edu/login?url=http://search.ebscohost.com/login.aspx?direct=true&db=aph&AN=26958003&site=ehost-live.

Selim, Yvette, and Tim Murithi. 2011. "Transitional Justice and Development: Partners for Sustainable Peace in Africa?" *Journal of Peacebuilding & Development* 6 (September 2014): 58–72. doi: 10.1080/15423166.2011.141478175834.

Szablewska, Natalia. 2015. *Current Issues in Transitional Justice: Towards a More Holistic Approach*. Edited by Natalia Szablewska, and Sascha-Dominik Bachmann. Cham, Heidelberg, New York, Dordrecht and London: Springer.

Teitel, Ruti. 2001. "Transitional Justice." *The American Journal of Comparative Law* 49: 363. doi: 10.2307/840816.

Teitel, Ruti G. 2003. "Transitional Justice Genealogy." *Harvard Human Rights Journal* 16 (69): 69–94. doi: 10.1021/ja051223y.

Teitel, Ruti G. 2015. *Globalizing Transitional Justice*. Oxford and New York: Oxford University Press.

United Nations Secretary General. 2010. *Guidance Note of the Secretary-General: United Nations Approach to Transitional Justice*. New York: United Nations.

Whiteman, Gail, and William H. Cooper. 2000. "Ecological Embeddedness." *Academy of Management Journal* 43 (6): 1265–82.

Wolfe, Stephanie. 2015. "The Politics of Reperations and Apologies: Historical and Symbolic Justice within the Rwandan Context." In *The Performance of Memory as Transitional Justice*, edited by Elizabeth S. Bird, and Fraser M. Ottanelli, Series on, 43–57. Cambridge, Antwerp and Portland: Intersentia.

Chapter 4

Construing Transitology in the Context(s) of Democratization, Transitional Justice, and Decolonization in Africa

A Legal Anthropology Perspective

Tapiwa Victor Warikandwa and
Artwell Nhemachena

INTRODUCTION

Transitology is generally accepted as referring to the study of changes from one political regime to another (Hermet 2000; Dobry 2000); primarily from authoritarian or uncivilized regimes to "democratic" ones (Israel and Mouralis 2014). Transitology therefore presupposes that from the post–World War I and II eras, there have been substantive efforts made toward addressing injustices perpetrated against innocent people through transitional justice (Grosescu 2015, 103). Emphasis in this regard was placed on the use of legal mechanisms to redress past abuses and/or injustices with a view to, "entrenching democratic stability and the rule of law" (Teitel 2000, 3). At the center of the transitional justice movement were the efforts of Eastern and Southern Europe as well as Latin America transitologists who sought to address the relationship between democratization and human rights accountability by governments (Linz 1978; Schmitter 1986; Huntington 1991). Transitional justice therefore accommodates different disciplines such as political sciences, history, law, psychology, sociology, and anthropology.

Issues of the relationship between concepts such as the rule of law, justice, and democratization have become fundamental concepts of transitional justice. It is in this regard that matters of decolonization become fundamental to the narrative of transitology and transitional justice. This view is informed by the fact that, to date, attempts and related processes aimed at addressing colonially induced past and present injustices, specifically in Africa, have largely been construed from the context of their measured impact on democratic consolidation (Kritz 1995; McAdams, 1977; Barahona de Brito et al. 2001; Olsen et al. 2010; Sikkink 2011). Theories of democratic transition and research related to efforts aimed at addressing historical injustices have often been sponsored by governments, in particular the United States of America, and international organizations such as the European Union, World Bank and the United Nations (Grosescu 2015, 103). These governments and international organizations have sought to develop the best practices and/or solutions for transitional justice, "in accordance with the political constraints of transition" (Kritz 2008, 1). It must be questioned as to how governments and international organizations which have presided over and have been complicit in or specifically responsible for human atrocities in Africa can be entrusted with the key responsibility of formulating principles of transitional justice and resultantly transitology itself, unless if the agenda is to inflict more pain of the victims of past injustices (Warikandwa et al. 2017).

This chapter therefore interrogates and/or questions the significance of transitology in developing fair and just transitional justice rules that can address colonial injustices in Africa. An analysis of methodological and theoretical methods that have been relied upon by transitologists and transitional justice scholars will be undertaken. Using a legal anthropology perspective, it will be pointed out that transitology has significant limitations which render it unsuitable to develop transitional justice rules in a decolonizing Africa. This is attributed to the fact that, whilst Western political control has on paper given way to African countries' self-governance, the legacy of Western domination in the political, cultural, and economic realms of African societies still remains. Transitology and transitional justice have supposedly provided short lived moments of false promises and inspiration in African societies, yet they have dismally failed to transform African political structures and economies to bring about real autonomy and sustainable socioeconomic development. Most African countries are still victims of the neoliberal economic order which inhumanely perpetuates colonial injustices and the impoverishment of Africans and evisceration of their moral values. Colonial injustices are still perpetuated regardless of the many toothless truth and reconciliation commissions ushered in supposedly as tools for realizing democratic transitions in Africa.

TRANSITOLOGY, LEGAL ANTHROPOLOGY, AND TRANSITIONAL JUSTICE: AN OVERVIEW

Transitology is generally accepted as the process through which "democratization" can be realized in varying contexts in specific societies (Rousso 2002;

Lebow et al. 2006), and is considered as a departure from authoritarianism and dictatorial tendencies which were synonymous with nature of political control exercised by colonial regimes on Africa. Such forms of dictatorship and authoritarianism were also common in post-communist Eastern Europe, Latin America, and Southern Europe (Gans-Morse 2004). As such, transitology has become a polarized debate in both political and scholarly spheres owing largely to the inexcusable generalization and overreliance on a Eurocentric narrative of transitology (Anders 2007). Such an approach negates the role of African history in informing policy makers on how to formulate an appropriate and/or acceptable formula as well as testable hypothesis for realizing transitional justice on the continent. As such, for plausible formulas for transitology and transitional justice to be realized, one would assume that anthropology and the law would have to be fused to remedy past injustices to indigenous Africans inflicted upon them by colonialists. Anthropologists have often studied and drawn justifiable conclusions on how the law can be used to reshape significant questions of justice. Anthropology of law therefore addresses fundamental ethical issues in the contemporary world in so far as past injustices are concerned. Sadly, the approach implicit in the anthropology of law has often been frustrated by international law and transitional justice (Goodale 2017).

The central claims of the law, its processes, and practices are fundamental legal instruments for shaping society (Kelly 2016). To that end, legal anthropology can be used as a fundamental tool for establishing the relationship between aspects of cultural, social, political, and economic life (Kelly 2016). It is also used as an essential tool for ascertaining the meaning and significance of the implications of socio-legal concepts such as transitology and transitional justice in the African context. Anthropology could thus be regarded to be a product of legal concerns of scholars who sought to understand the complex but reasonable legal systems employed by other cultures other than those in the Western countries (Kelly 2016). It is thus not surprising that anthropologists study issues such as property, citizenship, and human rights and how such concepts have shaped significant questions of biotechnology, indigenization and citizenship, transitology and transitional justice, amongst other issues (Von Benda-Beckmann 2008; Von Benda-Beckmann 1979; Von Benda-Beckmann and Von Benda-Beckmann 1994; Von Benda-Beckmann 2007; Von Benda-Beckmann and Von Benda-Beckmann 2013). Anthropology and law therefore provide a comprehensive examination of the methods through which anthropologists interact with, critique and study law (Goodale 2017). Law and anthropology examine structures for governmental action, moral norms, and enforceable rules in any given society (Goodale 2017). Regrettably, the value of law and anthropology has been unjustly undermined by skeptical academics who do not consider it as a viable and separate discipline (Collier 1997, 117–130; Geertz 1983, 170; Nader 2002,

72). However, Franz von Benda-Beckman (2008, 85) pointed to the significance of law and anthropology when he observed that

> scholars and practitioners from a wide range of academic disciplines engage each other in debates about law as one aspect of social and cultural life. In doing so, they simultaneously seek to develop a common language whilst being inevitably shaped by their respective disciplinary and national background. This entails multiple processes of translation, a constant seesaw between disciplines and idioms, straddling reflexivity and normativity that is challenging but ultimately rewarding as it pushes the law as well as the manifold ways of studying it to the limit.

Franz von Benda-Beckman's observation has been given little or no regard in the contemporary African context. Focus is largely placed on transitology and transitional justice, with little or no attention being given to historical events informing past injustices in Africa. Legal anthropology places significance on how history must shape any supposed forms of transition or transitional justice frameworks as may be proposed and deemed acceptable in any society. On the contrary, processes of democratization which promote transitional justice ideologies advance the view that history can be ignored to allow for transition into a "peaceful future." Grosescu (2015, 103) observed that

> within the framework of democratic transition and consolidation, one important question was: how should societies deal with crimes committed by the previous dictatorial regimes in order to ensure justice and democratic stability? Two different answers divided both scholars and political elites. The first one held that retributive justice for past abuses might jeopardize the new democratic project, and that an amnesty might be a more appropriate policy for ensuring a peaceful transition from authoritarian rule. Conversely, the second one argued that the arraignment of former dictatorial leaders would strengthen the democratic values of human rights and the rule of law, being thus an essential part of the democratization process.

Huntington (1991, 211–231) contended that in order to avoid antagonizing the previous regime which violated people's fundamental rights, trials and purges must be avoided. As such, to allow for transition into a new political dispensation, governments must limit trials if doing so endangers democratic sociopolitical alliances. Such practices have characterized the transition of power in Africa from dominant colonial military regimes or governments to African indigenes. In such instances, power was conditionally transferred to the African indigenes in return for the colonial leaders' amnesty and retention of the spoils of colonialism. The general reasoning implicit in such negotiated political settlements, as advanced by some scholars is that transitions from colonialism to postcolonial dispensations would not require prosecutions which would ensure that those who committed crimes against humanity are brought to justice (Katsikas 2014, 259–287). Instead, in order to avoid instability caused by the unrelenting colonial power, amnesties or just ignoring the past colonial injustices and/or abuses are considered as plausible approaches to achieving peace and democracy (Snyder and Vinjamuri 2003–2004, 5–44). The moral worthiness and legal viability of the approach proposed by Snyder and Vinjamuri (2003–2004) is subject to debate. Warikandwa, Nhemachena, and Mtapuri (2017) problematize the notion of paying a blind eye to the past misdeeds of colonialists when they continue to benefit at the expense of the victims. In return, and in a manner that is devoid of Ubuntu, the colonialists consistently expect African indigenes to turn a blind eye to their immoral theft of African materialities and the subsequent violation of African indigenes' human rights (Nhemachena, Warikandwa and Nauta 2017; Nhemachena and Warikandwa 2017). In fact, the descendants of colonialists have merely changed the nature of their stranglehold on Africa from a physically violent dispensation to a subtle and structurally violent economic order underlined by a neoliberal economic order.

The neoliberal economic order continues to impoverish African indigenes and regards them as lesser beings not fit to inherit their entitlements. What manner of transition is this? What transitional justice is there to talk about? Whose transitional justice is it anyway? The colonialists who have transitioned to capitalists now call for the need to recognize a contemporary democratic project which is supposedly underlined by the rule of law and letting bygones be bygones. According to this transitional justice perspective, "states should thus not focus on backward-looking measures, but on forward-looking goals such as the establishment of a constitutional regime, and institutional and economic reform" (Ackermann 1992). Such an approach is consistent with the act of a thief who steals and does not return what he/she unlawfully obtained subsequently crafted a law to protect such illegal ownership of property. Is this what transitional justice implies? Morality dictates that returning what you unjustly assumed ownership over is a plausible concept of transition into the future. Sustained theft and dispossession property without returning the same to the victims cannot be qualified as quantifying legitimate transitional justice. It cannot be justice to turn a blind eye to colonial injustices and the gross violation of human rights which were associated with the processes of colonization (Warikandwa and Nhemachena 2017).

In order to promote African peoples' confidence in the contemporary rule of law ideology, there is need to uphold principles of justice and undermine the culture of Western impunity in matters related to colonial violence and contemporary structural socioeconomic violence. Disregarding the need to address colonial injustices will buttress the notion of a Western elitist agenda that seeks to undermine African people to the extent of characterizing them as lesser legal subject. Grosescu (2015, 105) observed that

> theories of democratic transitions, and transitional justice studies inspired by them, adopt a short-term perspective on the post-dictatorial transformations. They do not take into account the fact that, *arrangements that seem to have positive effects in the first phase of transition may have negative consequences in the longer run.*

It is therefore evident that the relationship between democratization and justice, as inherited from transitology, is excessively inflexible to social phenomena. Instead of addressing social phenomena based on the instructive historical contexts, as is the case with Africa and its colonial past, transitology frequently seeks to justify the unjustifiable "proper solutions" advanced in attempts to address colonial injustices. Little emphasis is placed on providing legitimate, comprehensive and historically informed solutions to colonial injustices in Africa. Such an approach is informed by the Western-oriented tendencies to, "dehistoricize social facts and to ignore the influence of long-term historical processes" (Grosescu 2015, 105). The downside of this approach is that problems emanating from historical injustices are not addressed in the name of transitology and "transitional justice." The net result of this ill-informed approach is that society rejects such illegitimate and immoral settlement which then leads to social upheavals. Classic examples of social upheavals being prompted by the so-called democratic transition in society are the land reclamation initiatives that took place in Zimbabwe (*Campbell and Another v Republic of Zimbabwe* (SADC (T) 03/2009) [2009] SADCT 1 (5 June 2009); *Von Abo v President of the Republic of South Africa* (CCT 67/08) [2009] ZACC 15; 2009 (10) BCLR 1052 (CC); 2009 (5) SA 345 (CC) (5 June 2009); Human Rights Watch 2002, 1–44)) and the recent march toward expropriation of land without compensation in South Africa (Walther 2017; Hall 2018). History will point out that white farmers held over eighty (80) percent of all prime farmland in both Zimbabwe and South Africa. The remaining, often barren and unproductive land was then shared amongst the natives. The processes of transitional justice seem to ignore the fact that this pattern of property ownership deprived the rightful owners of what was legally theirs. In total contempt of the rights of the natives, the willing-seller-willing-buyer principle has been employed as a mechanism for facilitating the return of the land violently grabbed from African indigenes. Such an approach puts an unjust burden on the victims to buy back what was unjustly stolen from them. What is the justice in compensating the perpetrators violent land theft from Africans and their successors in title for a heinous crime they are yet to account for?

Should those that unduly enrich themselves be rewarded? Where is the rule of law in such practices? It is therefore evident that the concept of transitional justice as informed by transitology is greatly flawed, if applied in the African context.

DEMOCRATIZATION AND TRANSITIONAL JUSTICE IN AFRICA

Democratization is a highly debatable concept within the African context (Larok 2011). The debates against democratization in Africa emanate from plausible concerns relating to the imposing of Western value systems on Africa. Evidently, democracy should be defined by the societal context within which it is applied. Democracy should be understood as a way of life informed by the cultural values, norms and creeds of a specific grouping of people. It should not be defined by processes of acculturation in which norms and values of an alien society are superimposed on a grouping of people that are regarded as being "inferior" to such supposedly superior alien societies. It must therefore be accepted that different societies in the world have varying cultures, norms and creeds which translate to unique ways of life. It is therefore trite to conclude that Africa, based on its unique history, beliefs, and cultural practices, should shape its way of life and democratization concept underlined by an Ubuntu philosophy. Africa must be allowed to develop its unique sense of democracy as informed by its historical context, socioeconomic arrangements, and distinguished cultural conditioning.

The notion that Western forms of democracy, as developed in ancient Greece ought to be the hallmark of democracy in Africa, must be dismissed with the contempt it deserves. Often, comparative law has been used as an instrument of lawfare to manipulate African societies to conform to the hypothetically "civilized" Western laws and reject their customary norms and practices. Such dangerous forms of acculturation of Africans to destructive western value systems characterize the concept of transitional justice on the African continent. Transitional justice, as an academic discipline, is largely informed by theories of democratic transition (Grosescu 2015, 105). At the center of the transitional justice concept is the western countries' "vision of the rule of law . . . by a teleological perspective on transitions supposedly bound for democracy" (Grosescu 2015, 105). From the context of liberal Western democracies, human rights law is thus used (and not the African principle of Ubuntu) to address past injustices in societies.

International conventions on crimes against humanity, war crimes, and genocides have been crafted by the United Nations (UN) to facilitate the prosecution of any parties that commit the aforementioned infringements on human rights (see, for example, the UN Convention for the Prevention and Punishment of the Crime of Genocide of 1948; the International Covenant of Economic, Social and Cultural Rights of 1967; UN Convention on War Crimes and Crimes against Humanity of 1968; UN Convention on the Suppression and Punishment of the Crime of Apartheid; UN General Assembly, Rome Statute of the International Criminal Court, July 17, 1998 (last amended 2010)). Interestingly such international conventions, in particular the Rome Statute, have been selectively applied against African countries' leaders which gives the impression that Westerners are biased against African governments (Warikandwa 2017, 91). Such developments fuel arguments to the effect that transitional justice is a Western concept that is being employed to circumvent the accountability of Western countries for crimes against humanity and past colonial injustices.

DEMOCRACY AS A SYMBOL FOR NEOLIBERALISM DRIVEN EXPLOITATION IN AFRICA

Democracy or neoliberal democracy was employed in Europe to fight against absolute rule of monarchs (Larok 2011, 3). The same autocratic monarchs orchestrated the scramble for and colonization of Africa and championed the theft of African materialities (Nhemachena, Warikandwa, and Nauta 2017). Neoliberal democracy was advanced during the period of transition from feudalism to capitalism (Larok 2011, 3). It is pertinent to point out that democracy was perfected during the era of industrialization in Western countries. Such era was characterized by the exploitation and theft of natural resources from Africa by the west, slave trade, and land grabs in Africa (Warikandwa, Nhemachena and Mtapuri 2017). Such neoliberal democracy resultantly spread all over the world through Western expansionist policies such as colonization and investment activities informed by free market policies (Nhemachena and Warikandwa 2017). Such free market "investment" policies have often given little or no regard to human rights in Africa, with emphasis by the "investors" being placed on profiteering (Warikandwa and Osode 2016, 102; Chidede and Warikandwa 2017; Warikandwa and Osode 2017; Warikandwa and Osode, *Law, Democracy and Development* 2014; Warikandwa and Osode, *Speculum Juris* 2014; Warikandwa and Osode, *Comparative and International Law Journal of Southern Africa* 2014). The liberal business activities which have led to the impoverishing of past and present African societies are supposedly driven by "democratic" principles. It is therefore not out of place to conclude that liberal democracy-capitalism and resultantly democracy itself are questionable Western practices which have no place in Africa.

For example, as a key feature of democracy, leaders must be appointed subject to free and fair elections being conducted. As such, no leader can rule a country without being given the mandate and/or authority to rule or act in trust of the public. However, Africa has hardly experienced free and fair elections (Abuya 2010; Lepapa 2017). In most instances, elections are rigged in favor of presidential candidates who will assist western countries exploit a specific African country with relative ease. Legitimate transitions of power are also fraught with challenges. Recently, Mr. Emmerson Mnangagwa rose to power in Zimbabwe through a coup which deposed Mr. Robert Mugabe from being the country's constitutionally elected president (Palin 2017). Regardless of the African Union's stance against illegal power grabs, the world did not intervene in order to address the illegal power grab by Mr. Mnangagwa with the unconstitutional assistance of the Zimbabwe National Defense Forces. When the military interferes with constitutional democratic processes, one cannot consider the resultant government legitimate. However, due to the fact that the western countries and Asia were not comfortable with Mr. Robert Mugabe's plausible yet robust indigenization program which interfered with the Western and Chinese business interests in Zimbabwe (Chidede and Warikandwa 2017; Warikandwa and Osode 2017), the "smart" yet evidently dirty and immoral coup was sanctioned as a legitimate transition of power. The transition of power was thus justified on the basis that Mr. Robert Mugabe had caused untold suffering to Zimbabweans yet the same people who took over from him were the architects of such suffering. To be accepted by the Western countries, Mr. Mnangagwa has undertaken to undo all Mr. Robert Mugabe's indigenization policies in order to attract foreign "investment" in Zimbabwe. As such, a power transition in Africa is only illegal if it does not serve the best interests of the western countries and China.

Democracy also promotes the doctrine of individual choice through a secret ballot. Larok (2011, 4) points out that

> the assumption here is that with some conditioning, the individual voter has the level of consciousness to decide for society, sometimes even without any consensus on what societal needs are. This tyranny is probably the most un-transparent manner in which societal needs can be responded to, devalue debates, surrenders rights and enslaves minds.

Africa does not place emphasis on individual interests but the best interest of the collective grouping of people. It is Western countries which have the tendency to focus on individual interests at the expense of the [African] masses. This serves as reason why the West and China sanctioned the illegal military coup orchestrated by Mr. Mnangagwa in his quest to settle personal differences with Mr. Robert Mugabe who had relieved the former of his duties as the Deputy President of Zimbabwe for plotting to oust the later from power. Mr. Robert Mugabe's decision to fire Mr. Mnangagwa was meritorious as the later did topple the former, as stated in the grounds for his dismissal. It is therefore dangerous to presuppose that an individual can make informed decisions in the best interests of the society. Furthermore, it is not surprising that the ruling party ZANU-PF's primary elections in preparation for the 2018 presidential elections have been marred with controversy and irregularities (Koni 2018). ZANU-PF leaders (who were part of the coup orchestrated by Mr. Mnangagwa and the military) who lost primary elections (Zhangaza, Ndebele and Sibanda 2018; Admin 2018), were clandestinely afforded a re-run in order to enable them to win such elections thereof (Staff Reporter 2018; Gondo 2018). It must be questioned as to how free and fair elections will be conducted under the leadership of the illegal power grab merchants in Zimbabwe. It is evident that Western democracy in Africa creates a good foundation for anarchy which allows the former colonialists to pillage natural resources from Africa. They are evidently not keen on a government that focuses on ensuring that African indigenes benefit from the exploitation of their natural resources (Nhemachena and Warikandwa 2017). This serves as reason why there is a smear campaign against the opposition leader Mr. Nelson Chamisa regarding his remarks which suggested that he was going to review all "investment" agreements the Mnangagwa illegal government entered into with China. How can an African leader be vilified for trying to ensure that African indigenes benefit from the exploitation of their natural resources? What manner of democracy is this? Africa certainly is suffering from a political and legal disease caused by an overdose of toxic Western democracy-capitalism which places emphasis on the self and not the collective.

Another democratization narrative is that multi-partyism in Africa signifies the existence of alternative political ideologies and programs which lead to societal well-being (Larok 2011, 4). In traditional African societies, there was no multi-partyism as people were led by kings through a system of kingships. However, this system of kings was deconstructed by colonial powers as part of their divide and rule strategies in Africa. The traditional African society was characterized by unity under one leader and cooperation. The flawed concept of democratization erroneously places emphasis on unnecessary differences and celebrates selfish and counterproductive competitive behavior over cooperation. The net result of the supposed democracy in Africa is that there is an upsurge of elite rule and tyranny over the majority. As such, state capture is on the rise. Africa has more captured leaders who represent Western interests than the best interests of the African indigenes. The cases of Jacob Zuma in South Africa and lately Emmerson Mnangagwa in Zimbabwe are prime examples. Africa does not need uncle Toms but visionary leaders who grow economies on the basis of home-grown solutions underlined by principles of Ubuntu. Democratization does not suit African realities as is the case with transitional justice.

DEMOCRATIZATION: A WESTERN PRINCIPLE IMPOSED ON AFRICA TO DISEMPOWER IT

Democracy in Africa has often been connected to free market policies which are implemented in Africa to impoverish the African indigenes in the guise of foreign investment. Claude Ake (1994; 1996) accused Western countries of working toward globalizing Africa's political culture and market ideology as part of global homogenization. This serves as reason why Julius Nyerere's African socialism was fiercely resisted by the west and dismissed as being archaic, barbarous and anti-developmental (Larok 2011, 5). Any narrative, advanced by African leaders, which was and is contrary to the ideology of liberal democracy has led to such leaders being taken out of power in rancorous manner. This serves as reason why Pan-African-oriented leaders such as Patrice Lumumba of Zaire (now the Democratic Republic of Congo) and Thomas Sankara of Burkina Faso were savagely assassinated by Western imperialist forces working in collusion with African sell-outs. African scholars have constantly argued that liberal democracy is not ideal for Africa's realities. For example, Nyamnjoh (2005, 25) has argued that liberal democracy has a hyperbolic emphasis on the self-determining individual, a development which is not realistic in Africa which has an overriding collective spiritual ideology. Nyamnjoh pointed out that

> implementing liberal democracy in Africa has been like trying to force onto a body of a fully figured person, rich in cultural indicators of health with which Africans are familiar, a dress made to fit a slim, de-fleshed Hollywood consumer model of a Barbie-doll entertainment icon ... then when the dress fails to fit the African body, instead of blaming the tiny dress or its designer, the tradition has been to fault the popular body for emphasizing too much bulk, for parading the wrong sizes, for just not being the right thing. Not often is the experience of the designer or dress maker questioned. Such high levels of insensitivity are akin to the behavior of a Lilliputian undertaker who would rather trim a corpse than expand a coffin to accommodate a man-mountain or a carpenter whose only tool is a hammer and to whom every problem is a nail.

The sentiments of Nyamnjoh are echoed by Claude Ake (1996) who observed that

> the political arrangement of liberal democracy makes little sense in Africa. Liberal democracy assures individualism but there is little individualism in

Africa ... it assumes abstract universalism, but in Africa that would apply only to the urban environment, and finally political parties of liberal democracy do not make sense in societies where associational life is rudimentary and interest groups are essentially primary groups.

It is thus evident that the African system of democracy does not rest on the assumption of individualism or conflict of interest but on the collective approach to democracy, a development which underlines the social nature of human beings and Ubuntu (Ake 1994). Africa thus has its own functional narrative of democracy which regrettably is being unjustifiably undermined by western notions of democracy. The net result of this approach is that Africa is being disenfranchised and impoverished due to the continued loss of identity and materialities at the behest of Western ideologies (Rodney 1972; Kah 1992; Tandon 2015). The more Africa continues to embrace Western norms and practices for socioeconomic purposes the weaker its institutions will continue to be and the more its citizens will continue to be impoverished. African leaders and academic scholars must endeavor to develop a new narrative toward African democratization and growth initiatives. Sadly, there is hardly any indication to this effect as more African leaders continue to be used as puppets of the West in return for their stranglehold on power. This explains why incidences of State Capture are on the rise in Africa.

TRANSITIONAL JUSTICE AND DECOLONIZATION: A TALE OF TWO UNLIKE POLES WHICH DO NOT ATTRACT

Discourses on transitional justice have often paid fairly little attention to the effect of history on transitology in Africa. However, it is evident that "historical approaches to memory and transitional justice illustrate the fact that the past can continue to 'irrupt' in the present" (Rousso 2002). It is therefore imperative that any forms or narratives of transitional justice in Africa must be connected to the continent's historical context and not aim at downplaying the atrocities of the past in pursuit of a fallacious reconciliation and transition. Wouters (2014, 408) points out the dangers of attempting to pacify history and its substantive developments when he observed that

> even in societies that have a strong national consensual regime, memory incidents stay present right under the surface . . . . Alternative memories were never buried or forgotten but simply dominant or invisible (meaning not easily perceivable).

Wouters' views are augmented by Bevernage (2008, 166) who plausibly observed that " the past continues to disrupt the present, simply because historical processes resist 'being frozen' and always contain 'delays, survivals, and unfinished projects.'" Therefore, even if the concerns of realizing justice based on the historical narratives are often erroneously substituted by western driven sociopolitical agendas, in Africa, claims for accountability for past injustices will not simply vanish. The passage of time does not translate to the eradication of Africans' bitterness over colonial injustices. Transitional justice in Africa should thus not place emphasis on the so-called "negotiated settlements" that disregard pertinent issues of restoration for the theft of African materialities by colonialists.

It is surprising that the contemporary constitutional dispensations in Africa sanctions property rights regimes across the continent which retain rights of land and mineral ownership in the hands of colonialists and their successors in title (Warikandwa, Nhemachena, and Mtapuri 2017; Nhemachena and Warikandwa). Such an approach, in the name of realizing a "peaceful" transition into the postcolonial dispensation, turns a blind eye to the present truths concerning the suffering of African indigenes owing to the legacy of colonialism. The legacy of colonialism remains embedded in the national borders, trade networks, educational systems, and economies of an underdeveloped African continent (Warikandwa, Nhemachena and Mtapuri 2017). The current regrettable status quo in Africa was facilitated by the so-called transition arrangements for a postcolonial Africa. No justice has been realized for the ordinary African indigenes. This unjust development in which the colonialists and their successors in title continue to benefit from an unjust enrichment facilitated by colonialism has led to calls for decolonization in Africa. What this implies is that transitional justice ideologies have failed Africa as there has been no marked improvement in their general welfare of ordinary African indigenes in the postcolonial era. Those that have realized an improvement in their standards of living are African politicians and the middle class who are often beneficiaries of the crumbs that fall from the table(s) of their colonial masters. Fanon (1964) observed that "every former colony has a particular way of achieving independence. Every new sovereign state finds itself practically under the obligation of maintaining definite and deferential relations with the former oppressor." Transitional justice has been used as a tool for maintaining the relations between former colonies and the colonizers. Decolonization thus seeks to unyoke Africa from the injustices of the past without paying a blind eye to the legacy of colonialism. Where transitional justice focuses on negotiated settlements that leave the colonialists and their successors in title benefiting from the unjust transitional arrangements, decolonization seeks to address the legal injustices through restoration. This serves as reason why the African National Congress–led South African government has adopted a policy of expropriation without compensation. Whilst the policy is regarded as a threat to economic stability in South Africa, it allows the victims of colonial injustices to get back what is rightfully theirs (the land and control of the economy). Transitional justice and decolonization are therefore not complimentary but competing interests. Africa needs to rethink the western concept of transitional justice as it has no room in Africa's Pan-African oriented developmental agenda.

TRANSITIONAL JUSTICE AS A SECULARIZATION IDEOLOGY

Transitology is premised on the problematic assumption that complete democracies can only be realized if countries adopt liberal policies which are secular (Pfeifer 2013, 6). Secularization is composed of different facets but can generally be condensed in the conceptualization that it is a component of modernization (Shah 2012, 3). Secularization dangerously assumes that Western-driven "economic development" would lead to the degeneration of individual religious and belief systems of communities a development which would lead to the weakening of cultural influences on the overall developmental agenda of a nation (Shah and Philpott 2011, 28). Casanova (2012, 25–26) posited that

> because in Europe the three processes of secular differentiation, religious decline, and privatization have been historically interconnected, the tendency has been to view all three processes as intrinsically interrelated components of a general teleological process of secularization and modernization, rather than as particular contingent developments.

The above view therefore implies that liberal theories regard modernization as a, "liner process in which liberal formations such as capitalism, secularization, and democracy all progress together" (Snyder 2011, 18). As such a monist view exists with regard to the paths to modernization. Secular modernization places emphasis on science and rationality as a basis for fueling a gradual decline of religious, cultural and moral values in order to give way to secular societies and polities (Hayes 2009, 293). It is this conceptualization of modernization that has led to transitional justice being used as a tool to usher in a new sociopolitical dispensation in which the Western countries do not account for their historical atrocities as they are "enablers" of modernization. Any attempts at realizing retributive justice are regarded as being premodern and therefore an anachronism to the modern state.

Rawls (1993) argued that all principles and theories of "the good" life belong to the private sphere whilst the political and public sphere must be guided by pure practical reason. The modern African society, due to the influence of Western ideologies of "the good" life is thus characterized by a plurality of beliefs by citizens as opposed to the collective beliefs that shaped their societies in precolonial Africa. The negative result of this approach is that African societies no longer share one collective view of what is good. As such, whilst restoration of African materialities is a good objective for the African society, westernized African minds consider such an approach as being anti-developmental. As such, that which is good for all Africans is now being rationalized away and regarded as not being good for the general populace or the public. Such a development signifies how transitional justice dovetails into the secularization ideology in order to advance the modernization agenda which will culminate in the realization of the new world order. The new world order places significance on the interests of a few global elites at the expense of the planetary majority. This serves as reason why true transitional justice has been undermined by a globalization agenda which does not consider retributive justice as a fundamental component of a capitalist society. As such, Africans who suffered at the hands of colonialists must just forget about what happened and focus on the future in the hope that they will have a better life in the future. Secularization does not promote justice in Africa but only serves as a mechanism to enlarge the western empire on the African continent.

LEGAL ANTHROPOLOGY: A TOOL FOR DEVELOPING A NEW NARRATIVE FOR JUSTICE IN AFRICA

True justice for victims of colonial injustices can no longer be realized in Africa through the use of western models of transitology such as transitional justice. Regardless of how the Western countries consider transitional justice as a tool for democratization, it must be accepted that African societies are victims of prolonged periods of conflict and colonially induced social, political, and economic injustices, for which a new narrative apart from transitional justice must be sought to address such injustices. Whilst transitional justice has been celebrated as a viable mechanism for addressing past injustices (Kent 2016), it has failed in the African context to achieve its set objectives. African indigenes are eager to realize the resolution of colonially induced injustices. This has led to the adoption of radical economic policies in Zimbabwe, Namibia and South Africa, in an attempt to address structural injustices prompted by the colonial regimes which were operating in different African countries. It is in this regard that we propose that African countries should now look beyond the concept of transitional justice to address colonial injustices and decolonize their institutions and cultures.

Legal anthropology offers a good platform for developing an ideal concept for addressing colonially induced injustices in Africa. A social-scientific study of law characterized by the convergence between law and anthropology (Von Benda-Beckmann 2008), will offer practical solutions to addressing past injustices as opposed to the artificial concept of transitional justice. Africa needs critical legal thinking that is shaped by the telling historical and contemporary influence of fields of social science such as anthropology (Nader 2002). The importance of a legal anthropology approach is that the legal solution adopted to address past injustices such as those inflicted by colonialism will be informed by the findings of humanities scholars who locate their work in practical national and international situations. As such, a critical analysis of the impact of colonial injustices in Africa will inform the ideological undergirding of the legal mechanism to be adopted to address the past injustices. One cannot prescribe Western solutions to African problems. The situation in western countries differs from that prevailing in Africa. As such, anthropology must inform the law as to what it has to address insofar as colonially induced injustices are concerned. The African narrative can no longer be informed by Western countries whose proposed solutions to the problems they caused in Africa do not provide lasting solutions but create more complex problems such as civil unrest on the continent. Restoration and retribution, which are also aspects of Ubuntu, must be strongly considered as dominant mechanism for realizing true transitional justice in Africa. Anything less is a facade and mere window-dressing that does not offer lasting solutions to impoverished and marginalized Africans who continue to be victims of a western driven brutal capitalist agenda.

CONCLUSION

Transitional justice is still being celebrated and promoted as a viable mechanism for addressing colonially induced injustices in Africa. However, as argued in this chapter, transitional justice is not a sufficient legal or quasi-legal mechanism for addressing the complex legacies of colonialism and postcolonial structural socioeconomic violence that is still being inflicted on the impoverished African indigenes. Due to the limited reference to the historical concepts informing Africa's current challenges as informed by colonial injustices, transitional justice is merely a tool of choice for use in prosecuting African leaders and other leaders from developing continents who fall short of western countries' expansionist agenda. Transitional justice has failed to address historical issues which perpetuate and/or exacerbate the underlying colonial and capitalist ideologies that promote structural violence in Africa and mask the ongoing structural violence on the continent which is a colonial legacy. There is need to critically reflect on transitology, democratization, and transitional justice as western concepts aimed at undermining Africans' attempts to redress past and present colonial injustices. Africa and its academic scholars need to decolonize its legal and social systems in order to develop viable and lasting solutions aimed at addressing the unending effects of the colonial legacy. Legal anthropology could be employed as a plausible mechanism for developing an alternative to the Western façade of transitology, democratization, and transitional justice. We hope that this chapter will promote or evoke critical debates and reflections on transitology and its application in the contexts of decolonization, democratization, and transitional justice in Africa.

BIBLIOGRAPHY

Abuya, Edwin Odhiambo. 2010. "Can African States Conduct Free and Fair Presidential Elections?" *North-western Journal of International Human Rights* 8 (2): 122–64.

Ackermann, Bronwen. 1992. *The Future of Liberal Revolution*. New Haven: Yale University Press.

Admin. 2018. "Mutsvangwa Loses Norton Primary Election." *My Harare Times*, 16 May 2018.

Anders, Aslund. 2007. *How Capitalism Was Built. The Transformation of Central and Eastern Europe, Russia, and Central Asia*. New York: Cambridge University Press.

Barahona de Brito, Alexandra, Gonzalez-Enriques Carmen, and Aguilar Paloma. (eds.). 2001. *The Politics of Memory: Transitional Justice in Democratizing Societies*. Oxford: Oxford University Press.

Bevernage, Berber. 2008. "Time, Presence, and Historical Injustice." *History and Theory* 47 (2): 149–67.

Campbell and Another v Republic of Zimbabwe. 2018. (SADC (T) 03/2009) [2009] SADCT 1 (5 June 2009).

Chidede, Talkmore, and Tapiwa.V. Warikandwa. 2017. "Foreign Direct Investment and Zimbabwe's Indigenisation and Economic Empowerment Act: Friends or Foes?" *Midlands State University Law Review* 3: 25–45.

Claude, Ake. 1994. *Democratization of Disempowerment in Africa, Centre for Advanced Social Science Occasional Monograph No. 1*. Lagos: Malthouse Press.

Claude, Ake. 1996. Is *Africa Democratising?* Centre for Advanced Social Science. Lagos: Malthouse Press.

Collier, Jane. F. 1997. "The Waxing and Waning of 'Subfields' in North American Sociocultural Anthropology." In *Anthropological Locations: Boundaries and Grounds of a Field Science*, edited by Akhil Gupta and James Ferguson, 117–30. Berkeley: University of California Press.

Dobry, Michel. 2000. "Les voies incertaines de la transitologie: Choix stratégiques, séquences historiques, bifurcations et processus de la Path Dependence." *Revue Française de Science Politique* 50 (4–5): 585–614.

Fanon, Frantz. 1964. *Toward the African Revolution*. New York: Grove Press.

Gans-Morse, Jordan. 2004. "Searching for Transitologists: Contemporary Theories of Post-Communist Transitions and the Myth of a Dominant Paradigm." *Post-Soviet Affairs* 20 (4): 320–49.

Geertz, Clifford. 1983. *Local Knowledge: Further Essays in Interpretive Anthropology*. New York: Basic Books.

Gondo, Talent. 2018. "Mutsvangwa suddenly Wins Norton Primaries." *ZimEye*, 13 May 2018.

Goodale, Mark. 2017. *Anthropology and Law: A Critical Introduction*. New York: New York Press.

Grosescu, Raluca. 2015. "The Use of Transitology in the Field of Transitional Justice: A Critique of the Literature on the 'Third Wave' of Democratization." *Historein* 15 (1): 103–15.

Hall, Ruth. 2018. "Land Expropriation without Compensation: What Does It Mean?" *News 24*, 4 March 2018.

Hayes, James. 2009. "Religion and Foreign Policy." In *The Routledge Handbook of Religion and Politics*, edited by James Haynes. New York: Routledge.

Hermet, Guy. 2000. "Le charme trompeur des théories: un état des travaux." In *Démocraties d'ailleurs. Démocraties et démocratisations hors de l'Occident*, edited by Christophe Jafferot. Paris: Karthala, pp 585–614.

Human Rights Watch. 2002. *Fast Track Land Reform in Zimbabwe* 14 (1A): 1–44. Available on: https://www.hrw.org/sites/default/files/reports/zimbabwe1003.pdf

Huntington, Samuel. P. 1991. *The Third Wave: Democratization in the Late Twenty Century*. Oklahoma: University of Oklahoma Press.

Israel, Liora, and Guillaume Mouralis. (eds.). 2014. *Dealing with Wars and Dictatorships: Legal Concepts and Categories in Action*. The Hague: Springer.

Kah, Gary. H. 1992. *En Route to Global Occupation*. Louisiana: Huntington House Publishers.

Katsikas, Stefanos. 2014. "Transitional Justice after the Collapse of Dictatorship in Greece (1974–2000)." In *Transitional Justice and Memory in Europe (1945–2013)*, edited by Nico Wouters. Cambridge: Intersentia, pp. 259–288.

Kelly, Tobias. 2016. "Political and Legal Anthropology." *PoLAR* 1: 47–73.

Kent, Lia. 2016. "Transitional Justice in Law, History and Anthropology." *Australian Feminist Law Journal* 42 (1): 1–11.

Koni, Leonard. 2018. "ZANU-PF Primaries Marred with Violence, Irregularities and Candidate Imposition." *News 24*, 1 May 2018.

Kritz, Neil. J. (ed.). 1995. *Transitional Justice: How Emerging Democracies Reckon with Former Regimes*. Washington, DC: United States Institute of Peace Press.

Larok, Arthur. 2011." Democratising or Africanising Democracy: Which way Africa?" *Reflections by Arthur Larok for a seminar on electoral Democracy by MS TCDC*, 11 January. Available on: www.actionaid.org/sites/files/actionaid/arthur_democratizingafricaoroafricanisingdemocracy.pdf

Lebow, Richard. N., Wulf Kansteiner, and Claudio Fogu (eds.). 2006. *The Politics of Memory in Postwar Europe*. London: Duke University Press.

Lepapa, Naipanoi. 2017. "Challenges to Holding Free and Fair Elections in Africa." *The African Exponent*, 28 April.

Linz, Juan. J. 1978. *Crisis, Breakdown and Re-Equilibration*. Baltimore: Johns Hopkins University Press.

McAdams, James. (ed.). 1997. *Transitional Justice and the Rule of Law in New Democracies*. Notre Dame: University of Notre Dame Press.

Nader, Laura. 2002. *The Life of the Law: Anthropological Projects*. Berkeley: University of California Press.

Nhemachena, Artwell, and Tapiwa.V. Warikandwa. (eds.). 2017. *Mining Africa: Law, Environment, Society and Politics in Historical and Multidisciplinary Perspectives*. Bameda: Langaa Research and Publishing Common Initiative Group.

Nhemachena Artwell, Tapiwa V Warikandwa and Asteria Nauta. 2017. "Materialities and Human Rights in Contemporary African Higher Education: The Case of the 'Fees Must Fall Movements" in Southern African Universities." In *Decolonization of Materialities or Materialisation of (Re-)Colonisation? Symbolisms, Languages, Ecocriticism and (Non)Representationalism in 21st Century Africa*, edited by Artwell Nhemachena, et al. Bameda: Langaa Research and Publishing Common Initiative Group, pp. 89–120.

Nyamnjoh, Francis. 2005. *Africa's media – Democracy and the Politics of Belonging*. London and New York: Zed Books.

Olsen, Tricia. D., Leigh. A. Payne, and Andrew. G. Wreiter. 2010. *Transitional Justice in Balance: Comparing Processes, Weighing Efficacy*. Washington, DC: United States Institute of Peace Press.

Palin, Michael. 2017. "'Gucci Grace': Zimbabwe's First Lady's Lavish Existence Polarises Country." Available at www.news.com.au/world/africa/gucci-grace-zimbabwes-first-ladys-lavish-existence-polarises-country/news-story/6988a9c455b98b15e86f070c4e4710ec.

Pfeifer, Hanna. 2013. "Transitology, Liberal Democracy and Religion: Democratization and the 'Arab Spring'." A paper presented at the ECPR Conference in Bordeaux, France on the 5th of August.

Rawls, John. 1993. *Political Liberalism*. New York: Columbia University Press.

Rodney, Walter. 1972. *How Europe underdeveloped Africa*. United Kingdom: Bogle-L'Ouverture.

Rousso, Henry. 2002. *The Haunting Past: History, Memory and Justice in Contemporary France*. Philadelphia: University of Pennsylvania Press.

Shah, Timothy. S. 2012. "Religion and World Affairs. Blurring the Boundaries." In *Rethinking Religion and World Affairs*, edited by Timothy. S. Shah, Alfred Stephan, and Monica. D. Toft. New York: Oxford University Press, pp. 24–59.

Sikkink, Kathryn. 2011. *The Justice Cascade: How Human Rights Prosecutions are Changing World Politics*. New York: WW Norton.

Snyder, Jack. 2011. "Introduction." In *Religion and International Relations Theory*, edited by Snyder, Jack. New York: Columbia University Press, pp. 1–22.

Snyder, Jack, and Leslie Vinjamuri. 2003–2004. "Trials and Errors: Principles and Pragmatism in Strategies of International Justice." *International Security* 28 (3): 5–44.

Staff Reporter. 2018. "Mnangagwa Saves Mutsvangwa as ZANU-PF Politburo Orders Re-run in Norton." *The Zimbabwe Mail*, 6 May 2018.

Tandon, Yash. 2015. *Trade is War: The West's War against the World.* New York: OR Books.

Teitel, R. G. 2000. *Transitional justice.* Oxford: Oxford University Press on Demand.

United States Institute of Peace. 2008. *Transitional Justice: Information Handbook.* Available at www.usip.org/sites/default/files/ROL/Transitional_justice_final.pdf.

Von Abo v President of the Republic of South Africa (CCT 67/08) [2009] ZACC 15; 2009 (10) BCLR 1052 (CC); 2009 (5) SA 345 (CC) (5 June 2009).

Von Benda-Beckmann, Franz. 1979. *Property in Social Continuity: Continuity and Change in the Maintenance of Property Relationships through Time in Minangkabau, West Sumatra.* The Hague: Martinus Nijhoff.

Von Benda-Beckmann, Franz. 2008. "Riding or Killing the Centaur? Reflections on the Identities of Legal Anthropology." *International Journal of Law in Context* 4 (2): 85–110.

Von Benda-Beckmann, Franz, and Keebet Von Benda-Beckmann. 1994. "Coping with Insecurity." *Focaal: Tijdschrift voor antropologie* 22 (23): 7–31.

Von Benda-Beckmann, Franz, and Keebet Von Benda-Beckmann. 2007. *Social Security Between Past and Future: Ambonese Networks of Care and Support.* Münster: LIT Verlag.

Von Benda-Beckmann, Franz, and Keebet Von Benda-Beckmann. 2013. *Political and Legal Transformations of an Indonesian Polity: The Nagari from Colonialism to Decentralisation.* Cambridge: Cambridge University Press.

Walther, Tessa. C., 2017. "Land Reform: Will Zimbabwe's Economic Downfall be Repeated in South Africa?" Available at www.dw.com/en/land-reform-will-zimbabwes-economic-downfall-be-repeated-in-south-africa/a-41972001.

Warikandwa, Tapiwa.V. 2017. "African States' Threats to Withdraw from the Rome Statute: A Legal Masterstroke or Poisoned Chalice?" *Namibian Law Journal* 9 (1): 91.

Warikandwa, Tapiwa V., and Artwell Nhemachena. 2017. Colonial Land Dispossession and Restorative Justice after Genocide: An appraisal of the Practicality of the Nama and Herero Reparation Claims." In *Transnational Land Grabs and Restitution in an Age of the (De-)Militarised New Scramble for Africa: A Pan African Socio-Legal Perspective*, edited by Tapiwa V. Warikandwa, Artwell Nhemachena and Oliver Mtapuri. Bameda: Langaa Research & Publishing Common Initiative Group, pp. 327–360.

Warikandwa, Tapiwa V., and Patrick. C. Osode. 2014. "Forging Institutional Cooperation to Protect Core Labour Standards in Trade: Are a World Trade Organisation and an International Labour Organisation Joint Dispute Settlement System Practical?" *Comparative and International Law Journal of Southern Africa* 47 (3): 490–508.

Warikandwa, Tapiwa V., and Patrick. C. Osode. 2017. "Regulating against Business 'Fronting' to Advance Black Economic Empowerment in Zimbabwe: Lessons from South Africa." *Potchefstroom Electronic Law Journal* 20 (1): 1–43.

Warikandwa, Tapiwa V., and Patrick C. Osode. 2014. "Human Rights, Core Labour Standards and the Search for a Legal Basis for a Trade-labour Linkage in the Multilateral Trade Regime of the World Trade Organisation." *Law, Democracy and Development* 18: 240–63.

Warikandwa, Tapiwa V., and Patrick C. Osode. 2014. "Legal Theoretical Perspectives and their Potential Ramifications for Proposals to Incorporate a Social Clause into the Legal Framework of the World Trade Organisation." *Speculum Juris* 28 (2): 41.

Warikandwa, Tapiwa V., and Patrick C. Osode. 2016. "Chinese Companies' Trade Practices and Core Labour Standards: A South African, Zambian and Zimbabwean Perspective." *African Nazarene University Law Journal* 4 (1): 102.

Warikandwa, Tapiwa V., and Patrick C. Osode. 2017. "Exploring the World Trade Organisation's Trade and Environment/Public Health Jurisprudence as a Model for Incorporating a Trade-Labour Linkage into the Organisation's Multilateral Trade Regime: Should African Countries Accept a Policy Shift?" *African Journal of International and Comparative Law* 25 (1): 47–65.

Warikandwa, Tapiwa V., Artwell Nhemachena, and Nkosinothando Mpofu. 2017. "Double Victimisation? Law, Decoloniality and Research Ethics in Post-colonial Africa." *Africology: The Journal of Pan African Studies* 10 (2): 64–81.

Warikandwa, Tapiwa V., Artwell Nhemachena, and Oliver Mtapuri. (eds.). 2017. *Transnational Land Grabs and Restitution in an Age of the (De-)Militarised New Scramble for Africa: A Pan African Socio-Legal Perspective*. Bameda: Langaa Research & Publishing Common Initiative Group.

Wouters, Neil. (ed.). 2014. *Transitional Justice and Memory in Europe (1945–2013)*. Cambridge: Intersentia.

Zhangazha, Wongai, Hazel Ndebele, and Nkululeko Sibanda. 2018. "Zanu-PF risks General Elections Defeat." *News 24*, 6 May.

Chapter 5

Operation Murambatsvina, Transitional Justice, and Discursive Representation in Zimbabwe

Umali Saidi

INTRODUCTION

Discourses on transitional justice generally call for practical redress to human rights violations exerted on the weak. Much of these discourses refer to violations pinned heavily on violence, war, gross human rights violations from which a cocktail of reforms are recommended in order for targeted societies to regain their dignity, visibility, and honor. While authoritarianism and wars are cited as chief causes of human rights violations, these at times overshadow some aspects that seemingly qualify as conditions at the center of violations to human dignified survival without a record to loss of human life. Against these, transitional justice in its current form may be found wanting given its objectives which are at times adequate to handle such situations.

In post-independent Zimbabwe, aspects of human rights violations are centered largely on the *Gukurahundi* as well as political disturbances ushered in by the formation of the opposition party, the Movement of Democratic Change (MDC) in 1999 and the subsequent Fast Track Land Reform Program (henceforth "the Land Reform") of 2000. This chapter explores discourses of transitional justice in Zimbabwe in a bid to assess the success or otherwise of transitional justice; or whether social activities such as the *Operation Murambatsvina* (henceforth "the Operation") can foresee transitional justice playing a role in sustainable peace-building in the country.

BACKGROUND TO *OPERATION MURAMBATSVINA*

In post-independent Zimbabwe, discourses on Gukurahundi have sort first to establish as well as pin the blame on the government of the day while singling out individuals seen as having led the massacres of Zimbabweans in Matabeleland and Midlands Provinces. On the other hand, discourses on the Land Reform Program of 2000 reveal debates around the land question as an unfinished "decolonization" business to which its undertaking witnessed gross human rights violations on opposition political party members, white settlers and all those who opposed the manner in which the program was handled. However, amid these political developments, in 2005 Zimbabwe experienced *Operation Murambatsvina* (Restore Order) from which millions of Zimbabweans, mostly the urban populace, lost their property and livelihoods as the ZANU (PF) government embarked on an operation to "cleanse" the "filth" which it said had accumulated in the urban and peri-urban centers. A body of discourses on the operation followed. Subsequently, *Operation Garikai/Hlalani Kuhle* (henceforth *Garikai/Hlalani*) (Live Well), a scheme rolled out to mitigate the effects of Operation Restore Order, further ushered in discourses on both the Operation and "Live Well" posing serious questions on issues of transitional justice in the country.

Using Critical Discourse Analysis (CDA) (Van Dijk, 2001, Fairclough, 1992), this chapter explores discourses of transitional justice with reference to *Operation Murambatsvina* to assess whether transitional justice in Zimbabwe is possible in an effort to redress realities such as those created by the Operation. It is hoped that knowledge generated will help broaden first our view of transitional justice in general. Secondly, the chapter suggests that localized assessment of social activities that lead to violations should be used to model pillars of transitional justice or any form of social justice for that matter in given contexts. Further, policy formulation and efforts to foresee transitional justice especially in Zimbabwe should be all encompassing and designed to mitigate future scenarios likely to promote human rights violations; scenarios which could otherwise be avoided since prevention is better than cure.

Understanding Transitional Justice

There has been interest in understanding transitional justice over the years. Africa has become the major focus in as far as aspects of transitional justice are concerned largely because of wars, violence, oppression, and general human rights violations especially as perpetuated by notable African governments. It is as though Africa is a laboratory of transitional justice from which all aspects of human rights violations are used to model solutions for implementation in Africa and elsewhere in the world. Fischer (2011, p. 406) observes that

> judicial proceedings and prosecution of individuals suspected to have committed gross violations of human rights, truth commissions designed to establish a record of wrongdoing, reparations to the victims and vetting or dismissals of

persons from certain positions have become central ingredients in the 'menu' of reforms recommended by international organizations, donor agencies and outside experts for societies in transition from war or authoritarianism.

Crucial in this view is the context of human rights violations perpetuated by wars, authoritarianism, and politically powerful individuals. From these, judicial proceedings, human rights commissions are/were established against the recommendations by outsiders with the hope of promoting reparations and justice to the victims. Hence, transitional justice has been analyzed and explored by foreign observers through their agencies who recommend models of justice provision for the affected people by their own perpetrators.

As if to justify this "foreign" approach to transitional justice, Fischer (2011) says the concept of transitional justice stems from the international human rights movement. This means any view or discussion of transitional justice should borrow its basic definition from the dictates of international human rights movements. While meaning of transitional justice has its internal pockets of views recognizing judicial processes of addressing human rights violations committed by repressive regimes; and that aspects of processing war crimes and massive human rights violations committed during violent conflicts, transitional justice has thus become a term used by peacebuilding agencies mostly working in prominent war-torn societies across the globe—especially in Africa.

When references are made to tribunals, truth commissions, instances of settlements on reparations, as well a political and societal initiatives "devoted to fact-finding, reconciliation and cultures of remembrance" (Fischer, 2011, p. 19), transitional justice appears to fit without any diverging contradictions. The reason is simply that the sources of the human rights violations which are wars or violent conflicts (usually politically and religiously inclined); the call is that of maintaining sustainable peace, establishing truths, as well as seeking reconciliation. These are the major ingredients of transitional justice as spearheaded by international agencies on human rights on behalf of the victims.

This view of transitional justice places victims as objects rather than subjects of transitional justice. It means, both the victims and perpetrators of human rights violations view transitional justice as a commodity designed to shift and define blame. It may be seen as a systematic transfer of power from "perpetrators" to victims in times of "peace" with the expectation that victims will be served justice, regain, symbolically, those things such as freedoms, lives of their families, parents, and children, etc. they could have lost; and possibly repossess the material resources such as land, property, and so on. In return, victims are expected to "forgive" and accept perpetrators as reformed members of their own society for the purpose of peace and sustainable development in order to define "reconciliation."

There is no doubt, therefore, that such a limited approach on transitional justice has seen much of legal and international law scholarship being used in the establishment of international tribunals specifically on certain gruesome developments such as in Rwanda, former Yugoslavia, Sierra Leone, and Lebanon even the International Criminal Court (ICC) (Fischer, 2011) as implemented under the auspices of the United Nations (UN). Research has shown that most victims feel that justice is not often served. When victims speak of "visitor's justice," it is against the failure of transitional justice in bearing fruits within the actual contexts of where violations would have taken place since it is the international agencies who define the conflict, victims, perpetrators and are topical in spearheading transitional justice as per their definitions and thus exclude the affected themselves. Victims are only brought in as "witnesses" to the crimes and violations. Thus, the expectations of the affected communities should be the first account to be taken into consideration in matters of transitional justice. Lambourne (2014, p. 19) concludes that

> in determining the specific path to take in any particular transitional justice context, it is therefore critical to take into account the needs, expectations and experiences of the perpetrators, victims, survivors and other members of society directly affected by the violence and who are intimately involved in reconciliation and peace-building.

The other aspects regard truth, peace, and justice to which legalist discourses call for criminal justice with a view of deterring future human rights violations in independent contexts to ones under discussions. This is hoped to support peace-building in the world. Further, the elite who are singled out and have to bear the blame as perpetrators of conflict are singled out as a way to "help separate individual from collective guilt" thus "breaking the cycle of violence" (Fischer, p. 409). While these appear to call for accountability in conflict perpetuation, there is no agreement of the best model as no situation, cause, context, society, and conflict is similar to another hence the polarity of transitional justice itself. The above view heavily emphasizes backward-looking considerations leading scholars to rethink and have now come to argue that transitional justice is in fact a future-oriented project. For instance, Ramírez-Barat (2014, p. 27) says,

> transitional justice measures are also future-oriented projects to the extent that redressing past violations is precisely understood as a way of contributing to the construction of a democratic and peaceful future.

This entails that measures employed in realizing transitional justice are and should be symbolic, designed to break with the past in order to forge ahead a peaceful future. Hence, institutions established to foresee this break are deliberately mandated to document and create an inventory of what could have transpired in the past. This is a way of accomplishing their immediate functions. In Zimbabwe, the Catholic Commission for Justice and Peace in Zimbabwe (CCJPZ) established in 1972 is a very good example of an institution which was topical in documenting and created an inventory of human rights violations during the Gukurahundi era in Zimbabwe.

It is this information which continues even today in shaping the discourses of transitional justice with reference to Gukurahundi in Zimbabwe. Today, the UN Anna Tibaijuka "Report of the Fact-Finding Mission to Zimbabwe to assess the Scope and Impact of *Operation Murambatsvina*" produced in 2005 plays a similar role on *Operation Murambatsvina*. Further, transitional justice is thought to require political credibility while at the same time the involvement of the public is vital if transitional justice is to have an impact. Ramírez-Barat (2014) gives examples of Argentina and Peru where the public where involved with respective governments providing the political will hence the notable concrete and durable legacies of transitional justice.

Ramírez-Barat (2014) argues for the public's participation in transitional justice. Public understanding of transitional justice is thus crucial from this perspective as in order to deal with unrealistic high expectations which may arise from the onset since these, if allowed to stand or are ignored, may lead to disappointment or betrayal. Thus, transitional justice will easily support novel inclusive processes. This is because, as Ramírez-Barat rightly observes,

> Transitional justice processes involve novel institutions with complex mandates, rules, and procedures that can be technical and difficult to understand. It should not be assumed that they will function in public discourse in the same way as consolidated institutions with which populations are already familiar through everyday channels of socialization. Moreover, the legacies of previous conflicts or regimes—including deep social divisions and poor traditions of transparency, accountability, and democratic interaction, with a subsequent general lack of civic trust in public institutions—may also pose severe challenges for transitional justice measures that seek to gain popular acceptance and support. (Ramírez-Barat, 2014, pp. 28–29)

Hence, societies in which transitional justice takes place needs to be enshrined within the various socio-political realities to involve the public. Further, transitional justice in this instance thus demands financial investment. However, in most African contexts financial investment is an enormous challenge explaining why transitional justice has excluded the public and has been in most cases been the role of the international human rights agencies who in seeking to safeguard their financial investments also dictate and make use of victims as their objects in processes of transitional justice.

At a very broad scale, transitional justice aims at promoting social transformation in matters such as peace, democracy, rule of law, fostering reconciliation, and basic human development all of which are expected to take hold within a specified population. Involving the public or affected population in transitional justice allows creation of lasting legacies in matters of transitional justice hence sometimes recommendations form the rolling out of what Ramírez-Barat (2014, p. 31) calls "outreach programs." The advantage of outreach programs Ramírez-Barat says that they,

> generate this sort of informed public discussion around transitional justice measures and the abuses to which they are responding, to the extent that they are conducted by institutions or bodies established within the political and juridical spheres. (Ramírez-Barat, 2014, p. 31)

This is on the assumption that the designed programs center the public as the subjects who first and foremost are empowered through measures such as public's access to information, discussions and participation from which mass media, cultural practices, as well as educational frameworks (Ramírez-Barat, 2014) are designed to empower and prepare the public for the programs.

The claim that transitional justice does not happen in a vacuum holds true in that the social and historical contexts are crucial in defining the success or failure of any transitional justice endeavor. The media, education, artists, intellectuals, and the discourses produced carrying the narratives as well as the appropriation of the said discourses will by and large define the direction of transitional justice and subsequent processes in a given country or society. Societies often use expressions and codes such as academic research, journalistic chronicles, artistic work, popular culture, sport, day-to-day communicative interactions as a way to interpret, configure, as well as bring the past events to the present. It is the politics of the day that sometimes may define the tone of these expressions and codes. Either the politics may suppress or promote expressions as well as allow the public to access the information. Promotion often sees production of new sources of knowledge, triggering further reflections and discussions (Ramírez-Barat, 2014), thereby marking out the boundaries of the operations of images created which have a bearing in defining the future of the society.

In Africa, matters of transitional justice are often heavily linked to gruesome human rights abuses undertaken at a very large-scale or as mass abuses. Africa is characterized as prone to war and conflict as well as characterized by mass abuses. This alone has made the continent an appropriate candidate for debates around transitional justice more, so Africa lacks the financial resources to invest in the transitional justice processes. This deliberate view of Africa as conflict and war torn, has justified international human rights agencies to recommend models mostly outside the continent for implementation in Africa.

As such, submissions that Africa, because it has been confronted "by decades of impunity that have spiraled into civil wars, regional conflict, genocide and oppressive rule" (Villa-Vicencio, 2001, p. 34) makes the international human rights agencies and the international community at large insist "that perpetrators of such deeds have their day in court" (Villa-Vicencio, 2001, p. 34) as a way of promoting transitional justice to foresee and achieve peace building. The challenge, however, lies, as scholars rightly observe, for instance Villa-Vicencio (2001), in that, efforts to promote transitional justice as spearheaded by international agencies may fail to harness the local initiatives with the international ones thereby resulting in the peace-building initiatives and peace processes sliding back into conflict or creating new conflicts. At this point, we then realize that

> peace cannot be restored in conflict situations by persecutions alone. Nor can the international demand for an end to impunity be ignored or played down by less than decisive action being taken against those principally responsible for acts of genocide, crimes against humanity or war crimes. (Villa-Vicencio, 2001, p. 34)

These are the realities transitional justice has to battle with, that is, harnessing local initiatives, defining conflicts as well as boundaries on which international and local processes begin and end. Further, victim demands should be incorporated primarily if TJ is to mean and support any sustainable peace-building in conflict societies. There is a general view that conflicts in Africa are political, hence the resultant "similar" human rights violations. Examples often given are those historical realities in DR Congo, Uganda, and Sudan to mention a few.

Against the above, to have a glimpse of transitional justice, often scholarship has alluded to literature that attempts to theories transitional justice. The basic view by theorists is that transitional justice is a very politically sensitive subject as it deals greatly with situations and realities in post-conflict or post-authoritarian eras forcing a return to the past; that is, to the conflict or authoritarian periods to unearth narratives of realities during the conflict era, perpetrators of human rights abuses and so on. Questions that we often have to ask, therefore are, how best should we understand transitional justice? Should it be from a pragmatic perspective where we have to follow the Human Rights Agencies and even International Organizations such as UN's definitions? Alternatively, we should start from theoretical perspectives and engage scholarship on transitional justice.

It is my conviction that a theoretical perspective should begin in order to demarcate, understand, and incorporate the pragmatic views advanced by international agencies in a bid to provide a holistic understanding of transitional justice. It should be noted that defining transitional justice should be able to accord anyone handling issues around transitional justice with opportunities to interpret specific contexts nursing transitional justice issues, attempt models in the implementation of transitional justice if anyone hopes to judge if transitional justice has been successful in a given context. Broadly speaking, what cannot be denied is the fact that transitional justice "has gained global significance as an umbrella term for approaches to deal with the past in the aftermath of violent conflict or dictatorial regimes" (Buckley-Zistel et al., 2014, p. 1).

Buckley-Zistel et al. (2014) noted that the term "transitional justice" came to prominence in the 1990s and ever since it has been an umbrella term to describe mechanisms and institutions designed to redress past wrongs, vindicate the dignity of victims at the same time providing justice in times of transition (Buckley-Zistel et al., 2014, p. 1). Identified mechanisms and institutions include tribunals, truth commissions, memorial projects, and reparations to name but a few. Notably, is the observation that despite a large body of literature on TJ from the 1990s to present, Buckley-Zistel et al. (2014) say transitional justice lacks theoretical frameworks. Instead, the discourses and practices are observed as,

> largely based on implicit assumptions about transition and/ or justice that are often commonsensical in Western thinking. These assumptions are strongly influenced and shaped by particular historical experiences, such as the Nuremberg and Tokyo trials after the Second World War, the transitions of South American countries from dictatorship to democracy, international criminal tribunals, such as the tribunals for the former Yugoslavia and Rwanda, or the Truth and Reconciliation Commission (TRC) in South Africa. Thus, the challenge is both to reveal what these underlying assumptions entail and how they influence—or limit—the practice of transitional justice. (Buckley-Zistel et al., 2014, p. 1)

Faced by the above challenge, especially when dealing with specified contexts such as Zimbabwe in which displacement was done through a systematic operation, the *Operation Murambatsvina*, which exhibits unique and different historical experiences, it follows that a theoretical framework is needed to contextualize discussion of transitional justice against say the *Operation* in Zimbabwe. Such a view makes us acknowledge that transitional justice is very heterogeneous, which probably could explain why it may also be difficult to establish a common transitional justice theoretical framework. Attempting a theoretical approach to transitional justice will help establish knowledge on what it is and get to appreciate how it functions. In addition, generally, theories do improve one's ability to explain phenomena, allows one to predict and understand processes and developments. Theories also generally provide the language that can be used in communicating issues at stake thus giving a visible parameter of any discursive endeavor.

Some scholars claim that we should situate transitional justice within the context of peace-building rather than mere promotion of human rights, democracy, and rule of law (Lambourne, 2014). This approach allows us to view transitional justice as a mechanism or as mechanisms systematically to promote socioeconomic, political, and legal redress and discourage a culture of impunity and guarantee human rights and the rule of law. This way, peace-building is thought to be addressed. This is thought to be the only sustainable way to establish "security, legal, political, economic, structural, cultural and psychosocial conditions necessary to promote a culture of peace in place of a culture of violence" (Lambourne, 2014, p. 22). What we learn from the above is that transitional justice should be approached from the peace-building perspective. This explains why Lambourne (2014, p. 20), for instance, calls transitional justice "transformative justice incorporating political, economic and psychosocial as well as legal dimensions."

The aspect of psychosocial or reference to it in the context of transitional justice allows encapsulation of the dimensions of justice that calls for the truth in terms of both knowledge and acknowledgement of the violations, its human, and relational impact (Lambourne, 2014). It follows therefore, that the knowledge in our context of the Operation would be establishing who was responsible for authorizing the demolitions, how did it happen, what were the implications in humanitarian as well as economic costs and can perpetrators acknowledge the loss, pain, hurt and suffering caused? It is hoped that from this perspective, knowledge and acknowledgement can contribute to a psychological process of healing and building of inner peace. Once the inner peace is built, the psychosocial may easily be observed.

TRANSITIONAL JUSTICE IN POST-INDEPENDENT ZIMBABWE

Zimbabwe has not been spared the call for peace-building given its historical realities. Atrocities and mass human rights violations undertaken by the colonial administration as well as the ZANLA (and ZIPRA) forces during the periods of the liberation struggles have been well documented. At independence in 1980, Robert Mugabe's reconciliatory speech appears to have become a lid to the establishment of institutions to deal with gross human rights violations during the war. In other words, Mugabe's reconciliatory speech can be taken as a lid placed on TJ at independence. Partly, this could be taken in that, because both parties, the Natives and Settlers were equal perpetrators in the killings that took place during the liberation struggle between 1966 and 1980 as well as that there had been human rights violations on both sides hence there was no need of any form of setting up tribunals to reprimand perpetrators. Ian Smith was not dragged to court or international tribunals or punished for any wrongdoing.

However, the independent government spearheaded mechanisms of re-writing the history of the Second Chimurenga. National days such as the Independence Day (April 18) and Heroes Day (August 13) witness the reclamation of narratives linked to realities about the war. War jingles are played on national television and radios from the few days before the said holidays to days well after the said days.

Today, every Sunday bulletin on national television, ZBCTV, always carry a section where the "war" and various other narratives are revisited. The twenty-first-century land reform program was presented as a mechanism to redress the injustices of the past, specifically access to land and anything connected to it. Not all these developments have been very clear, especially if one is to take the propagated international stance on transitional justice. The war of liberation did not witness establishment of tribunals for instance in which the white settlers and those responsible for the bombing say of Chimoio and Nyadzonia camps were brought to book either by local systems or international courts. Zimbabwe, one can argue that, probably the narratives characterizing constant reference to the war, the land reform program could be interpreted as subtle ways or models the country adopted to deal with the past in peace-building. At independence, post-independent Zimbabwe was quickly plunged into a conflict in from 1982 to 1987, what has come to be known as the *Gukurahundi*. For Ndlovu-Gatsheni (2012) *Gukurahundi* was a violent strategy deployed by the then Mugabe government against the Ndebele speaking people accused of harboring dissidents in Matabeleland and Midlands regions. Hence, *Gukurahundi*

> was the name for an exclusive Korean-trained ZANLA force (Fifth Brigade) that was deployed in Matabeleland and the Midlands regions in the period 1982–87, leaving more than twenty thousand civilians dead. (Ndlovu-Gatsheni, 2012, p. 4)

During *Gukurahundi*, thousands of people in the Matabeleland provinces were massacred to which the North Korean-trained ZANLA brigade is said to have been at the service of the government. The signing of the Unity Accord in 1987 marked the "end" of *Gukurahundi*. Attempts to deal with the era of Matabeleland disturbances resulted in the nation recognizing the Unity Day (December 22) and Robert Mugabe merely commented on it as "A moment of madness." Today, the *Gukurahundi* issue has not been dealt with and a Peace and Reconciliation Commission was established recently by the Emmerson Mnangagwa led administration to deal with the "past" that is, the *Gukurahundi* issues and any other conflicts of the past.

Politically, the ZANU (PF) has over the years, especially at the turn of the twenty-first century when the main opposition party, the Movement of Democratic Change (MDC) was formed and challenged the Mugabe regime; rolled out an ideology pinned on disqualifying anyone "without war credentials" from running the country later alone becoming the president of the country. This probably explains the discourses around ZANU(PF)'s efforts in blocking the then leader of the MDC, Morgan Tsvangirai, in 2008, from assuming power having won "73%" of the vote. Instead, they allowed a marginally below 51 percent to force a rerun, which, sadly, ended up becoming a one man show as violence made Tsvangirai boycott the poll leading to the formation of Government of National Unity (GNU) in early 2009.

If we follow Ndlovu-Gatsheni's (2012) views, one may submit that the ZANU (PF)'s favored ideology is hinged on its purported "solo" participation in the liberation struggle. This has made the party advance claims through rhetoric designed to legitimize it as a sole player which ushered independence to Zimbabweans from colonial rule. We note that this unfortunate development is key in the blocking of pragmatic implementation of mechanisms of justice to victims of the liberation either struggle or post-independent conflicts. The ruling party, in part, was also a perpetrator of the human violations hence its unwillingness to foster inclusive and serious mechanisms of TJ. It also explains the dominance of ZANU (PF)'s ideology in the writing of Zimbabwean history as well as commanding what it deems as "recollectable" in memory building or reconstructions of the past, leaving victims without social or economic justice. As such, we note that there have not been any notable efforts in realizing TJ in Zimbabwe.

One can further submit that, with reference to the *Gukurahundi*, the conflict could not have received due attention due to lack of political will or it was a deliberate attempt to buy time with the hope that victims would eventually forget past memories and appropriate instead those the government ideologically advanced. International involvement in recommending the government of the day through various agencies could have been more foreign than local. Lambourne (2014) asserts that Western liberal traditions of revisiting the past in an attempt to produce accountability have a tendency of promoting adversary since models used are prosecutorial and use retributive models of formal legal justice instead of models of peace-building. According to international standards, the *Gukurahundi* has not been solved and no attempt has been put in place to resolve it. Hence, Ndlovu-Gatsheni (2012) concludes that lack of TJ to past conflicts especially linked to the ideology of Chimurenga and *Gukurahundi*, explains the continued conflicts in Zimbabwe due to the unresolved "early manifestation of the culture of violence that today is affecting the whole country" (Ndlovu-Gatsheni, 2012, p. 4).

RESTORING ORDER—AN OPERATION OF HUMAN RIGHTS VIOLATIONS

Much of the literature on transitional justice has a basic bias toward conflict-ridden circumstances that have resulted in gross human rights violations foreseeing loss of life, property and freedoms of people as tribal groups sort political power or authoritarian regimes sort to extinguish opposition from rivalry parties. The bias that the discourses offer or provide are quick to suggest restorative justice from which the past is recollected through tribunals, courts, and various institutions designed to provide justice to the victims.

In Zimbabwe, *Operation Murambatsvina* offered a very complex instance of a conflict in which the government of the day, which over the years had impoverished its populace through various authoritarian policies leading to economic collapse. Related issues also pointed to the poor urban planning initiatives, poor land management, and allocation as well as strict legal systems in purchasing land by citizens. Suddenly, the government turned on its people mostly the urban populace not on political, tribal, or religious grounds as both ZANU (PF), MDC, the non-partisan were equally affected. Perhaps it could have been based on class as the capitalist elite pushed for a quick solution to arrest the dwindling profits from their interests as the "informal' economy seemed now to be controlled by the "poor." Much of the losses, therefore, was property and settlements; judged to have been illegally constructed or established such as residential dwellings, makeshift commercial, and economic establishments. These had become sources of livelihoods as they provided and defined the livelihoods of the people who had mostly migrated from the rural and remote areas in search of survival in the cities and towns.

Operation Murambatsvina was rolled out in May 2005 by the government of Zimbabwe. This was a wide range operation to demolish mostly the informal sector infrastructure. The operation was code named *Operation Murambatsvina,* described by the populace as, *chamupupuri* or Tsunami, "a whirlwind" given the speed in which it was implemented and the trail of destruction it left behind. Musoni (2010) says it was a government sponsored "program," Potts (2006) says it was a "campaign" to cleanse the urban landscape of the informal businesses and illegal activities in the cities while Potts (2008) further described it as a "Tsunami"—revealing the trail of destruction that the operation left behind. The ActionAid International Southern Africa Partnership Program (SAPP-Zimbabwe, 2005, p. 1) reported that the operation, witnessed the destruction of urban poor dwellings, livelihoods, the destruction of vending stalls and the confiscation of goods and property of informal traders. It is estimated that over 55,000 households in 52 sites across the country and between 250,000–500,000 have been rendered homeless or forced to migrate to the rural areas. Furthermore, more than 30,000 people were arrested and fined in the process.

An armed contingent of the Zimbabwe Republic Police (ZRP) having teamed up with Municipal Police, in cities and towns; operationalized the "Tsunami" by ordering informal traders to demolish their infrastructure and "owners of backyard cottages, tuck-shops and street-side market stalls" (Musoni, 2010, p. 301) were ordered to destroy their buildings. Kamete (2009) also says intelligence operatives and the militia assisted in the rolling out of the operation.

Traders, who attempted to resist Musoni (2010) claims, were beaten up by the ZRP. The demolitions were carried out under the auspices of a "nation-wide government sponsored urban 'clean-up program'" Musoni (2010, p. 301). In some cases, cranes and mechanized graders were used to pull down beautiful residential houses purported to have been built in violation of the Urban Council's Act. Hundreds of people were forced to migrate while others were subjected to in situ displacement. In the clean-up project in question, the government of Zimbabwe became both the problem and subjected itself as a provider to the solution on informal trading in Zimbabwe. Musoni (2010, p. 303) traces the Zimbabwe's informal sector as having been created by colonialism. He says,

> During the colonial period, unemployed urban dwellers resorted to street vending, beer brewing, market gardening, prostitution, and other income-generating activities. In addition to the general repression to which the colonized people were subjected, the colonists imposed stiff by-laws to curb the growth and autonomy of what has been dubbed the 'African economy'. However, the informal economy survived into independent Zimbabwe, where it experienced a steady growth until the late 1980s. Under the auspices of the neo-liberal Economic Structural Adjustment Programs (ESAP), the 1990s saw a rapid expansion of informality in urban employment and housing as hordes of people who lost jobs in the shrinking formal sector established their own small and medium enterprises. The central government and authorities in most of the country's urban areas were also failing to cope with the rising demands for accommodation, leading to the mushrooming of several unauthorized housing structures.

By the time that the *Operation* was rolled out, either the informal sector had become effectively the economy which had in part forced the complete closure of several major companies or seriously downsized operations as products from the informal sector had dominated the market. The government of

Zimbabwe defended the operation, insisting that it was an operation to deal with crime and squalor that had characterized much of the urban landscape. In place, it was argued that the government was rebuilding and reorganizing urban settlement as well as coming up with the Small and Medium Enterprises (SMEs) through means that would, it was argued, bring economic sanity, dignity, order, as well as prosperity to all stakeholders.

The United Nations (UN) Tibaijuka (2005) report is perhaps one of the commonly referred to document on the *Operation* which extensively gave character to the impact of *Operation Murambatsvina* in Zimbabwe. The report analyzes the mechanics of the operation. It is respected, as it was a United Nations sponsored study done in the country by the UN Special Envoy, Anna Tibaijuka. The report reveals the suddenness of the implementation of the Operation. Descriptions of where it started in Zimbabwe and the trail of destructions to other parts of the country are presented. Statistics marking the magnitude of the impact are also provided. Central to the report are the submissions that senior key members of the Zimbabwean society across the political, social, religious, and even economic divide were involved and information was provided from them. Based on this study, key findings that stand out are that the operation,

> was carried out in an indiscriminate and unjustified manner, with indifference to human suffering, and, in repeated cases, with disregard to several provisions of national and international legal frameworks . . . . Operation Restore Order turned out to be a disastrous venture based on a set of colonial-era laws and policies that were used as a tool of segregation and social exclusion. . . . The humanitarian consequences of Operation Restore Order are enormous. It will take several years before the people and society as a whole can recover. (Tibaijuka, 2005, p. 7)

> Any humanitarian response can only be meaningful and sustainable if it contributes to the long-term recovery and reconstruction efforts of the Government and of its people. Zimbabwe is not a country at war, and it remains peaceful. (Tibaijuka, 2005, p. 8)

These are part of the key findings on the Operation which point to the fact that the Operation was a deliberate move by the government of Zimbabwe to violate human rights for reasons that are assumed or inferred based on the economic, political, social, and historical realities that characterized the country at the time. It also explains one of the conclusions the report makes which explicitly points a finger to the government of Zimbabwe that

> the Government of Zimbabwe is collectively responsible for what has happened. However, it appears that there was no collective decision-making with respect to

both the conception and implementation of Operation Restore Order. Evidence suggests it was based on improper advice by a few architects of the operation. The people and Government of Zimbabwe should hold to account those responsible for the injury caused by the Operation. (Tibaijuka, 2005, p. 76)

This is perhaps the rallying point which supported the varying reactions to the UN Tibaijuka (2005) report. While human rights organizations and institutions, opposition parties and civil groups welcomed the report, the government of Zimbabwe was adamant that the report had not captured truthfully issues around the operation. Through the then minister of foreign affairs, Simbarashe Mumbengegwi, and the government dismissed the report as heavily biased and was more in opposition to the efforts of the government. While acknowledging the demolitions, the government of Zimbabwe insisted that demolitions were done to structures and settlements which had been illegally established in violation of the laws of the country and that the exercise was to restore legality and sanity in the urban centers.

Operation Garikai/Hlalani Kuhle (Live Well) was instead extensively cited as ongoing and designed to mitigate part of the challenges the report had cited. The media reported that even the then Minister of Local Government and Housing, Ignatius Chombo, defended the operation at the same time sidestepping any criticism by focusing on the government's new corrective program, *Operation Garikai/Hlalani Kuhle* and was cited as having said "Our people are much happier because the government is giving them land, they are getting stands, and are getting government assistance" (The Solidarity Peace Trust. 2006). Against, aspects of TJ therefore, it is pertinent to revisit what the government of Zimbabwe extensively cited in its defense of human rights violations during the Operation to assess the agility of the government of Zimbabwe's defense as it too appeared to play victim of international community's politicking.

OPERATION GARIKAI/HLALANI KUHLE AS FAILED REDRESS

The only way to read *Operation Garikai/Hlalani Kuhle* is to refer to the *Operation*. This came about as a response by the then Mugabe government to offer some breathing space for the urban populace following the "whirlwind" or the "Tsunami" of the *Operation*. *Garikai/Hlalani Kuhle* was a scheme that involved a speedy construction of dwellings from the purported victims of the Operation who had lost their homes. The scheme at its infancy was presented by the Government of Zimbabwe as a pragmatic solution to most pockets of criticisms leveled against it during the Operation. It appeared as though the government would live to its word, but the scheme too proved to have been a smokescreen the government was blowing in the face of huge criticism on its record of human rights abuses.

Given the "failure" of *Garikai/Hlalani Kuhle*, international agencies came in to also assist pragmatically either to push government to address housing challenges as well as create space in assisting those who had been affected by the government of Zimbabwe's policies most of which had affected the poor urban populace as reflected by much of the *Operation* discourses.

Hammar (2017) speaks of constructions of homes in New Mazwi (a location 20km from Bulawayo CBD). The constructions, Hammar (2017) submits that, was funded by the International Organization for Migration (IOM) "which had become more actively present in the country following the politically motivated ZANU (PF) party-state campaign of mass urban displacement in mid-2005 called *Operation Murambatsvina*" (Hammar, 2017, p. 81). She further states that the dwellings were being given free of charge to new settlers although in the long term recurrent costs and challenges were a reality. Hammar (2017) describes the allocation of the land on which the houses were built as a "gesture" given by the Bulawayo City Council following pressure from the "squatters" themselves, religious groups and other pressure groups.

For Hammar (2017), however, focus has been a community of urban dwellers who had for years had an experience of evictions, as they had been "squatters" in Bulawayo. *Operation Murambatsvina* is taken as merely having worsened their situation as they too had long been defined as 'illegal' citizens and the relocation and dwelling constructions at Mazwi became a broad aspect of gaining citizenry from the years of "squattership." Thus, using these groups of people to assert and assess TJ may require another broad context which is that of general urban displacement which had over the years been characteristic of the Zimbabwean landscape.

The Solidarity Peace Trust (2006) documented the mass demolitions in Zimbabwe during the Operation and the effects of the aftermath of the operation. The report first establishes the context of *Operation Murambatsvina* and analyzed it as above other things having been a systematic criminalization of the informal sector by the Government of Zimbabwe. More importantly, the report reflects that the government of Zimbabwe had no official line Ministry or individuals who claimed responsibility for ordering the Operation, which the report found very ironic as the involvement of the armed police and army as well as the magnitude of the demolitions would not have been possible without authorization from the highest offices in the country.

The UN is claimed to have recommended the prosecution of perpetrators and the government of Zimbabwe has not acted on the recommendations. However, the report refers to Garikai/Hlalani Kuhle described by the Solidarity Peace Trust (2006) as "a scandal of dismal delivery." The Solidarity Peace

Trust (2006) describes the scheme as a suddenly announced "biggest housing scheme in the history of Africa was hastily made to cover up for the cruelty of the demolitions, which threw 560,000 people out of shelter in the middle of winter." The report further notes that the government promised to build close to 300,000 housing units by the end of 2005, and each subsequent year up to 2008 would witness the building of up to 250,000 units. Inter-Ministerial units are reported to have been set up, most of which were headed by high-ranking army officers effectively taking over the responsibilities from the expected local government in terms of allocation of stands and houses. The report claims that

> in October 2005, it was already clear that no building targets had been met, and that in fact they had been dismally failed. And by June 2006, the failure of OGHK to deliver to more than a handful of homes to those displaced is unmistakable. (The Solidarity Peace Trust, 2006)

Scandals and corruption characterized the scheme. Some scandals included collapse of the built houses proving that material as well as unskilled labor had been used. There was failure to lay sewer reticulation systems such as in Bulawayo as some areas where the houses were built were on bedrock and blasting could not be done in the areas as houses already now stood thus exposing poor planning to the project. Hired constructors pulled of the project citing non-payment of materials and labor and in response incomplete homes were allocated to beneficiaries leaving the burden of completing building to the occupiers who ironically were already been financially crippled. Further, beneficiaries were expected to pay registration fees and the report notes that

> the greatest scandal surrounding OGHK involves allocation of the handful of houses built—every town has reported gross irregularities, with houses being allocated to government officials, children of cabinet ministers, police, army, multiple house-owners and others who were not on any official housing list. (The Solidarity Peace Trust, 2006)

It meant that *Garikai/Hlalani Kuhle* had a further blow on the actual victims of the Operation as the scheme became a self-enrichment exercise for the well placed and powerful government officials. The conclusion that the scheme was a flop as victims of the *Operation* were placed with circumstances that either required them to fork out money for registration or to finance the incomplete poorly built homes without any sewer and water reticulation, or they faced a strict bureaucratic system that favored government officials and other multi-home owners. *Garikai/Hlalani Kuhle* was thus an extension of the *Operation* which gave false hope to the affected and further disfranchised them. There was not audit done by the government to assess the success or failure of the scheme. The project one can submit that it merely proved to have offered economic opportunities to well-placed civil servants to further enrich themselves either by using government resources or by further accommodating the displaced for a fee using the houses the poor were expected to have benefited in the first place. Hence, to put the above context, that is, the *Operation* and *Garikai/Hlalani Kuhle*, into the perception of transitional justice, I refer to Critical Discourse Analysis below in order to weigh mechanisms of transitional justice in Zimbabwe.

THE HIDDEN DIMENSIONS OF THE *OPERATION*: A TRANSITIONAL JUSTICE IN PERSPECTIVE

Tibaijuka (2005) reported that victims submitted views that the operation was a smokescreen, that is, a cover-up by the Government of Zimbabwe which wanted to preempt a possible uprising in light of deepening food insecurity and other economic hardships (Tibaijuka, 2005, pp. 20–21) which had characterized the country for years. In terms of the effects, the government of Zimbabwe through its officials claimed that the operation significantly reduced criminality in Zimbabwe's urban areas; however, they "acknowledged that the operation had undesirable effects on those who lost their houses and businesses" (Musoni, 2010, p. 309). There have not been substantive figures to ascertain the actual number of people who lost their homes and businesses given the manner in which the operation was rolled out hence the statistical wrangle best summarized by Musoni (2010, p. 309) who says,

> Whereas, in July 2005, the government indicated that about 133,534 households were directly affected when 92,460 housing structures were demolished and 32,538 small-to-medium enterprises were destroyed, a month later the government's report maintained that only 2,695 households were temporarily made homeless. A joint study by the Action Aid International and Combined Harare Residents Association estimates that 'over 55,000 households in 52 sites across the country and between 250,000–500,000 people have been rendered homeless or forced to migrate to the rural areas' Providing a slightly different set of figures, UN report says about 700,000 people in the country's major cities were directly affected while a further 2.4 million suffered indirectly from the impact of *Murambatsvina*.

What is evident is the fact that a considerable percentage of the urban poor populace was affected directly or indirectly. Further, the operation unnecessarily caused hardships and generally violated people's human rights. To support this fact, the international community lambasted the operation in various ways. As has been indicated above, the Tibaijuka (2005) report exposed the government of Zimbabwe. Opposition parties led by the MDC partnered human rights groups in an alliance that called for a mass stay away in protest. The New Zealand cricket team which was due to travel to Zimbabwe in 2006 was called upon to boycott the match in protest to the humanitarian violations of the *Operation*, and it hid the call.

To avert the pressure, the government of Zimbabwe rolled out a reconstruction scheme code-named *Operation Garikai/Hlalani Kuhle* designed to assist victims affected by the *Operation* promising to build over 300,000 housing units but pragmatically the scheme failed dismally. Ironically, the same government, through the then Minister of Local Government and Urban Development, Ignatius Chombo, moved quickly to allow some victims of the *Operation Murambatsvina* to construct temporary shelters in some areas that had ironically been 'cleansed' or cleaned-up (Musoni, 2010, p. 311).

> They have been discourses produced during and after the Operation. The discourses documented the various realities connected to the operation. Musoni (2010) explores the strategies taken by traders affected by the operation using Glen View as his case. He shows the gravity of the effects on traders in one of Harare's suburbs indicating that as a political group negotiated for space using mechanisms informed by their understanding of the sitting government's political mood.

Potts (2006) blamed the Government of Zimbabwe for the urban poverty experienced at the turn of the twenty-first century. Potts observes that in the 1990s the urban population was less poor. She cites a 1991 survey that revealed that 10–15 percent of households in the city had incomes, social services functioned well and the vast majority of the urban population against their income had access to clean water and electricity. But, by 2003, the same urban population, Potts (2006) says, 72 percent of the urban population was classified as poor including 51 percent deemed as very poor (Potts, 2006, p. 274). It is this situation; which Potts says created informalized urban employment as the populace sort to service the harsh economic realities. Thus, Potts (2006) says *Operation Murambatsvina* was a campaign by the Government of Zimbabwe targeting this impoverished section of the population, spanning a period of three months, from May to July 2005. She describes the operation as,

> "massive"—nothing on this scale in such a short duration has ever been witnessed in urban Africa, not excluding apartheid South Africa—and spread right throughout the urban hierarchy from the capital city down to small "growth centers" in communal areas. The government was as good, or rather as bad, as its word: the vast majority of the informal sector enterprises and trading locations and houses (and other buildings) that were destroyed had contravened some

by-law or another although, as the condemnation of the campaign mounted, many were swift to point out that some "legal" buildings were being destroyed too. (Potts, 2006, p. 275)

What follows is a narration of the effects and the statistics given of the numbers of households and people affected. She too fails to give a substantive figure but refers to statistics provided by the UN 2005 Report (Tibaijuka, 2005), as well as results of the surveys published by international agencies on human rights. Potts describes poverty and economic challenges as having created what most scholars have come to identify as an informal economy. Bottom-line, scholarship and discourses reveal that Zimbabwean urban populace sort to irk out a living against the conditions that now characterized their country. What is key is that Zimbabweans are said to have been "forced into the informal sector as self-employed entrepreneurs operating at different scales and skill levels, or as, usually poorly paid, employees of such entrepreneurs" (Potts, 2006, p. 288).

Hence, Potts (2006) gives a narrative of the realities of the time and her study qualifies as documenting what had become day-to-day realities as well as rights to survival prior to *Operation Murambatsvina,* from which when the campaign was rolled out those rights were taken away from the very people who had been forced into the socioeconomic situation only to lose even the little that they had created. The magnitude of the violations is visible here given the background that characterized the urban populace. ActionAid International Southern Africa Partnership Program (SAPP-Zimbabwe, 2005, p. i) carried out a survey and reported on the impact of the Operation from day one of operation to the period of reporting. Their claim was to enhance the national information base. In other words, they intended to document realities around the operation mostly on the damage it had left on the urban landscape. The report squarely placed the actions of the Government of Zimbabwe which resulted in the suffering of "millions of Zimbabweans." Central to the report is the call that the document claims to be,

> an advocacy tool to remind the nation and the international community of its humanitarian and developmental priorities as well as to alert the nation and other stakeholders of the emerging challenges. (ActionAid International Southern Africa Partnership Program [SAPP-Zimbabwe, 2005, p. i])

Hence, reading the report we gain an insight into the impact of *Operation Murambatsvina* on individuals, communities, and households affected by the operation. The report provides statistics of the affected populace from those communities and household studied.

The report confirms that approximately 70 percent of the urban dwellers' livelihoods was affected, 70 percent again lost shelter and 76 percent are reported to have indicated that they lost their sources of income. For other groups such as children, 22 percent of them dropped out of school while 44 percent struggled to fund education (ActionAid International Southern Africa Partnership Program (SAPP-Zimbabwe, 2005). Bottom line, every aspect of the urban dwellers life and rights was affected. From employment, shelter, education, health, property, disruption of family unity, status, and dignity leaving various people vulnerable to disease, abuse, and even death. And while the operation was initiated in Harare, the capital city of Zimbabwe in May 2005, by July of the same year Kamete (2009) notes that "virtually every urban center had been emptied of the 'filth'" (Kamete, 2009, p. 897).

Hammar, McGregor and Landau (2010) viewed the operation from a broad perspective of displacement to which the operation is seen as merely an instance of the government's "militaristic 'Operations' through which the state sort to assert control" (Hammar, McGregor, & Landau, 2010, pp. 269–270). They further situate the Operation within the dictum of African's post colony characteristic conditions in which economic reforms, such as the Economic Structural Adjustment Program (ESAP) of the 1990s, resulted in a combination of flourishing informal economies and heavy-handed state response to urban unrest, legitimated through rhetoric of modernization, cleanliness and restore order—hence, *Operation Murambatsvina*.

Kamete (2009) locates *Operation Murambatsvina* within the broad spectra of urban planning and social control. He says, aspects of planning generally promoted capitalist interests and thus the need to suppress and control the minority while promoting state security. Characteristic to this were repressive projects, use of force and violence usually by state institutions such as the police. He further asserts that usually capitalist authoritarian regimes,

> In their bid to tackle informality and restore order to urban spaces, authorities use or manipulate planning to justify two state-directed activities—namely, eviction and demolition, as well as the attendant violence. (Kamete, 2009, p. 899)

This appears to be directly characterizing the government of Zimbabwe, hence, Kamete sees the Operation as a capitalist move to implement its urban planning projects. To achieve its goal, it is Kamete's (2009) conviction that the then Mugabe regime impoverished the urban populace in defense of its capitalist interests which were dwindling in the face of a deteriorating economy due to ESAP of the 1990s, involvement of the government of Zimbabwe in the Democratic Republic of Congo (DRC) 1998–2003 conflict, the 1997 payments of unbudgeted gratuities to war veterans, as well as the meltdown caused by the radical land reform program rolled out in February 2000.

Further, the urban planning system itself, Kamete (2009) observes that, it was too legalistic and tough hence contributed to housing problems

Zimbabwe faced leading homeowners to construct unauthorized extensions to their homes, erected backyard shacks for letting out to desperate home seekers. Central government's 'transitional camps' set up for people evicted from other parts of town especially in Harare, experienced a huge influx of people into these areas leading the government losing control and the areas degenerating into permanent slums. Again, Kamete (2009) points the blame of the effects of the Operation to the Government of Zimbabwe by alluding to socio-economic, urban planning and even political realities leading to *Operation Murambatsvina*.

Benyera and Nyere (2015) simply found *Operation Murambatsvina* as the inaction of ZANU (PF)'s statecraft defined by violence considered by the government as an instrument of governance. They cite the First & Second Chimurenga of 1896–1897 and 1965–1980, respectively, *Hondo Yeminda* (Fast Track Land Reform Program of 2000, *Gukurahundi, Operation, Makavhotera Papi?* (Operation on where did you place your vote?) of 2008.

While their focus is particularly the effects of the Operation on women and children, what is central is the characterization of the operation as violent and not different from other operations the government of Zimbabwe. There is no doubt that the *Operation* in their conception, violated the rights of people, in this case that of women and children. Against the above, therefore how can we unpack aspects of transitional justice given the internal dynamisms of the operation that hugely violated human rights in Zimbabwe?

One obvious way of implementing transitional justice is mechanizing reparations. Reparations generally consist of civil remedies (as opposed to criminal remedies) that are designed to redress harm resulting from an unlawful act that violates the rights of a person. However, in Zimbabwe, almost the entire society was affected one way or the other and there hasn't been any court case from which reparations can be done later alone a report detailing who lost what and where? Given the levels of corruption, how can documentation of such losses be done, and will all forms of loss be documented for instance loss of relations, psychological effects, and even life due to depression caused by the operation? The Zimbabwean situation hence requires administrative solutions to foresee reparations of the victims of the *Operation*.

The scheme *Garikai/Hlalani Kuhle* was rolled out in an attempt to ease the burden caused by the government but this too did not yield tangible results as, poor planning and corruption promoted the undeserving from benefiting the poorly constructed few houses built for the purported affected. Reparations were expected to be hinged on moral and ethical grounds. The general backward-looking aspect with the hope of allowing calculating the loss has been challenging in Zimbabwe. First, the government rejected the Tibaijuka UN Report citing that it did not reflect the actual situation as the government instead took a political perspective rather than a civil and humanitarian one in interpreting the report. There has not been any research done at the behest of the government to ascertain the cost caused by the Operation in terms of humanitarian costs, property, and economic opportunities for the individuals who were already suffering economically. This means the government of Zimbabwe has not had any political will hence has been unwilling to promote transitional justice in general.

While reparations can be viewed as a justice mechanism, it appears that undertakings on reparations are easily dwelt with directly in tandem with situations where the conflict has had a legal or court process for resolution. In our case, how can the *Operation* be subjected to a court case, where and which perpetrators are supposed to take the stand when from the ultimate outlook a considerable chunk of the urban population were affected by the Operation. In addition, how, under such a scenario, can the government of Zimbabwe compensate all in the spirit of transitional justice more so when the country is also characterized by corruption which became topical in blocking the successes of the *Garikai/Hlalani Kuhle* scheme reported to have benefitted even the perpetrators and people who were not affected by the Operation?

LINKING CRITICAL DISCOURSE ANALYSIS AND TRANSITIONAL JUSTICE

Discourses either in the form of reports, research, or surveys and even media reports act in most cases as discursive representational tools. With reference to Zimbabwe, a great deal of discursive representational tools was produced during and after the Operation. The UN Tibaijuka (2005) report, the Action-Aid International Southern Africa Partnership Program (SAPP-Zimbabwe, 2005) survey and other human rights agency reports, media reports both local and international; and other researches on the same are examples in point. It should be noted that nobody elected, from the perspective of the victims of course, to represent them and these are not formally accountable to the victims of the *Operation*. Some victims may not have an idea that they are being represented or were represented by the said groups. However, in terms of these groups representing the discourses of the Operation against human rights violations and justice in general, the victims were projected in a well-calculated manner as victims of an unjust sociopolitical and economic space in Zimbabwe. Therefore, what we read is that, the corpus of literature produced during and after Operation reveals some notions of representing individuals and groups affected by the operation in Zimbabwe. This representation was deliberately made within the broad context of transitional justice. Had it not been for the dictates of transitional justice, the discourses become invalid. We thus take "discourse" here, following Dryzek and Niemeyer (2008, p. 481) as a set of concepts embodying specific assumptions, judgements, contentions, dispositions, and capabilities. It enables the mind to process sensory inputs into coherent accounts, which can then be shared in intersubjectivity meaningful fashion.

Further, we note that discourses rely heavily, from a communicative point, on metaphors and rhetorical devices. In doing so, discourses assume power to manipulate, judge, dictate, and generally constrain thought, speech, and action (Dryzek & Niemeyer, 2008, p. 482). However, discourses must assume some qualities; for instance, they must embody acceptable knowledge and should not exist in a vacuum. They must take a side from which some interests are deliberately given, venting and treated as valid while suppressing or repressing those that may be considered invalid. This formulation helps discourses move beyond a surface manifestation of interests to constituting identities and their interests (Dryzek & Niemeyer, 2008, p. 482). Thus, having located and established the boundaries of discourses, we then move to exploring Critical Discourse Analysis (henceforth CDA) in order to appreciate discursive representation in the context of transitional justice in Zimbabwe with reference to the Operation. CDA was developed within linguistics. CDA, therefore, is an

> analysis of the dialectical relationships between discourse (including language but also other forms of semiosis, e.g. body language or visual images) and other elements of social practices. (Chiapello & Fairclough, 2002, p. 185)

The *Operation* and transitional justice are both social practices which created identifiable discourses as such the role of discourses in such an instance of a social practice should not be taken for granted. Analyzing discourses around the *Operation* as a social practice can thus lead us to understand better some aspects of transitional justice as played out in Zimbabwe and this should be established through some form of analysis. This approach is hoped to bring richer insights into transitional justice as well the *Operation* or any other form of human rights violations. Further, "social practice" means "a relatively stabilized form of social activity" (Chiapello & Fairclough, 2002, p. 193). While the *Operation* was a short term "social activity" with politically and capitalist charged motives, it has had long-term effects making it qualify as a social activity, however, divorced from the usually accepted activities such as classroom teaching, family meals, medical consultations, and so on. Because this activity resulted in the articulation of diverse social elements, it naturally had to include or have discourses.

Chiapello and Fairclough (2002) note that discourse figure in three basic ways; as part of the social activity involving use of language in a particular way, figures in representations because social actors within a social practice produce representations of even other practices. For instance, international human rights agencies in Zimbabwe during and after the *Operation* do qualify as social actors given their mandate of policing aspects of justice around the world. The same applies to Zimbabwean intellectuals all of who produced representations (or misrepresentations) of human rights violations in Zimbabwe, where violations are practices not required in safeguarding democracy and peace in the world. The lives of the poor urban populace in Zimbabwe at the time of the *Operation* was/is thus represented in the social practices of governance. Lastly, they figure in the ways of being constituting the identities of the victims of the Operation.

Van Dijk (1993) discusses the principles of CDA and submits that CDA studies the relations between discourses, power, dominance, social inequality, and the position of the analyst in such social relationships. This means that CDA challenges the dominance or exercises of social power by elites, institutions or groups. This makes us appreciate that the *Operation* as an operation should be broadly viewed as an instance of human rights violations or the inaction of authoritarian power by the then Mugabe government on the socio-economically pressed urban populace in the twenty-first century.

In reaction, international agencies and national ones responded to the domination by the capitalist elite not militantly but by producing reports and studies that exposed the violations in order for them to have voice in the post conflict era. It is by studying these discourses today, do we appreciate and make inroads into the basic call for transitional justice as the discourses exist not only to expose injustice and its perpetrators but also to side with victims and represent them even if the victims are/were not aware that they are/were being represented in matters of social justice.

If we are to follow Van Dijk's (1993) views, it follows that national and international human rights agencies as well as scholars of TJ alike are in fact critical discourse analysts. Van Dijk (1993) says critical discourses "(should) take an explicit socio-political stance: they spell out their point of view, perspective, principles and aims, both within their discipline and within society at large" Van Dijk (1993, p. 252). This means, the discourses they produced were critically analytical of the social activities aligned to human rights and justice issues within a Zimbabwean context which over the years has been proven to be heavily characterized by systems that have resulted in the abuse of human rights hence a call for justice and subsequently social justice.

OF DISCOURSES AND TRANSITIONAL JUSTICE IN ZIMBABWE

It has been shown above that transitional justice involves mechanisms of meeting or promoting social justice to societies affected by conflict. The mechanisms, generally, begin in as well as call for reconstruction of the past, thus, redefining what was done, by who and with what effects. Such is a linear view of establishing or building peace, tolerance, and creating mechanisms of avoiding future conflicts of a less magnitude. Here, we have a similar role laid out by the discourses on the *Operations* as represented by the reports and studies cited above. Hence re-reading such discourses from a CDA perspective, therefore, reveals that producers of such discourses are critical discourse analysts who have systematically documented a social activity in Zimbabwe—the *Operation*, that had its historical roots in the economic and political policies of the government of the time.

What appears common in the discourses is the explicit side they take of representing the ordinary, poor, politically and economically disadvantaged urban people in the country. How else could the voice of these people have been heard in the context of transitional justice if such discourses did not represent them? As has been noted, the representation was deliberate, and sides taken appear to have been influenced by the basic history of the Government of Zimbabwe and ZANU (PF)'s well-documented history of lack of respect for the rule of law and an ugly record of accomplishment of human rights violations.

In other words, the authoritarian nature of the then Mugabe government as well as its total rejection to recognize the relevancy of the opposition and its unwillingness to entertain any constructive criticism, even from within, made it easier for the discourses to side with the people. There is no doubt, therefore, that the discourses, even without using the term "victim" explicitly suggest that every poor urban person affected one way or the other, regardless of political affiliation, was a victim not only of *Operation* but of Mugabe's authoritarian capitalist rule.

Tibaijuka (2005) indicated that Zimbabwe was a peaceful country. This was very deliberate and well calculated to reveal that the nature of conflict in Zimbabwe at the time was not one to which opposing sides wedged guns or machetes. Thus, the conflict at hand could not be described or equated to "war." What we read instead is the notion that the situation in Zimbabwe at the time and the *Operation* itself was a resultant economic meltdown which the Government of Zimbabwe had failed to solve for years whose effects could even be mistaken to effects that are normally observed in war torn contexts. Displacements, demolitions, arrests, psychological and economic effects, breakdown of family unions and so on are characteristic of effects of war. When discourses speak of "criminalization" of the urban populace by its government, which ironically was expected to protect them, shows the ruthlessness of the government and the hidden agenda to justify the "demolitions" as well as displacement of people from the urban centers. Kamete (2009, p. 897) analyses this process of criminalizing the populace by saying,

People became filth if they occupied or used urban spaces in violation of planning and property laws; activities became filth if they happened in undesignated areas; informal business and residential structures were filth because they did not have requisite planning and building permission.

Discourses, therefore, begin by critically exposing the deliberate process of criminalizing the poor to justify the actions that followed. They further go on to justify elements of criminalization making it even difficult for the Government of Zimbabwe or scholars who defend the government's actions. The *Operation* itself, code named "Restore Order" is also given two meanings, that is, the idea of restoring order as well as "cleansing filth." Kamete (2009) choses "filth" and uses it as if to lampoon the government of Zimbabwe for characterizing its people as filthy and disorderly. This alone reveals that human rights violations went beyond physical demolitions and displacements as the whole urban population was characterized as "filthy" by their own government. How, then, under such identity creations do we deal with restoration of dignity of the people in the context of TJ when first there is a deliberate ideological undertaking to characterize and negatively portray the poor before physically violating their rights?

During the colonial era, colonial discourses ideologically portrayed Africa as a dark continent. The people of Africa were characterized as backward, uncivilized, defeated, and grotesque especially when one refers to Conrad's (1902) *The Heart of Darkness*. Such an ideological portrayal was deliberately made to justify imperialism as Europe descended heavily on Africa in the name of civilizing it, and today imperialist results are there for all to see. This appears to be a similar jinx used by the government of Zimbabwe to first portray, ideologically, and characterize its own people as filthy and disorderly to justify even with reference to the Urban Council's Act its human rights violations during the time. This can be worse than imperialism as imperialism was hinged on racial grounds, which grounding was the government of Zimbabwe hinged on when it characterized its own people as filthy and disorderly. Hence, recording the hidden as well as subtle reasons and motives of the then Mugabe government during the time in this way is to awaken people's memories of the past in the context of transitional justice.

The government of Zimbabwe acknowledged that the country was peaceful as captured by Tibaijuka (2005). But what the report for instance further drives us to is the contrast is created which the Government of Zimbabwe even as it sorts to distance itself by asserting that the demolitions were those of illegal settlements in terms of the laws of the country, the trail of destruction left by the operation was enormous which one could easily equate to destructions caused usually by war-related conflicts. In a peaceful country like Zimbabwe, such mega destruction could mean far much more than a mere cleaning up exercise of the illegal settlements. This explains the description of the exercise as a "Tsunami" (Potts, 2006), or "whirlwind."

Discourses further show that the government had been responsible in the impoverishment of the urban populace and its laws on urban planning as well as urbanization had been too strict; and unaccommodative of the expanding urbanization. In some cases, the same government had created holding centers on the outskirts of cities but moved in too slowly to find space for them resulting in the spaces degenerating into "slums" which it came back to define as "dirty" or filth and spaces of economic insanity posing a serious risk to public health. The government of Zimbabwe used legality, public health risks, and disorder to justify its stance yet the decision to clean up the exercise is even presented as not having been discussed or planned by cabinet (Tibaijuka, 2005). Hence, lack of a specific government department responsible for the operation, yet a militarized police force acts on the orders from the highest echelons of power. Thus, Tibaijuka (2005) is explicit in naming the government as the perpetrator.

But, the government of Zimbabwe had its defenders such as Mahoso (2008) who extended rejection of the report by placing it within a regime change ideology to which he questions why the report magnified a cleaning exercise equal to similar exercises done even internationally elsewhere. He views the *Operation* as "a routine event, namely slum clearance" (Mahoso, 2008, p. 159) and accuses Tibaijuka (2005) of having magnified *Operation Murambatsvina* by turning it into,

> a "global" incident, with the writer or writers wondering aloud how the event could qualify for UN Security Council attention and even for the International Criminal Court. (Mahoso, 2008, p. 159)

For Mahoso (2008), therefore, *Operation Murambatsvina* exposed what he suggests as what had become the popular condemnation of the Mugabe government. Here, the government of Zimbabwe is presented as a victim of global politics to which the popularity of the UN Tibaijuka (2005) report is seen as deliberately biased and produced by the powerful forces "as a basis for interference and intervention in the affairs of other countries" (Mahoso, 2008, p. 161).

Mahoso (2008) suggests that to represent "the filth," "disorderly," or "criminal" elements that made up the urban populace is to side with forces, which had long campaigned against the Zimbabwean government. The historical interpretation of the *Operation* is thus given a contrasting view to which the actions of the Zimbabwe government are taken as normal and appropriate and the suffering, if any, of the people of Zimbabwe is in fact a result of international interference in governance issues in the country.

While discourses that analyze the *Operation* refer to the failure of economic policies employed by the government, Mahoso (2008) takes a political dig instead of the international politicking, as having shaped specifically the UN Tibaijuka (2005) as such it should be rejected as not a true reflection of the *Operation*. Mhiripiri (2008) exposes the Government of Zimbabwe's responses to the Operation. These responses Mhiripiri (2008, p. 149) rightly notes that the Government of Zimbabwe was aware of international practices to developments of human nature with a bearing to human development. He says,

> Internationally, it is now generally accepted that any government's responses to critical human rights condemnations should be taken seriously because they are a strong marker and indicator of the level of concern, tolerance and therefore democracy in that particular country. It also has strong implications for a country's reputation and image.

This exposes the consciousness of the government of Zimbabwe to this fact and thus responded mainly through "public briefings, press releases and official statements to more restricted channels such as direct letters and meetings with delegations, and communications in regional or global agencies" (Mhiripiri, 2008, p. 149). For the government of Zimbabwe, as Mhiripiri rightly notes, became more of rebuttals in some cases conversion of defensive positions into an attack on the part of the constructive critic. It appears to be this behavior which influenced Mahoso (2008) greatly, as he attacked the UN and anyone who agreed with them.

The medium used by the Government of Zimbabwe was mainly its state-owned media such as *The Herald* and *The Sunday Mail* and the ZBC Radios and TV Station. In responding to criticism of its actions to the *Operation*, the Government of Zimbabwe placed itself as a victim to international politics and vilification to which it claimed to have been demonized by the west largely due to its agrarian reform program. But, Mhiripiri (2008, p. 152) summarizes the texture of the Government of Zimbabwe's responses to *Operation Murambatsvina* thus,

> three forms of denial appear in the discourse of official responses to allegations of human rights violations. These are (1) literal denial which is an insistence that 'nothing of the sort ever happened'; (2) interpretive denial which insists 'what happened is really something else'; and (3) implicatory denial which argues that 'what happened is justified'. The Zimbabwean government has used all forms of denial in varying degrees.

Mhiripiri (2008) further gives instances of situations as well as statements in which the Government of Zimbabwe through its officials, and even the then

President Mugabe, either literally denied, interpretively denied or implicatorily denied and wrong doing or its role in human rights violations during the *Operation*.

It is not surprising that even references to *Garikai/Hlalani Kuhle* also took a similar stance. There is no difference in representations and linguistic description to the actions of the government in responding to the destructions of the *Operation*. New terms are incorporated especially by The Solidarity Peace Trust (2006) who explicitly show that corruption further worsened the situation of the already affected poor people. Due to lack of a significant paradigm shift in human rights violations, much of these discourses are quick to show that *Garikai/Hlalani Kuhle* although a "scheme" undertaken by the government in response to the pressure exerted on it during the Operation, it merely became an extension of *Operation*. Hammar (2017) for instance, indicates that the City of Bulawayo presented land for the construction of houses for the "squatters" as a "gesture" more as its mandate and responsibility to create space for urban settlements.

When taken together, the discourses that provide evidence and voice of the victims of the *Operation* and the responses of the government which was the perpetrator or expected protector of the people, we learn of the complexities that characterize characterization of agreeing on "what actually" happened in the past? This undermines any efforts to transitional justice because transitional justice assumes that the wrong doer accepts their actions, or some tribunal should at least proclaim and point out the wrong doer in order for victims to deal with the past psychologically or internally with external actions such as reparations and so on coming in to cement and promote reconciliation with the hope of building sustainable peace.

Two hostile camps are created by the discourses. On one hand, we have discourses that use a humanitarian interpretation of the *Operation* as a social activity within a very politically charged country. On the other, we have discourses of rebuttal by the government and its supporters who use instead a political interpretation of the social activity and subsequent discursive representational voices of the *Operation*. The government appears to be less worried with humanitarian effects of its people prompting Mhiripiri (2008, p. 152) to conclude that such a behavior is not surprising as it is

> usually used by repressive regimes that care little about their democratic credentials—regimes somewhat self-insulated from outside scrutiny and insensitive to their own inter- national image or reputation.

This, therefore, calls for redefining and retheorizing transitional justice especially when faced with the *Operation* and the representations of voices by the discourses created. First, the social activity itself reflects a great deal and evidence of human rights violations and *Operation* actually led to a serious humanitarian crisis. Nevertheless, this crisis was not enshrined or caused by war but by elite capitalist economic policies that caused poor people to devise mechanisms of survival without militantly confronting the central government. When the government had failed in its control even in promoting its elite capitalist economy given the informal economy which directly challenged the formal one; it used its authoritarian hand to stop "informalism" mechanisms of which had a huge impact on the poor.

Even, under pressure, *Garikai/Hlalani Kuhle*, also failed to meet its objectives and to date there is no government position in the form of reports or discourses that reveal an effort by the government to recollect the *Operation*. New economic policies such as the ZIMASSET as well as a wide range of initiatives to which local authorities have been pushed to work with land developers in selling land for residential and commercial purposes to people have been topical in government discourses. These appear to have been taken as automatic reparations to those that were affected by the *Operation*. There have been scandals involving land developers to which so called land "barons" (and government officials have been fingered in the schemes) have sold availed land for personal enrichment and beneficiaries losing their contributions.

NON-STATE TRANSITIONAL JUSTICE MECHANISMS USEFUL IN ADDRESSING *OPERATION MURAMBATSVINA* VIOLATIONS

Social justice is difficult to ascertain as having been rendered to victims of the *Operation*. The poor urban populace has instead, following Musoni (2010), devised mechanisms of rebuilding their small scale businesses destroyed by the *Operation* while churches and other civil organizations have assisted the populace with food, shelter and other forms of help to help them cope. The assistance has been short term and necessary.

For the affected, who have dusted themselves as noted by Musoni (2010), what we read is the nature of the populace's ability to read the political mood of their government. It means they have not demanded reparations in the political sense of the term or as defined by mechanisms of transitional justice. Instead, they appear to have used "silence" in advancing their demands but practically devising means to rebuild their livelihoods. Partly, this is because, in transitional justice, as has been noted above, representations are done by foreign human rights agencies and not by the affected themselves. For the foreign agencies to demand reparations on their behalf is, in the case of Zimbabwe, to invite the government's wrath of accusations.

In 2005, the government stood firm to rebut and defend its actions and claimed it had cleaned up the cities with respect to its laws and that there was nothing sinister as the clean-up exercise was in tandem with international practices (Mahoso, 2008). Today, the same cities are still considered dirty and informal traders continue to run battles with local authorities especially in Harare and elsewhere. There continues to be a call from government and the City of Harare to return the city to its "sunshine" days, but no sustainable solution has been found to date. Most people now make a living out of "vending" right at the city center. Somehow, the government has diplomatically attempted to engage and persuade the "informal" traders to "formalize" their operations. This stance may be partly an effort to appease the urban populace and avoid the 2005 demolitions or displacements.

Broadly, however, more still needs to be done especially by the government. While it is challenging to address every individual, who may have been affected, the economic stance of the whole population needs to be addressed to which the government is expected to come up with concrete long-term economic policies that can uplift people from poverty. The government should allow and open up spaces for people to discuss and engage each other, especially the government, on the past, specifically the *Operation* era in order for memories to find an outlet. The involvement of the government in this endeavor is required to bring in political will since transitional justice requires political will to succeed.

There are non-state transitional justice mechanisms that might bring about peace building in the country with reference to the *Operation*. Given the long history and record of the ZANU (PF) treatment of the population, one can note that the population has lost trust in their own government. This created a culture in which the populace has come to find ways of dealing with their condition of absurdity deliberately created by the then Mugabe government. Hence, if the government is to play a key role in funding or initiating transitional justice mechanisms victims are likely to take the government's stance with suspicion. Given this reality, non-state mechanisms may have better results as compared to state mechanisms of transitional justice.

Music and arts can be used to promote dialogue from which developments of the past especially during the *Operation* can be allowed to freely be made in the media and various other platforms. The arts (music, film, painting, dance, etc.) will help bring the populace to a dialogue and advance a culture of tolerance as well as a leeway of evoking memories of the *Operation*. If reconstruction of the past is the generally accepted first stage of TJ, the arts will play this pivotal role of recreating that past. This way, the psychologically affected may have ways of venting out internalized hatred or disdain. The arts can thus give hope and motivate them to rebuild their relations, work on whatever may now be available and move on into the future.

Comprehensive studies can also be done, and recommendations suggested for implementation. The civic society such as churches can play a major role to fund or carry out such studies to document what happened as well as come up with programs of engaging and empowering groups affected by the Operations. Churches are normally trusted by the populace and in Zimbabwe the Church has a significant role to play in peace building as one end it deals with matters of the spirit while on the other it is expected to deal with pragmatic day-to-day issues that affects its congregates. If the then minister of higher and tertiary education Jonathan Moyo, pushed for a formal study of the impact of sanctions on Zimbabwe, a similar aspect can be done to which a studies funded by government as well as civic organizations can be done to assess the impact of the Operations and also audit *Garikai/Hlalani Kuhle* to create a body of discourses that allow victims recreate the past, deal with it and promote reconciliation and thus promote sustainable peace development.

CONCLUSION

This Chapter has explored discourses *Operation Murambatsvina*, a campaign rolled out in Zimbabwe in 2005 against aspects of transitional justice through discursive representations. It has noted that the discourses created by virtue of the *Operation*, represented the victims and exposed the government of Zimbabwe as the major perpetrator of a very complex campaign which in outlook was nothing but a serious instance of human rights violations. While transitional justice is an idealistic notion with the objective of foreseeing sustainable peace-building around the world, its usual approach is weakened by the texture of "one jacket fits all approach." The *Operation* proved that human rights could be violated outside the obvious definitions of conflicts which normally foresee mass graves. The *Operation* instead witnessed mass destructions in a short space of time, the urban populace regardless of political affiliation were all subjected to the "Tsunami" of 2005. A scheme, *Garikai/Hlalani Kuhle* was rolled out by the government partly in response to the pressure exerted on the government to stop the violations. This too was also seen here as having become an extension of the *Operation* as corruption, poor planning where structures were either poorly built or were given to so-called beneficiaries in their incomplete state. The already impoverished populace was further subjected to economic violations in this manner.

The discourses produced, the chapter has shown that, represent the victims in as much as they appear as a record of the social activity in the form of the *Operation*. However, the problematic nature of this representation is observed in fulfilling aspects of transitional justice which apart from reconstructing the past, to which the discourses rightly fulfill this role, the call for reparations and bringing perpetrators to book are not fulfilled making it difficult for the cycle of transitional justice to be complete.

It has thus been suggested that non-state transitional justice mechanisms require primacy to which civic institutions in Zimbabwe can play a significant role. The church or other social organizations appear to have the trust of the populace as compared to the distrust that the government has due to its long history of betraying its own people. Music, films, and the other arts can be conditioned or used to promote social justice in the country; from recording and recreating the past to calling for reparation as well as foreseeing promotion of sustainable social justice. These areas are the cheaper discourses of representing their own people to which the represented can also participate actively through singing, dancing, and in other performative arts.

BIBLIOGRAPHY

ActionAid International Southern Africa Partnership Program (SAPP-Zimbabwe) PREFACE. 2005. "The Impact of "Operation Murambatsvina/Restore Order" in Zimbabwe.

Benyera, Everisto and Chidochashe Nyere. 2015. "An Exploration of the Impact of Zimbabwe's 2005 Operation Murambatsvina on Women and Children." *Gender & Behaviour* 13 (1): 6522–34.

Buckley-Zistel, Susanne, Teresa Koloma Beck, Christian Braun, and Friederike Mieth. 2014. "Transitional Justice Theories: An Introduction." In *Transitional justice Theories*, edited by S. Buckley-Zistel, T. K. Beck, C. Braun, and F. Mieth. New York: Routledge, pp. 13–28.

Chiapello, Eve, and Norman Fairclough. 2002. "Critical Discourse Analysis and New Sociology of Capitalism." *Discourse & Society* 13 (2): 185–208.

Conrad, Joseph. 1902. *The Heart of Darkness*. London: Elegant Books.

Dryzek, John S., and Simon Niemeyer. 2008. "Discursive Representation." *American Political Science Review* 102 (4): 481–93.

Fairclough, Norman. 1992. Discourse and text: Linguistic and intertextual analysis within discourse analysis. *Discourse & Society* 3 (2), 193–217.

Fischer, Martina. 2011. "Transitional Justice and Reconciliation: Theory and Practice." *Advancing Conflict Transformation. The Berghof Handbook II*, pp. 405–430.

Hammar, Amanda. 2017. "Urban Displacement and Resettlement in Zimbabwe: The Paradoxes of Propertied Citizenship." *African Studies Review* 60 (3): 81–104.

Hammar, Amanda, Jo Ann McGregor, and Loren Landau. 2010. "Introduction. Displacing Zimbabwe: Crisis and Construction in Southern Africa." *Journal of Southern African Studies* 36 (2): 263–83.

Kamete, Amin Y. 2009. "In the Service of Tyranny: Debating the Role of Planning in Zimbabwe's Urban 'Clean-up' Operation." *Urban Studies* 46 (4): 897–922.

Lambourne, Wendy. 2014. "Justice After Genocide: Impunity and the Extraordinary Chambers in the Courts of Cambodia." *Genocide Studies and Prevention: An International Journal* 8 (2): 29–43.

Mahoso, Tafataona. 2008. "Reading the 2005 Tibaijuka Report on Zimbabwe in a Global Context." In *The Hidden dimensions of Operation Murambatsvina*, edited by M. T. Vambe, 159–68. Harare: Weaver Press.

Mhiripiri, Nhamo. 2008. "The Zimbabwe Government's Responses to Criticism of Operation Murambatsvina." In *The Hidden dimensions of Operation Murambatsvina*, edited by M. T. Vambe, pp. 147–68. Harare: Weaver Press.

Musoni, Francis. 2010. "Operation Murambatsvina and the Politics of Street Vendors in Zimbabwe." *Journal of Southern African Studies* 36 (2): 301–17.

Ndlovu-Gatsheni, Sabelo J. 2012. "Rethinking Chimurenga and Gukurahundi in Zimbabwe: A Critique of Partisan National History." *African Studies Review* 55 (3): 1–26.

Potts, Deborah. 2006. "Restoring Order'? Operation Murambatsvina and the Urban Crisis in Zimbabwe." *Journal of Southern African Studies* 32 (2): 273–91.

Potts, Deborah. 2008. The urban informal sector in sub-Saharan Africa: from bad to good (and back again?). *Development Southern Africa*, 25 (2), 151–167.

Ramírez-Barat, Clara. 2014. *Transitional Justice, Culture and Society: Beyond Outreach*. Edited by C. Ramirez-Barat. New York: Social Science Research Council.

Solidarity Peace Trust. 2006. *'Meltdown' Murambatsvina One Year On*." (August).

Tibaijuka, Anna. K. 2005. Report of the Fact-Finding Mission to Zimbabwe to Assess the Scope and Impact of Operation Murambatsvina. Harare and Geneva: United Nations

Van Dijk, Teun Andrianus. 1993. "Principles of Critical Discourse Analysis." *Discourse & Society* 4 (2): 249–83.

Villa-Vicencio, Charles. 2001. *Transitional Justice and Human Rights in Africa*. Accessed from: http://citeseerx.ist.psu.edu/viewdoc/download?doi=10.1.1.573.424&rep=rep1&type=pdf

Chapter 6

"Healing the Dead" in Matabeleland, Zimbabwe

Combining Tradition with Science to Restore Personhood after Massacres

Shari Eppel

INTRODUCTION

Zimbabwe is a nation with a long history of state-organized violence, dating back to the imposition of the colonial state in the 1890s in what was then called Rhodesia. The white colonial government ruled by racist laws and oppressive forms of social control, as well as by outright violence against the black majority (Auret 1992). This led, by the 1960s, to organized resistance and a war of independence, which ended with majority rule in April 1980. However, since 1980 there have been other eras of state-organized violence, which have impacted variously on millions of lives in Zimbabwe. In no instance has there been any formal accountability or truth for victims, by early in 2018 at least.

The intention of this book is to examine the ways in which communities have found alternatives to formal "transitional justice" mechanisms, either alongside or instead of state mechanisms. The term "transitional justice" (TJ) assumes that a transition has taken place. However, in 2018, it could be argued that Zimbabwe is still waiting for a true political transition, apart from that which undoubtedly took place in 1980 in the changeover from colonial to majority rule in Zimbabwe. The decision of Robert Mugabe at Independence in April 1980 was to "draw a line through the past," and not to examine the crimes of colonialism and the war of independence (Mugabe 1980). He was praised at the time for his magnanimous ability to embrace his erstwhile enemies, and this appeared necessary then to maintain stability in the country, after a brutal civil war for independence. It is also true that 1980 was ahead of what became the international "norm"—the accompaniment of most peace deals with a package of transitional justice (TJ) commitments. However, by granting particularly the colonial government and also the guerrilla armies impunity, Mugabe set the stage for his reaction to all future human rights violations—the nation has been repeatedly battered under the Zimbabwe African National Union—Patriotic Front (ZANU-PF), and has been repeatedly told to forget about these crimes and move forward: the past is dead (ZBC 2018).

ERAS OF CHANGE SINCE 1980—AND STATE RESPONSE

Since 1980, there have been several eras of political upheaval leading to transitions in Zimbabwe, but none has been acknowledged officially by the state as a transition requiring any kind of justice, transitional, or otherwise. A true "transition" presupposes a genuine shift in political power, and in the early months of 2018, this has yet to happen in Zimbabwe. A November coup in 2017 finally replaced Robert Mugabe, after nearly 38 years of rule, with Emmerson Mnangagwa as president; however, this left both ZANU PF and the militarized state still firmly in control (Solidarity Peace Trust 2018). This chapter will list briefly the three "semi" transitions that have occurred since 1980, to place each in its historical moment, before returning to explore in more detail the so-called Gukurahundi era of the early 1980s.

In 1980, the integration of three armies—the Rhodesian National Army, the Zimbabwe African National Liberation Army (ZANLA), armed wing of ZANU-PF, and the Zimbabwe Peoples' Revolutionary Army (ZIPRA), armed wing of the Zimbabwe African People's Union (ZAPU)—was problematic. While ZANLA and ZIPRA jointly fought the war of liberation, there were antagonisms dating back to the breaking away of ZANU from ZAPU in 1963, and in the field, the two armies fought each other fiercely during the 1970s, even while sharing the aim of fighting the Rhodesian army (Alexander et al. 2000). In the first election in 1980, Mugabe's ZANU PF won most seats countrywide, but in the three Western provinces, ZAPU won overwhelmingly, which posed a threat to Mugabe's desire for political hegemony. It was therefore hardly surprising that during military integration there were some defections and armed banditry countrywide as anxious ex-combatants feared for their futures. In particular, there were stories of ex-ZIPRAs being "disappeared" by their commanders from the ranks of the "united" force and never being seen again, which led to other nervous ZIPRAs defecting (Alexander et al. 2000).

While defections and caching of arms by both ZIPRA and ZANLA occurred countrywide, this phenomenon was used selectively by Mugabe to build a case against ZAPU (Alexander et al. 2000). Retrospectively, it is clear that even while Mugabe spoke of "drawing a line through the past," he was intent on avenging grievances from the 1970s and crushing ZAPU and its support base, to ensure a one-party state. In August 1980, within months of the first election, and before there were any disturbances in the nation, Mugabe flew to North Korea and commissioned them to train for him what effectively became a hit squad, the 5 Brigade.[1] In 1982, Mugabe himself named this the "Gukurahundi Brigade" at their passing out parade. "Gukurahundi" is a Shona word meaning the "first rain of summer that washes away the chaff from the last season" (CCJP and LRF 1997). The Ndebele and ZAPU supporters came to see themselves as the "rubbish" to be washed away. Between 1983 and 1985, an estimated 10,000 to 20,000 civilians in Matabeleland and the Midlands are estimated to have died at the hands of 5 Brigade, with tens of thousands more raped, tortured, and beaten. This era has been treated with silence and denial by the state and is not referenced in official histories in Zimbabwe. There has been no accountability, no truth-telling, and no reparations.

The Unity Accord, which ended this era in 1987, simply entrenched the power of both ZANU PF, which now officially ruled in the context of a de facto one-party state, and of Robert Mugabe, who transitioned from being a prime minister to be an all-powerful president through a constitutional amendment that coincided with the Unity Accord. ZAPU officially ceased to exist, being absorbed into ZANU PF, which now ruled with more powers and hegemony. This Accord could be seen to mark the first political "semi-transition" in Zimbabwe.

The second "transition" was that brought about by the land invasions during the post-2000 era. These were provoked by the rise of a new political opposition, the Movement for Democratic Change (MDC), the first formidable opposition since the demise of ZAPU. ZANU PF seized on real land grievances that had not been resolved since Independence to regain electoral support that was slipping away in the face of the MDC, by taking land from white commercial farmers and redistributing it (RAU 2009). The outcomes of this land redistribution are not the focus of this chapter, but suffice it to say, the land invasions literally changed the landscape of most of Zimbabwe in permanent and irreversible ways, with hundreds of thousands of new small-scale farmers taking up land as white commercial farmers were displaced. Much of this was violent, outside of both the law and the specifically revised constitution, but its outcomes have undoubtedly amounted to a transition, with some positive outcomes at the local level for the resettled farmers (Cliffe et al. 2011; Scoones et al. 2010).

It could be argued that the land redistribution program was in fact a form of delayed TJ—an outstanding issue not addressed at Independence because the Lancaster House peace deal placed a ten-year moratorium on land redistribution. While the state did not ever use the terminology of TJ, it was clear that reclaiming the land was a form of justified reparation to ordinary people for the crime of theft of their land by white settlers. However, it created a new slew of injustices including the allocation of more than one farm each to senior ZANU PF leadership, many of whom scavenged and then abandoned one farm after another, and the displacement of over one million indigenous farm workers and their families (RAU 2009; Sachikonye 2003). The state also used the cause of land redistribution to obfuscate the widespread abuses that were taking place against rural and urban MDC supporters, including torture, rape, murder, as well as politically motivated arrests and oppression (Physicians for Human Rights 2002).

After the 2005 election, in which urban residents voted solidly for the opposition, ZANU PF embarked on "Operation Murambatsvina," allegedly to punish urban voters and to head off any popular uprising in Harare (Potts 2008). As with the displacement of farm workers, targeting the urban poor was once again targeting those perceived to primarily support the MDC. This resulted in the displacement of over 700,000 people, who lost homes and livelihoods and were pushed into abject poverty (Tibaijuka 2005). Once more, there has been no reckoning of this act, which undoubtedly drove hundreds of thousands into despair and material loss from which they have never recovered. This could be considered an attempt at urban engineering and seen as part of the land redistribution process: many peri-urban commercial farms have been carved up into plots and given to ZANU PF supporters, thus changing the voting landscape of Harare in particular (Mongoma 2017; Solidarity Peace Trust 2018).

The election of 2008 ultimately resulted in the third almost-transition, with the formation of the Government of National Unity (GNU), after the late Morgan Tsvangirai won the first round of the Presidential election, but with less than 50 percent of the vote. This led to the intervention of the army and paramilitary forces loyal to ZANU PF, who killed more than 200 MDC supporters and beat thousands more during the presidential run-off period (Solidarity Peace Trust 2008a, 2008b). This moment was also a clear indicator that it is the military wing of ZANU PF rather than the political commissars that hold the real power in the country.[2] Tsvangirai withdrew from the run-off on grounds of the extreme violence, and the GNU was brokered by the Southern African Development Community (SADC), which led to politically shared government until 2013. During this time, the MDC battled to make headway in terms of reforming institutions and restoring the rule of law. Positively, a new constitution was passed, which among other changes, succeeded in institutionalizing, in theory at least, the existence of five independent commissions.

These included the establishment of the National Peace and Reconciliation Commission (NPRC), which was mandated to have a ten-year tenure (Constitution of Zimbabwe 2013). For the first time in nearly 40 years, it appeared the state was committing itself to some kind of formal transitional justice mechanism. However, at the time of its inclusion in the constitution, there was an assumption that the opposition MDC would win the elections of 2013, thus ensuring a space for some accountability for the past and the crimes of ZANU PF. That did not happen: ZANU PF swept to victory in 2013 with more than two-thirds of the seats. This left the NPRC in a strange space, in which it could be assumed that there will be very little space for official TJ, as it would mean ZANU PF would have to hold itself to account for all these series of abuses since 1980.

After Emmerson Mnangagwa's post-coup installation as president in November 2017, a few months later he surprised many by signing into law the NPRC Bill, which had been referred back for further revisions four times since 2014, at the insistence of civil society organizations and the opposition, to try and pull it in line with the constitution (National Transitional Justice Working Group 2017). While not a perfect Bill, as it still allowed for interference from the presidium instead of being totally independent (among other shortcomings) it was finally approved by parliament in late 2017, but Mugabe failed to sign it. Within weeks of Mnangagwa's signature bringing the Act into effect in late January 2018, the NPRC held provincial consultations in all ten provinces, creating at least some expectation that this heralded the opening of official political space to deal with at least some aspects of the past. In Bulawayo and Matabeleland North, meetings were disrupted with angry young activists challenging the authenticity of the commission's makeup and its intentions (Ncube 2018). How the commission will proceed in due course is uncertain at the time of writing this chapter and will depend in part on how much pressure is maintained on the state and the NPRC by civics and victims of abuses, and the degree to which the NPRC insists on some independence from the executive in government, who may have vested interests in the NPRC not achieving much. Now that the lid is slightly opened to release the countless stories of victimhood from all these eras going back to the war of liberation, will the state be able to control the direction and outcome of the NPRC entirely? What can be realistically expected of the state to help the thousands of victims move on into a better, more reconciled future, over and above some limited "truth telling"? Mnangagwa was constitutionally compelled to sign the Bill, but the fact he did so as one of his first acts in office suggests an awareness that the violence of the past has to be addressed. On the other hand, the complete lack of resources budgeted by the state for the NPRC is an indicator that it may not be intended to achieve much more than a few token glances at the past. The violence in the wake of the 2018 election, in which the army shot dead six people on the streets of Harare, also seemed evidence that when threatened in any way, ZANU PF will revert to type, and resolve problems with violence against civilians.

It is apparent that Zimbabwe is no stranger to major shifts in sociopolitical direction but has yet to experience a true transition since independence in 1980: ZANU PF has remained solidly in power for 38 years and has shown itself prepared to commit acts of violence to ensure this remains the case. Prior to 2018, they have also proved unprepared and unwilling to provide space for truth telling, even less so for justice or any other form of reparations, for any of the crimes occurring during their almost four-decade-long rule. It is also apparent that Zimbabweans, especially in Matabeleland, have reeled from one era of oppression to the next, without long, intervening periods of feeling stable and secure enough to address the past.

CONSEQUENCES OF VIOLENCE CONFLICT: AWAY FROM THE WESTERN AND TOWARD THE INDIGENOUS, CUSTOMARY AND NON-STATE

It has been inevitable that in the vacuum of government-driven reparation and healing policies, communities and civics working with communities, have nonetheless in some instances found their way toward making peace with the past and resolving some of the problems left behind by state violence. This has remained difficult, and experiences are isolated and have often not entered the public domain—the political situation remains fraught and threatening. In Matabeleland, formal requests to conduct commemorations or to discuss the massacres of the 1980s have routinely resulted in denials, police cordons, and beatings, if activists attempt to approach sites associated with this era (Mlotshwa 2016). This has finally begun to shift, with commemorations being authorized by the police for the first time in December 2017 and February 2018 (Ndlovu 2017; Nyathi 2018). This coincided with Mnangagwa assuming the presidency and appeared to herald a more open space in which talking about the past is possible.

This chapter will focus on the experiences of one nongovernmental organization (NGO), operating initially as Amani Trust and later as Ukuthula Trust (both meaning "Peace" Trust). This NGO interacted with communities to find their way forward in dealing with the terrible pain and practical problems left behind by the 1982–1985 Gukurahundi massacres in Matabeleland and the Midlands Provinces. Amani's mandate was to rehabilitate victims of human rights abuses. As a Western-funded and Western-oriented NGO, Amani's initial impulse in the 1990s was to use the "standard" medical model as the most appropriate lens through which to assess the damage of Gukurahundi on rural populations (Eppel 2014). The organization focused on training nurses to ask questions about histories of torture, and to offer counselling and documentation for victims. Those affected by violence would typically present at the rural clinics with somatization of psychological distress—complaining of symptoms from multiple organ systems, such as headache combined with back ache, stomach ache, and/or sleep disorders (Reeler et al. 2001). Aches and pains are real, long-term physical consequences of beatings, but a wide range of vague, insistent symptoms can also indicate what in other cultural contexts has been labelled as mixed anxiety-depression disorder, for example. Posttraumatic Stress Disorder (PTSD) is another commonly found, Western diagnosis after epidemic violence.

However, Amani was literally pulled away from this medical model by rural leadership in a small community in Matabeleland South, who, when they had the opportunity to speak openly, revealed that the worst problem left behind by the violence was the angry dead: the community leaders reported that those murdered and buried without ritual in disrespectful or clandestine graves, were causing hardship and illness for their living family members. Discussions with affected families established that infertility, marital problems, failed development projects, and a host of other misfortunes were being laid at the feet of the improperly honored dead (Eppel 2010, 2014). In Ndebele belief systems, as elsewhere in Zimbabwe, a monotheistic belief system has the ancestral spirits playing an integral part in mediating between the living and God (Mlilo). According to their belief systems, it is the ancestors who offer advice, punish and guide them on a regular basis, and whom they have to consult when making family decisions. In order for the spirit of the dead to enter the spirit hierarchy, it is necessary for certain rituals to have taken place, before, during and after burial, as well as for a key ceremony to take place a year after the burial, called *"umbuyiso."* This involves calling the spirit home: senior family members approach the grave of the deceased with a goat, at night. Traditional beer is poured onto the goat, and when it twitches its back, this indicates the spirit is now riding on the goat. The goat is taken back to the homestead and the spirit is introduced to the living family elders, and also to the hierarchy of the dead who have gone before. The spirit can now enter the ancestral world and become a benign and helpful force. The next morning, the goat is slaughtered, cooked, and shared with the community. If this final ceremony does not take place, the spirit is perceived to remain in some version of "limbo," where s/he is disturbed and will keep reminding the living of the need for these rituals via repeated misfortunes (Eppel 2014). Even though Christianity has become widespread in rural Zimbabwe, many still retain their ancestral belief systems in tandem with Christianity.

Between 1998 and 2002, Amani Trust was shown multiple graves in this rural area, including alongside the primary school playing field and one next to a cattle dip. It was obvious that to resolve the problems, exhumation of the human remains was needed rather than some form of western psychotherapy! It was clearly not acceptable to have human remains buried in a school playing field, where unknowingly, children ran and played on the bones, while the mother of the young dead man was unable to visit and mourn her son. He had been tied hanging head down to a tree and was then publicly kicked and bayoneted to death, in February 1984. His crime? Being a so-called dissident. He left behind two young sons aged 3 and 1 respectively. His manner of death and burial amounted to enforced disappearance and denied the family the basic human right to honorably mourn their dead—a right now enshrined in many Latin American Bills of Rights.

Amani Trust contacted the Argentine Forensic Anthropology Team (EAAF) who came to Zimbabwe every year from 1998 to 2001, both to exhume a limited number of graves and to train our team in the skills of forensic anthropology. Thus, paradoxically, *modern scientific skills became the route to allow for ancient mourning and healing systems to fall back into place.* A "new tradition"—exhumations—became incorporated into village life in a certain geographically limited part of southern Matabeleland. Family after family came forward to the Amani team, as did those who had been forced at gunpoint to clandestinely bury the dead. Often, those forced to bury had been themselves threatened with death if they divulged where the graves were. Neighbors involved in burials thus felt unable to let families know where their dead were, leaving these dead as disappeared persons, their spirits completely dishonored.

Between 1998 and 2001, around 23 individuals were exhumed, mostly without the engagement of the state, other than to gain burial orders from local officials. Permissions were granted by traditional leadership, who considered the "bones in the forest" to fall under their jurisdiction. In each case, Amani worked extensively with families and affected village communities, establishing and documenting the facts of what happened in each case, and ensuring that the Trust was dealing with eyewitnesses to, or participants in the burials. Over the decades, hearsay complicated and misled families as to where bones actually lie, and in three cases, Amani exhumed empty graves as a result. But in the vast majority of cases, Amani exhumed people who were returned to families for reburial. After 2014, ad hoc exhumations resumed, under the auspices of Ukuthula Trust, which was approached by families in urgent need of recovering their loved ones from clandestine graves on ledges, in caves and crevices in the hills of Matobo.

The exhumations were always extremely intense, emotional affairs for the community: at last, they were being allowed to recover their historical memory. While it can be traumatic to be confronted with skeletal remains rather than fleshed individuals more clearly recognizable as the person once loved and remembered, personal effects tend to be well preserved in the soils of Matabeleland, serving to vindicate and revive memories of the dead. A well-cherished silver cigarette lighter, wedding rings, a white patent leather belt, spare buttons and thread lovingly kept in a shirt pocket—these items have spoken for and named the dead at times. Each exhumation has restored memory, and restored personhood to those long lost and never adequately mourned and honored (personal communication 2018).

Forensic anthropology techniques used by the trained team serve to indicate sex, age at time of death, approximate stature, and the history of trauma of each recovered individual. This facilitates identity of the recovered bones: DNA testing can also be used when considered necessary, for example, where there is no surviving eyewitness who knows with certainty who is in the grave. It is for this reason that only fully trained persons should be involved in exhumations, as they can ensure that all the bones are recovered without postmortem trauma;[3] that associated evidence such as bullet cases are identified at the scene; that in graves of more than one individual, the bones are not commingled; that the full story of the bones is recorded to ensure identity and the narrative of what happened at the time of death, and since. A trained expert can tell the difference between a fracture to a bone close to the time of death (peri-mortem blunt force trauma), as opposed to a fracture caused by an animal digging or walking on the bones postmortem. A trained expert can reconstruct bones shattered by a bullet, or damaged by roots, to reveal at times bullet entries and exits, or minimum numbers of blunt force blows in the hours leading to death. This can all serve to vindicate eyewitness testimonies and restore the voice of the dead as to who they are and what happened to them. Forensic anthropologists act as interpreters for the bones:

> Bones make great witnesses, they speak softly but they never forget, and they never lie. (Clyde Snow quoted in NLM 2006)

At exhumations and reburials, children now in their 20s and 30s hear anecdotes of long-dead fathers and mothers for the very first time. It is Ukuthula's observation that families themselves effectively "disappear" those murdered by the state from the family tree and lexicon. How do you talk of somebody without inevitably having to talk about the terrifying, undeserved and unresolved death of that person? It becomes simpler not to refer to that person at all, except in whispers in corners, often linked to the aggrieved spirit. We have witnessed how at reburials, charming and happy anecdotes of the deceased are finally brought out into the light of day, putting flesh back onto the bones. At a reburial in 2015, the chief of the community reminisced about the man who was being reburied:

> D was a wonderful dancer and drummer, I remember now how he used to dance and drum at events in the community. (personal communication 2015)

His two sons, a few months old at the time of their father's death, were deeply moved and grateful to imagine their drumming, dancing father for the first time. The uncle who had raised these boys—now men in their 30s—commented to us:

> I could not talk to D's sons then because it was painful. But now we have got proof of how it ended and so I feel free to fill in the gaps of their father's history and the type of man he was. (personal communication 2015)

This same uncle produced photographs of his dead brother for the very first time, a few days before the reburial: these had never been seen by the children of the deceased since his murder, because of the silence that surrounded him. These photos literally gave a face to a father that had been a shadowy figure for decades.

> Yesterday, when one of his daughters saw the photos for the first time, she said that she had never seen her father before—although she used to dream about her father a lot, he had no face in her dreams. (personal communication 2015)

These exhumations have remained entirely family- and community-driven. The state has not been directly involved in any of these activities, apart from certain officials issuing letters of "no objection" to the exhumations, or burial orders to families to facilitate reburials. Nobody questioned the issuing of burial orders for those already dead for more than one or two or three decades, depending on when the exhumation occurred: in Matabeleland, officials have at times tacitly and unofficially acknowledged that these problematic graves are in need of resolution, and so have "allowed" the exhumations, without consulting the authorities in Harare who might have denied them.

Traditional leadership have been the prime officials who have sought out the Ukuthula team and requested these exhumations, on the grounds that it is their responsibility to ensure that these "bones in the forest" are properly relocated to the right places. In Matabeleland, every year in August before the summer rains arrive, traditional leadership organize for the forest to be cleansed of bones and any elements of dead animals. This is to ensure the forest floor is clean and ready for the rain. If this is not done, the belief is it can lead to drought, which occurs often in Matabeleland. However, the shallow graves of murdered humans, and skeletal remains on ledges in caves in the hills, have long posed a particular dilemma for traditional leaders. They consider these bones in need of moving to cleanse the landscape but are afraid of handling the bones of the unknown dead, both because they do not want to risk disturbing an angry spirit, and because they are afraid of the state's response (Eppel 2014). In many instances, it has not always been clear to local leadership who the remains are of, meaning that there is no point in just moving them if they are still not going to be buried by their own relatives in the right place, which would be adjacent to the deceased's family homestead. Traditionally, men were buried near the cattle kraal, and women by the maize field, although now more often there is one family graveyard on family land. But, why exhume if there is no obviously more correct place to rebury?

The process of connecting remains with their living relatives has been a painstaking task of Amani Trust and now Ukuthula Trust, involving talking to many people, often over many years, to find the eyewitnesses who can speak with some certainty to the events and to the graves. In more recent years, new witnesses and requests for further exhumations have come forth at reburials: people attending a reburial may realize for the first time that professional exhumations are in fact possible, meaning that there is finally some point in unburdening themselves of memories they submerged years ago, to save themselves the pain of thinking about terrible events.

All the activities undertaken by Ukuthula in relation to exhumations are entirely dependent on the communities themselves driving the activities. Ukuthula is not the repository of what happened or who was buried where and can only respond to grassroots demands for action. At reburials, families with disappeared persons in their past, as well as the traditional leadership, make appeals to those present to come forward and speak of human remains or graves they may know about, in order to facilitate other families recovering their dead loved ones and moving on from the past. In some instances, families who have known for many years where their dead are lying—in a shallow grave or on the ledge of a cave, unburied—and who have tried to carry out rituals in these strange places in the hope of appeasing the dead, have asked for exhumations. It could even be noted that it is often those families that have tried to do the most to appease the dead where they lie, who are most-keen on exhumations, and who feel that these previous attempts to do rituals have not been sufficient to honor the dead (personal communication 2018).

In Zimbabwe, most of the dead, particularly in 1983, were murdered by 5 Brigade in front of multiple witnesses in their rural villages (CCJP and LRF 1997), and this is fortuitous in that as long as some witnesses remain alive, there is a good possibility of bones being exhumed and restored to the right families. But the passing of time will increasingly create difficulties for communities and leadership: it is now 35 years since the first massacres of 5 Brigade, and eye witnesses who were leadership aged in their 50s then, are now very old or already deceased themselves. There is urgency if thousands more who would benefit from being exhumed, reburied, and properly mourned are to have that chance: in many instances, they require the memories of the living to put them on the right path to recovery of voice and identity. The bones can vindicate living narratives as to their identity but are harder to read in the absence of this collaborative voice. In theory, it is possible to exhume and store remains and to hold these remains for years or decades if necessary, waiting for DNA matches from families who have a disappeared person in their family. Nevertheless, this process can be frustratingly slow, even in nations where the state is fully cooperative and massive outreach campaigns are undertaken appealing to relatives of the disappeared to come forward, and where the complicated procedure of recovering DNA from bones is in place—none of which is currently the case in Zimbabwe. In Argentina, for example, the EAAF have in their offices several hundred unidentified skeletons of individuals, disappeared during the 1980s junta, that they have failed to find DNA matches for, among the families of the disappeared. This is in spite of massive media outreach campaigns across Argentina; on the other hand, the EAAF have identified scores of these dead, and returned them to families (author's personal observations), and the bones have also been used in multiple trials to convict perpetrators of murder. In Zimbabwe, the taking of testimonies from those still alive needs to be made a priority, to avoid a scenario of exhuming those who have no families waiting to rebury and honor them. Prosecutions are not a realistic possibility in Zimbabwe, owing to the amnesty of April 1988, which prevents prosecutions linked to the Gukurahundi era, as well as owing to the prevailing politics, but exhumations are in and of themselves a form or reparation, allowing families to mourn their dead.

NON-STATE MECHANISMS ACHIEVING TRUTH AND "RECONCILIATION" AT THE LOCAL LEVEL

In Ukuthula's experience, every exhumation is a time and place-limited truth commission, a space in which villagers and traditional leadership can talk about the terrible events that led to this particular killing, the beatings other endured around that same time, and the community pain and lack of understanding of why this happened at all. Each exhumation truly breaks what remains a very intense and painful silence, which is perhaps the first step toward reconciling to the past. Families will usually opt to undertake traditional rituals on the day before an exhumation, and to explain to the spirit of the dead that strangers are coming to remove them, but they should not worry about this, as it is a first step to them finally lying in the right place with the right rituals. Families have the option to conduct further rituals during the exhumation, and to observe the process of exposure of the remains.

This is the time in which the testimonies of the living and the dead intercept, opening an intense space for relatives to grieve and reveal what they saw and what happened to themselves.

The reburial ceremonies are often almost celebratory—this is the day on which a wrong is finally being put right, in which someone who has been neglected and denied his/her need to be mourned is finally being honored and restored to the ancestral hierarchy. It has been salutary to observe that no expense is spared in honoring these extra-special dead, who have been awaited for decades. In one recent reburial, the family found scarce resources to enable them to buy a brand new suit and shirt to place over the skeleton of their father in his coffin, to assure his spirit how much he was loved and how important this moment of correcting the past was. An old woman at this funeral turned to me and said, "this is a very unusual day." Yes, it is unusual for someone to be buried for the first time more than 30 years after his death . . . ! The reburials are also events at which the truth telling space is extended beyond the immediate family to reach the much broader community, numbering into hundreds, as graveside speeches claim space and history not just for the deceased but also for the community affected by the killings more generally.

CONCLUSION

What Amani/Ukuthula Trust has shown from their longitudinal relationships with communities where exhumations and traditional rituals and reburials have taken place, is that in situations where the state is recalcitrant or hostile to acknowledging the past, communities can nonetheless find ways of claiming the truth on a localized scale. We have succeeded in "healing the dead" and therefore in healing some aspects of the tortured past associated with their living relatives and communities. To date, this has been done without the open collaboration of the Zimbabwean state. However, we have in the early months of 2018 met with the NPRC and have promising indications that they recognize that exhumations are an important form of reparation and recovery of memory. This may pave the way for exhumations on a much larger scale, by ourselves in collaboration with the NPRC. For such a collaboration to remain a healing space, it would be necessary for families and traditional leadership to remain in charge of the exercise, and for it not be subsumed in state bureaucracy and control (Stover and Shigekane 2002). Maintaining community control of how the dead are to be healed and remembered may be a new challenge going forward, as the quest to create some space for both truth and reconciliation continues in Matabeleland.

NOTES

1. The Zimbabwe National Army produced a magazine commemorating the formation of "Gukurahundi Brigade" and this refers to the 1980 agreement with North Korea.
2. The ability and determination of the military to drive the direction of the nation was to be made more obvious with the coup of November 2017.
3. In terms of International Committee of the Red Cross, the minimum standards for exhumation state that failing to collect all bones is the equivalent of deliberate dismemberment of the dead, which is a crime in international law. Commingling or mixing of remains also denies the right of individuals to recover their identity through DNA and other means. Remains are laid out in coffins in anatomical order by Ukuthula, and every bone is named and accounted for to the families, and any missing bones are explained, for example, as being scavenged by predators, or destroyed/ damaged at the time of death, depending on the evidence.

BIBLIOGRAPHY

Alexander, J., J. McGregor, and T. Ranger. 2000. *Violence and Memory: One Hundred Years in the Dark Forests of Matabeleland.* Oxford. James Currey.

Auret, D. 1992. *Reaching for Justice: The Catholic Commission for Justice and Peace, 1972–1992.* Gweru. Mambo Press.

Catholic Commission for Justice and Peace (CCJP) and Legal Resources Foundation (LRF). 1997. *Breaking the Silence, Building True Peace: A Report on the Disturbances in Matabeleland and the Midlands 1980–1988.* Harare. CCJP and LRF.

Cliffe, L., J. Alexander, B. Cousins, and R. Gaidzanwa. 2011. "An Overview of Fast Track Land Reform in Zimbabwe: Editorial Introduction." *Journal of Peasant Studies* 5 (38), 907–38.

Government of Zimbabwe 2013. Constitution of Zimbabwe Amendment (No. 20) Act, 2013. Retrieved from: https://www.refworld.org/docid/51ed090f4.html [Accessed 4 April 2019].

Eppel, S. 2010. "Repairing a Fractured Nation." In *The Hard Road to Reform*, edited by B. Raftopoulos, 1st ed. Harare: Weaver Press. pp. 211–250.

Eppel, S. 2014. "'Bones in the Forest' in Matabeleland, Zimbabwe: Exhumations as a Tool for Transformation." *International Journal of Transitional Justice* 2014: 1–22.

Mlotshwa, K. 2016. "Police ban Gukurahundi Commemorations." *Newsday*, Bulawayo. [Online]. Available at: www.newsday.co.zw/2016/12/police-ban-gukurahundi-commemorations/. Accessed on 24 April 2018.

Mongoma, T. 2017. "President to Unveil 20k Stands for Youths." *The Chronicle*, Bulawayo. [Online]. Available at: www.chronicle.co.zw/president-to-unveil-20k-stands-for-youths/.

Mugabe, R. 1980. *Zimbabwe Independence Day Speech.* Available at https://panafricanquotes.wordpress.com/speeches/robert-mugabes-zimbabwe-indipendence-speech-17-april-1980/. [Accessed on 29 August 2017]

National Library of Medicine/National Institute of Health (NLM/NIH). 2006. "Visible Proofs: Forensic Views of the Body." USA. [Online]. Available at: www.nlm.nih.gov/visibleproofs/galleries/cases/disappeared_image_2.html. Accessed on 24 April 2018.

National Transitional Justice Working Group Zimbabwe (NTJWGZ). 2017. "What Is Wrong with the NPRC Bill?" *NPRC Watch*, 3.

Ncube, L. (28 February 2018). "Mthwakazi Party Disrupts National Healing Consultative Meeting Again." *The Chronicle*, Bulawayo. [Online]. Available at: www.chronicle.co.zw/mthwakazi-party-disrupts-national-healing-consultative-meeting-again/. Accessed on 24 April 2018.

Ndlovu, N. 2017. "Another Gukurahundi Memorial on the Cards." *Zimbabwe Daily*, Bulawayo. [Online]. Available at: www.thezimbabwedaily.com/news/171577-another-gukurahundi-memorial-on-cards.html. Accessed on 24 April 2018.

Nyathi, P. 2018. "Mugabe Birthday Declared Day of Gukurahundi Commemorations." *My Harare Times*, Harare. [Online]. Available at: https://myhararetimes.com/mugabe-birthday-declared-day-of-gukurahundi-commemorations/. Accessed on 24 April 2018.

Physicians for Human Rights. 2002. *"We'll Make them Run": A Report on Post-election Violence in Zimbabwe, March to May 2002*. Physicians for Human Rights and Solidarity Peace Trust: Copenhagen and Johannesburg.

Potts, D. 2008. "Displacement and Livelihood: The Longer-Term Impact of Operation Murambatsvina." In *The Hidden Dimensions of Operation Murambatsvina*, edited by M. Vambe. Harare. Weaver Press, pp. 53–64.

Reeler, A.P., P. Mbape, J. Matshona, J. Mhetura, E. Hlatywayo. 2001. "The Prevalence and Nature of Disorders Due to Torture in Mashonaland Central Province, Zimbabwe." *Torture* 11: 4–9.

Research and Advocacy Unit (RAU) and Justice for Agriculture. 2009. *If Something is Wrong: The Invisible Suffering of Commercial Farm Workers and Their Families Due to "Land Reform"*. Report produced for the General Agricultural & Plantation Workers Union of Zimbabwe. [Online]. Harare. Available at: www.kubatana.net/html/archive/agric/091111gapwuz.asp?sector=AGRIC#download. Accessed on 30 August 2017.

Sachikonye, L. 2003. *The Situation of Commercial Farm Workers after Land Reform in Zimbabwe*. A Report Prepared for the Farm Community Trust. Ed CIIR. London. Available at: archive.kubatana.net/docs/landr/fctz_farm_workers_0305.rtf. Accessed on 30 August 2017.

Scoones, I., N. Marongwe, B. Mavedzenge, J. Mahenehene, F. Marimbarimba, and C. Sukume. 2010. *Zimbabwe's Land Reform: Myths and Realities*. Harare. Weaver Press.

Solidarity Peace Trust. 2008a. *Punishing Dissent, Silencing Citizens: The Zimbabwe Elections*. [Online]. Johannesburg. Available at: http://solidaritypeacetrust.org/133/punishing-dissent-silencing-citizens/. Accessed 30 August 2017.

Solidarity Peace Trust. 2008b. *Desperately Seeking Sanity: What Prospects for a New Beginning in Zimbabwe?* [Online]. Johannesburg. Available at: http://solidaritypeacetrust.org/326/desperately-seeking-sanity/. Accessed on 30 August 2017.

Solidarity Peace Trust. 2015. *Hoping without hope: Murambatsvina - Ten Years On*. [Online]. Available at: http://solidaritypeacetrust.org/1724/hoping-without-hope-murambatsvina-ten-years-on/. Accessed on 24 April 2018.

Solidarity Peace Trust. 2018. *Old Beginnings. The Political Context of Zimbabwe and a Report on Biometric Voter Registration (BVR): A National and Matabeleland Perspective*. Available at: http://solidaritypeacetrust.org/1791/old-beginnings-the-political-context-of-zimbabwe-and-a-report-on-biometric-voter-registration-bvr-a-national-and-matabeleland-perspective/. Accessed on 24 April 2018.

Stover, E., and R. Shigekane. 2002. "The Missing in the Aftermath of War: When Do the Needs of Victims' Families and International War Tribunals Clash?" *IRRC* 84: 845–66.

Tibaijuka, A. (2005). *Report of the Fact-finding Mission to Zimbabwe to Assess the Scope and Manner of Operation Murambatsvina*, Prepared by United Nations Special Envoy on Human Settlements Issues in Zimbabwe. New York: United Nations.

Zimbabwe Broadcasting Corporation (ZBC). 2018. Be united, be positive, says President Mnangagwa. Available at: www.zbc.co.zw/?p=72346. Accessed on 16 April 2018.

Chapter 7

The Aftermath of Gukurahundi

Dealing with Wounds of the Genocide through Non-State Justice Processes in Bubi (Inyathi) and Nkayi Districts, Matabeleland, North Province, Zimbabwe

Ruth Murambadoro and Chenai Matshaka

INTRODUCTION

Following periods of violence and unlawful killings—such as the Gukurahundi genocide which occurred in the early 1980s in Zimbabwe—Zimbabwean society is confronted with the predicament of deciding what to do about the perpetrators and how to help the victims move forward from this ugly past.[1] The decision taken in this regard is an integral part of postconflict transitional justice and reconciliation processes and is often a delicate balance between meeting the needs of the victims while ensuring stability and peace by managing the interests of former parties to the conflict, who may potentially threaten peace. This decision often boils down to whether to take a retributive approach which seeks punishment and the imposition of penalties that are commensurate with the crime committed (Amstutz 2006, Van der Merwe et al. 2009); or a restorative approach which focuses on repairing the damage done to the victims and attending to their needs, rather than punishing the offender (Johnstone 2013).

While there are no local words to explain the concepts of transitional justice and reconciliation as described in literature, an understanding of these two terms in this chapter is derived from the lived experiences of the research participants in the Bubi (Inyathi) and Nkayi districts who endured the Gukurahundi genocide, and from how they expect the past injustices to be addressed. Transitional justice for the research participants refers to processes of redress for the wrongs that took place during periods of disruption, and that reflect diverse practices of justice, thus enabling the society to transform incidents of past injustices into an environment that fosters social harmony. Moreover, reconciliation encapsulates the idea of an engagement that enables conflicting parties to deliberate on issues affecting them, thus fostering social harmony. These two meanings for transitional justice and reconciliation are informed by the understanding that the Gukurahundi genocide that occurred in the Matabeleland and Midlands provinces disrupted the living conditions of community members and eroded the social contract that binds people to live in harmony. This social contract is not codified, but it is binding, and it informs how local people relate with each other and manage their everyday life. It emanates from the moral values, practices, and code of conduct (*Imikhuba lenhlalo/Tsika Nemagariro*) bestowed upon each member of the community, and which inhibit people from committing any actions that violate social harmony. As one participant shared:

> Remember it is not in our nature to kill each other, *panoita nyaya yengozika nokuti upenyu chinhu chakakosha kumunhu wese* (that will bring a case of the avenging spirit because life is a precious thing for everyone). I cannot just treat another anyhow. (Harare, 07/07/2015)

The research participants reported that Gukurahundi had destroyed the social fabric (essence of humanity) of the community to the extent that some people are no longer on talking terms and they do not trust each other. This breakdown of social relations among family members or community members of various ethnic backgrounds and between the government and the citizens does not augur well for social harmony and stability in the country. It tramples on the *Imikhuba lenhlalo/Tsika Nemagariro* which are core values held by the people and that are embedded in their everyday lives to promote cooperation, social harmony, respect, interconnectedness, and collective responsibility. Hence, where atrocious acts have occurred in the community, processes of redress that can rebuild the social fabric (inner essence of humanity) of the community are required, as indicated by the research participants, and they have an array of practices they follow to render this.

Drawing from the narratives shared by 28 participants, this chapter responds to the question: What mechanisms, institutions and modes of everyday life were evoked by these communities in their endeavor to forge ahead with their lives? Further, are the victims healed, and have they managed to find closure? What lessons can be drawn from the way the Gukurahundi genocide victims have survived their past? Using perspectives from community members, this chapter shows that despite the passage of time, and given the recent political changes in the country, redress for the Gukurahundi genocide requires more than a statist approach such as that which has been offered by the government through various national justice and reconciliation initiatives.

HOW THE STUDY WAS UNDERTAKEN

The chapter draws from two independent fieldwork projects that were conducted by the two authors during the period 2014 and 2017. The research by the first author covered four areas, namely the Harare, Bulawayo, Bubi (Inyathi), and Nkayi districts, while the second author focused on participants in the cities of Bulawayo and Harare.

The research participants included government officials who served in the Joint Monitoring and Implementation Committee (JOMIC) and the Organ for National Healing, Reconciliation and Integration (ONHRI), civil society representatives, academics, and community members. Participants representing civil society organizations, academics, and government were interviewed in Harare and Bulawayo because they are the major cities in Zimbabwe where most of their offices are located. The Bubi (Inyathi) and Nkayi districts in Matabeleland North Province were purposively selected because the community members in these areas experienced the government-sanctioned *Gukurahundi* genocide in the early 1980s which, over the years, has created tensions between government and civilians and to some extent ethnic divisions between the Ndebele and Shona ethnic groups who were party to the conflict (Catholic Commission for Justice and Peace in Zimbabwe 1997—CCJPZ). Multiple research techniques were used for data collection, semi-structured in-depth interviews, focus group discussions, and participant observations at the public hearings for the National Peace and Reconciliation Commission (NPRC) Bill and the chief's court. A triangulation approach was adopted for this research (validating data through cross referencing from two or more sources) in the form of conducting archival studies (macro level), and interviews and focus groups (micro level), to enrich the output of the research (Babbie and Mouton 2001).

In addition, snowball and convenience sampling methods were used. Due to the small sample size, the research results cannot be generalized to reflect the whole population of Zimbabwe. However, the data gathered was useful in contributing to understanding the dynamics at play in addressing the *Gukurahundi* genocide at various levels of the society.

STATIST TRANSITIONAL JUSTICE AND RECONCILIATION PROJECTS IN THE AFTERMATH OF *GUKURAHUNDI*

Following Zimbabwe's independence in 1980, the government's approach for fostering justice among the racially and ethnically divided population groups that had experienced years of protracted war was to "sweep the past under the carpet" and move on with the future (Mashingaidze 2010). This precedent was set upon the inception of a "letting bygones be bygones" policy of reconciliation adopted by the then prime minister Robert Mugabe in 1980 and has largely continued to be used as an approach for transitional justice pertaining to the preceding periods of violence and political antagonism (Morreira 2014).

This has been achieved through various amnesties, both official and unofficial, and the failures of government institutions that are meant to deliver justice. Efforts toward transitional justice and reconciliation have thus remained an elitist project whereby the majority party in government has undermined any opportunity for redress, leading to a continued cycle of violence stirred by anger, revenge, and lack of remorse. As argued by Morreira (2014: 04), "in the ensuing years, Mugabe's insistence upon forgetting the past did not unfold as neatly as it was presented in his independence speech. Rather, the politics of remembrance and forgetting have been deeply politicized and strategic."

Hence, the government of Zimbabwe has tended to address the past by "letting bygones be bygones" through various policies and mechanisms including amnesties and the setting up of commissions of enquiry. During the *Gukurahundi* genocide, two Commissions of Inquiry into the Matabeleland Disturbances (viz., the Dumbutshena and Chihambakwe Commissions of Inquiry[2]) were established to investigate the 1980s violence. The findings of both commissions have never been made public and this has left the society without full knowledge about the genocide while the perpetrators have not been brought to account for their actions. The immediate response of the warring parties was to sign a Unity Accord on December 22, 1987, between the Zimbabwe African National Union (ZANU) and the Zimbabwe African People's Union (ZAPU), which ended the hostilities between the two parties and formed some form of cohesion between them. Unfortunately, this did not trickle down to the communities that had been affected by the conflict. Instead, the affected communities were left feeling cheated by the signatories to the Unity Accord because it was accompanied by an amnesty provision, *Clemency Order No. 1 of April 18, 1988*, which prevented prosecutions for the crimes committed during *Gukurahundi* (Human Rights Watch, 2011).

The *Clemency Order No. 1 of April 18, 1988,* which granted blanket amnesty to all parties who administered violence during the genocide, has made the government reluctant to release the findings of the commissions. The government has maintained that releasing the findings might fuel tensions between the Ndebele and Shona population groups, who were victims in or perpetrators of the conflict, over what happened in the past (Hayner 1994). This has resulted in the continued suppression of the truth and a lack of closure for the victims (Bosha 2014).

Other state-sanctioned mechanisms that could have addressed the *Gukurahundi* genocide and other episodes of violence in the country include the

Organ for National Healing, Reconciliation and Integration (ONHRI), or Organ, which was established in 2009 and the National Peace and Reconciliation Commission (NPRC) (Machakanja 2010), or the Peace Commission commissioned in 2018 (Chiromba 2015). The Organ was established to fulfill Article 7 of the Global Political Agreement (GPA) of 2008, which was signed by the Zimbabwe African National Union Patriotic Front (ZANU PF) and the two formations of the Movement for Democratic Change (MDC) following the electoral impasse and political crisis. According to Ndlovu-Gatsheni (2009) and Machakanja (2010), Article 7 of the GPA mandated the Government of National Unity (GNU) that was formed between ZANU-PF and the two MDC formations in 2008 to consider the setting up of a mechanism to advise the government on measures to be taken to achieve national healing, national cohesion, and unity.

The GPA which sanctioned the formation of ONHRI became the first official document to explicitly include justice, national healing, and cohesion as policy goals of the government (Machakanja 2010). The impact of the work of the Organ, however, was less fruitful, especially at the community level where most of the victims of the genocide are located. This was due to the lack of political will on the part of the government and the lack of adequate funding for its operations (Mbire 2011). Under the new constitution of Zimbabwe adopted in 2013, the National Peace and Reconciliation Commission (NPRC), or Peace Commission, was established to replace the Organ. Its mandate is to address the past injustices and to forge conflict prevention mechanisms and early warning systems. The NPRC has a predetermined lifespan of ten years, which seemingly commenced in 2013 when the new constitution was adopted.

At the time of writing this chapter, the Peace Commission had passed almost five years of its ten-year period and little work had been done in terms of giving citizens access to justice. The government spent almost three of these five years screening candidates suitable to serve as commissioners and another two years were spent on deliberations around the policy framework that would guide the functions of the commission (*NTJWG* 2016). After many years of waiting, the NPRC Act was commissioned in January 2018 but still little progress has been made regarding giving access to justice to victims of the *Gukurahundi* genocide (Muchadehama 2018). This delay in commissioning the NPRC seemingly suggests that there continues to be a lack of political will and commitment from government pertaining to state-led processes of addressing past injustices.

This can be observed from the public statements made by some government officials involved in state-led transitional justice projects, such as the former vice president Phekezela Mphoko who oversaw the National Reconciliation Ministry between 2013 and 2017. The former vice president, Mphoko, constantly labeled the *Gukurahundi* genocide a "western conspiracy," suggesting that external actors and not the ruling ZANU-PF government were responsible for the injustices that occurred in the 1980s (Sasa 2015). This narrative of the former vice president removes the government from taking the lead in addressing the atrocities that occurred during *Gukurahundi*, even though the report by the CCJPZ and LRF identified state-sanctioned intelligence and military officials as main perpetrators of the violence that occurred (CCJPZ 1997). Moreover, the research participants are aware that police intelligence and military officials were responsible for most of the atrocities committed during *Gukurahundi* and have been making constant demands for justice to be rendered and for truths about the whereabouts of their loved ones to be revealed for the people to gain trust in the government (CCJPZ 1997, Eppel 2006).

Therefore, the research participants remained pessimistic about the state-led transitional justice processes. They expressed doubt in the current Peace Commission because of the government's dismal track record where similar initiatives have failed to provide the justice required by the affected parties. One participant shared that

> we saw what they did with the Zimbabwe Human Rights Commission; the enabling legislation stripped it of all its powers that were provided for by the Constitution and clearly the same may be done to the NPRC. (Harare, 06/11/2014)

Some of the research participants maintained their lack of trust in state-led processes, citing that a precursor to justice is a high level of trust between the state and citizens; but in this case, the trust of civilians in the government has been eroded as some government officials implicated in the violence have continued to hold political office with impunity. Hence, these political elites may still be able to influence processes that seek to bring them to account.

Furthermore, the provision for the creation of the Peace Commission was made in 2013 in the new Constitution of Zimbabwe, but commissioners for the body were sworn in only at the beginning of 2016, and this amidst controversies. The NPRC has been marred by controversy that stems from a Bill that was passed by Parliament in December 2015 to regulate the operations and functions of the Peace Commission. The major criticisms cited by members of the civil society is that the Bill has taken away most of the Constitutional provisions made to safeguard the autonomy and credibility of the NPRC. An example can be drawn from changes made in the Bill determining that the NPRC is accountable to the Minister of National Healing, Peace and Reconciliation instead of to Parliament (ZHRNGO Forum 2016). Under clause 8 (7) of the Bill, this minister has been given authority to independently decide on how to handle the findings and recommendations of the commission, which compromises its independence and transparency.

The Constitution had also made provisions for the tenure of the commissioners to be secured like that of judges, but the Bill has given the president the power to terminate the tenure of a commissioner after five years, which jeopardizes the credentials of commissioners whose work opposes the interests of the government (ZHRNGO Forum 2016). More so, the bill has omitted provisions on how the services of the NPRC will be decentralized to be accessible to all citizens, a move that further alienates members of the society who do not reside in Harare where the NPRC is currently stationed (Heal Zimbabwe Trust and Zimbabwe Civic Education Trust 2016). These shortcomings raise questions about the political will of the government to see this institution fulfill the expectations of the populace, as shared by one participant,

> The resistance by the state to operationalize the NPRC as per the constitution is a resistance to accountability and justice. The state is not eager to open the past. Even if they do operationalize the NPRC, it will become a lame duck, an ineffective organ; because of the make-up of the current regime. (Harare, 6/11/2014)

The above sentiments also point to the lack of trust in both the institution and the personalities appointed to implement initiatives for postconflict justice. This lack of trust seemingly continues because the country has not yet undergone a full transition in its leadership. The ruling party ZANU PF has been in power for over three decades and a quasi-change of leadership was necessitated by a military coup that occurred in November 2017, leading to the removal of the long-standing president Robert Mugabe who was replaced by his previously ousted vice president, Emmerson Mnangagwa. However, the ZANU-PF party has maintained in office some of the political figures who were implicated in the *Gukurahundi* genocide and, through its dominance, it will likely continue to protect and preserve the political and personal interests of individuals in the party by silencing any threats to its hegemony. The unfortunate effects of this silencing among a people living in a predatory state[3] are the creation of anxiety and delayed justice.

Already, the amnesty provisions offered by the government over the various periods of violence have protected human rights offenders from prosecution by law and, consequently, developed the modus operandi for the ZANU-PF led government to override any further calls to prosecute offenders (ZHRNGO Forum 2012). The government's poor record of dealing with past injustices has created distrust of its processes and institutions among many Zimbabweans, as established by the fieldwork. The feelings of resentment among the victims of *Gukurahundi* have been worsened by the apparent lack of remorse from the government as featured in a speech made by the former president Robert Mugabe in 1999 at the funeral of the late vice president Joshua Nkomo (Murambadoro 2015). At this funeral, Mugabe announced to the congregates that the *Gukurahundi* era was a "moment of madness." which left many to wonder what they should make of the pronouncement. A participant in Bulawayo asked this question during the fieldwork,

> If *Gukurahundi* was a moment of madness, the question becomes, has the mad person regained sanity now? Has he atoned for the period of madness, and what should the aggrieved do about it? (Bulawayo, 22/04/2014)

As argued by Morrel (2003: 13), "The *Gukurahundi* . . . has left a festering wound in the psyche of the Zimbabwean nation." This was reaffirmed during the fieldwork as communities affected by *Gukurahundi* remain socially and politically divided, particularly along regional and tribal lines.

LIVED EXPERIENCES OF THE GUKURAHUNDI GENOCIDE AND THE NON-STATE JUSTICE PROCESSES IN BUBI AND NKAYI DISTRICTS

The Bubi (Inyathi) and Nkayi districts are both rural areas located in the Matabeleland North Province in Zimbabwe which experienced high records of attacks on civilians during the *Gukurahundi* era (CCJPZ 1997). During the fieldwork, the researchers gathered that these rural areas had been targeted by government-sanctioned security agents because they were presumed to be hiding grounds for the Zimbabwe People's Revolutionary Army (ZIPRA) ex-combatants ("so-called dissidents") that were being hunted down by the government. One participant shared that

> it was a Friday in April 1983. I remember that four men of the Fifth Brigade soldiers arrived at our compound early in the morning and called everyone out. They asked us [a family of eight] in Shona to tell them where the dissidents were hiding but no one could give an answer because we did not understand the language they were speaking [Shona]. They started calling us names; for example, *"mapenzi evanhu muchadura kwaari madissidents enyu"* (you rascals you are going to tell us where your dissidents are hiding), and they beat the whole family with the barrel of their guns calling us to tell them about the whereabouts of the dissidents. (Nkayi district, 16/04/2014)

The above narrative indicates that the military used excessive force on civilians who were in communities where the "so-called dissidents" were suspected to be hiding. The Fifth Brigade was a special task force (mainly comprised of Shona people and ex-combatants of the Zimbabwe African National Liberation Army [ZANLA]) which had been trained by North Korean forces to settle the rivalry between the Zimbabwe African National Union-Patriotic Front (ZANU-PF)-led government and ZIPRA ex-combatants (the armed wing of Zimbabwe African People's Union-ZAPU) who were largely comprised of the Ndebele ethnic group (CCJPZ 1997). The *Gukurahundi* genocide occurred in the Midlands and Matabeleland provinces where the majority of the population is Ndebele, which the government seemingly associated with the ZIPRA ex-combatants and ZAPU (Eppel 2003). Eppel (2009) argues that the stronghold of ZAPU in this region posed a geopolitical threat to the ruling ZANU-PF government due to threats of secession and that this may have influenced the regime to employ excessive force to gain control of the region.

Several scholars have argued that the administrative divisions in Zimbabwe between the Ndebele and Shona population regions, which were inherited from colonial rule, have continued to fuel the creation of political parties along ethnic lines (e.g., ZAPU with a Ndebele majority and ZANU-PF with a Shona majority) (Msindo 2012, Ndlovu-Gatsheni 2009). The administrative divisions between Mashonaland and Matabeleland, which host the majority of the Shona and Ndebele ethnic groups respectively, make it difficult for the government to create a well-integrated country. Hence the actions of the government during the *Gukurahundi* era and the systematic unequal distribution of resources to the Matabeleland and Midlands provinces after the genocide have resulted in deep resentments amongst the Ndebele in this region (Eppel and Raftopoulos 2008, Ndlovu-Gatsheni 2012). Ethnic divisions in Zimbabwe are a largely unacknowledged factor in the political discussions related to reconciliation and justice to date, to the detriment, we argue, of any successful transformation of the past.

Muzondidya and Ndlovu-Gatsheni (2007: 275), citing the repeated calls for secession made by the Umthwakazi group in Matabeleland, argue that "[although] Zimbabwe has since the days of the *Gukurahundi* genocide not experienced serious ethnic-based wars or political instability, there is serious ethnic polarization in the country and ethnicity remains one of the challenges to the survival of both the state and the country." One participant affirmed these concerns by stating that

> I grew up without a father because he was killed during *Gukurahundi*. My mother told me he was abducted and later killed for refusing to tell the soldiers where the dissidents had been hiding. I resent Shona people for what their soldiers did to my father because he was an innocent man. (32-year-old male, Nkayi community, 16/04/2014)

Msindo (2012) reiterates that the experiences of the *Gukurahundi* genocide have entrenched animosity in survivors, particularly the younger generation (aged 21–45). Many of the younger generation, particularly below the age of 30, have come to understand the issues of *Gukurahundi* from oral evidence. These stories continue to be shared from one generation to the other, harboring feelings of hatred and revenge-seeking among survivors who have not gone through any justice process to retain social harmony, accountability, and stability. This animosity, pain, and anger held by some survivors of the genocide perpetuates because the violence they experienced has not only impacted their physical space, but also the metaphysical space which they belong to as cosmological persons.

In the African setting, particularly sub-Saharan Africa (Zimbabwe included), a community is often made up of people who belong to the same ancestral family or bloodline and a village chief or family elder serves as a representative of the community (Gelfand 1973). These community leaders represent the community in the physical realm, but there is a metaphysical realm which is the backbone of the community, comprised of the ancestral family (Gelfand 1973). The ancestral family are—spirit beings of the departed members of the community—who form a generational pattern of communities that preceded the current living community. The ancestral community of the "living dead" serves as a protector and guardian of the "living living" (the people in the physical realm) and intercedes for the people to God, who is the creator of all beings, be it in the physical or metaphysical realm (Gelfand 1973, Nyathi 2015).

Within this setting, spirituality[4] has a significant bearing on the worldviews held by the people and their understanding of reality is shaped by both the physical and metaphysical realms (Nyathi 2015). The physical realm is a sphere of existence occupied by living persons (the "living-living") and the metaphysical realm is occupied by the "living dead" and "unborn living" (Gelfand 1973, Nyathi 2015). The "unborn living" (spirit of a person yet to exist in the physical realm) are future beings whose existence depends on the ability of the "living-living" and "living dead," to create a conducive environment. The "living-living" (spirit of the living person) are custodians of the physical realm and the "living dead" (spirit of deceased persons) oversee the metaphysical realm but both entities have an interdependent relationship that transcends to the unborn living (Gelfand 1973, Nyathi 2015).

This transcendental reproduction of the physical world in the metaphysical is, arguably, a fundamental component of life that brings social harmony to African communities (Ellis and Ter Haar 2004, Lan 2006). Resultantly, human dignity which is an underlying component enshrined in the customs, beliefs, and values of the people, is built on the principle of reciprocal recognition of human beings as entities within a cosmological community that have duties and responsibilities to both the physical and metaphysical social world (Setiloane 1978). This understanding of human dignity encapsulates the understanding of justice that informs the practices followed by the local communities to address injustices.

Thus, the research participants were unable to offer a local meaning of the concept of transitional justice, but instead gave definitions of justice in their vernacular languages of isiNdebele and ChiShona. They defined justice as *kuenzanisa* (creating a balance), *kunzwana nhunha* (listening to troubling issues), and *lunganisa* (making things equal). The research participants made it clear that the above meanings of justice are action words, in that they require one who is rendering *kuenzanisa* or *kunzwana nhunha*, to engage people in deliberations that allow conflicting parties to reflect on the impact of the injustice and then work together to foster social harmony. Social harmony in this context is crucial because it refers to a social phenomenon that describes the experience of being at peace with self and the social world in which people exist (Gelfand 1973, Nyathi 2015). Thus, *kuenzanisa* or *lunganisa* redresses the disrupted lives and harmony among conflicting parties because an injustice is understood as "deviant behavior" that destroys the essence of another human being.

Moreover, the local words for reconciliation shared by research participants were *yananiso* (bringing back together), *kugadzirisana* (fixing things), *kutaurirana* (engaging in dialogue), and *nokubuyisana* (making amends or restoring things). These words encapsulate the idea of an engagement that enables conflicting parties to deliberate on issues affecting them, which fosters social harmony. A 54-year-old man from Nkayi district who has been living in Matabeleland his whole life narrated how his surviving family has managed to cope with the experiences of the *Gukurahundi* genocide by exercising tradition-based justice practices. The man shared that

> dissidents came to our house and gathered us in the kitchen. They beat me, my mother, father and other siblings. When my father was bleeding to death from the wounds, they took out a gun and shot him. They instructed me to get an axe and chop my father into pieces. They told me to put my father's head in a box and take it to the soldiers to inform them that they have dealt with the sell-out/informant. Upon returning from the soldiers' camp, I found my mother dead; she had committed suicide by tying herself with a rope in the kitchen. (16/04/2014)

His father was murdered because the alleged dissidents suspected him of being an informant of the government military. The tragedy of losing both parents in one day has been a burden for this man because they died when he was still young. In his narration he shared that the untimely death of his parents caused problems for his family because, a few years after their deaths, they returned as avenging spirits and tormented the community. He stated that

Mushure mekufa kwevabereki vangu hapana kutora nguva, vakapfuka kuita zvipoko zvaigaro wonekwa pachi bhorani apo zvekuti vanhu vakanga vozeza kupfuura nepachi bhorani kana kunze kwasviba. Vanhu vaiti vakasiya migoro pachi bhorani apo kana kwakuvira pakunoedza vaiwana aine mvura, uye ukapfuura nepo kwasviba wainzwa mazwi ababa namai vachitaura zvinova zvinhu zvairatidza kuti mufi akaenda nechigumbu—it did not take much time after the passing away of my parents that people started to see their ghosts there by the borehole. It became difficult for people to use the pathway that passes through the borehole after dark because they would come across my parent's ghosts. If people left their water tins at the borehole during the sunset hours the following morning, they would find them filled with water. Also, if they passed by the borehole after sunset, they would hear my parents having a conversation and this ordeal revealed that the deceased persons where angry. (54-year-old male, Nkayi district, 16/04/2014)

This encounter of witnessing the spirit of a deceased person coming back to cause havoc in the space of the "living-living" is an experience the local people call *kupfuka kwengozi* (eruption of the avenging spirit). The *ngozi* (avenging spirit) mostly erupts in cases where a person has died unlawfully at the hands of another. As cosmological persons, the people in this community uphold the belief that a person in the physical form is a "living spirit" (living living) but when the person dies, they transcend into the realm of the "living dead" and become an ancestral spirit that guides and protects the "living living." More so, whereas birth is a rite of passage into the realm of the "living living," death is also a rite of passage into the realm of the "living dead." It is believed, therefore, that the premature death of a person violates their dignity, and there is need for the injustice to be addressed through the tradition-based practice of *kuripira ngozi* (appeasing the avenging spirit); without this atonement, the spirit of the deceased would return to fight for justice (Benyera 2014a, *The Standard* 2011).

Benyera (2014b) elaborates on this tradition-based practice by noting that, in the Zimbabwean African culture, an undignified death is shameful to the ancestral community because the deceased cannot assume the ancestral responsibility of protecting and blessing the family. He adds that the family of the deceased remains aggrieved because they have been robbed of the opportunity for their loved one to look after them. Eppel (2006) and Nyathi (2015) further state that death, in the Zimbabwean African culture, is a rite of passage that one ought to enter in accordance with the traditions and practices of one's ancestral family. Nyathi (2015) adds that the African people in Zimbabwe are devoted to maintaining the harmonious continuation of the cosmological community (physical and metaphysical realms) because that is the essence of their humanity, which guarantees the existence and expansion of their lineage. It is against this backdrop that the practice of appeasing avenging spirits has become a popular phenomenon of addressing injustices among the local communities.

In the above case, the research participant explained that the appeasement of the avenging spirits of his parents has not yet been done. Usually, when an appeasement is being conducted, the offender reaches out to the family of those who were wronged, asks for forgiveness and offers compensation in accordance with the demands of the spirit of the deceased. Often in *kuripira ngozi,* the offender compensates the family of the deceased with livestock and performs a ritual to cleanse the community. Some of the offenders in this incident have already died and the one whom the research participant could account for was said to be in a state of mental illness. Since the offender is insane and his family cannot afford to offer the compensation needed to perform *kuripira ngozi*, the family of the deceased settled for another tradition-based practice called *chenura* (cleansing) to allow the community to retain social harmony.

In accordance with the local customs, *chenura* (cleansing) is a cleansing ritual that is conducted to disinfect the community from the bad aura associated with the unlawful killing of a person. This cleansing ritual and ceremony involves the slaughtering of an animal (cattle, goat, or lamb) and smearing of the animal's blood mixed with traditional herbs at the spot where the person died. Here, the perpetrator or the family of the perpetrator is expected to offer an animal to the ancestors of the land (*masvikiro enzvimbo*) and to ask for forgiveness for polluting the environment. The animal is slaughtered according to custom and the blood of the animal is poured to the ground as the *homwe* (host of the spirit medium who is usually a family member) chants to the ancestors asking for forgiveness. This is followed by *pungwe* (celebration ceremony) in which community members gather all night to sing, dance, and share in traditional beer and eat the meat from the slaughtered animal. Some of the meat is also put in a traditional plate and placed *mumba mesvikiro* (the hut of the ancestral spirit) together with traditional beer for the ancestors to feast. The locals believe that *chenura* enables the spirit of the deceased to join the ancestral family and come back into their lives during the *umbuyiso/magadziro* (welcoming the spirit of the deceased) ceremony, in the form of a guardian that provides various services to the clan.

Magadziro/umbuyiso is a traditional ceremony in which the spirit of the deceased is welcomed back into the family as a guardian among the ancestral community. Here, a goat or sheep is used as an offering during the ceremony which involves the brewing of traditional beer and all-night celebrations (*pungwe*). Before the ceremony commences, the animal is brought into the compound and tied to a tree. The whole family and relatives gather about the tree and the selected family representative will lead the ceremony by pouring traditional beer on the animal and the ground for the ancestors to drink.

They also make use of *bute* (snuff) which they sprinkle on the ground as they chant to the ancestors, moving about the compound, to welcome the spirit of the deceased. The rest of the attendants will be singing, dancing, and chanting praise to the ancestors. It is expected that, once the spirit of the deceased has descended (*wasvika mumusha*), the animal will bow down and one of the family members will go into a trance. When this occurs, the deceased's spirit will address the gathering through the host (*homwe*), an act that symbolizes the return of the spirit being as a guardian that will remain in the compound protecting and providing for the family. Hence, it is important for one to have a dignified death because, as spiritual beings, death is a transition from one realm (living-living) to another (living dead). These practices facilitate psychosocial and spiritual healing for the affected parties while simultaneously bringing social harmony to the whole community.

While commenting on the efficacy of tradition-based justice practices, a 46-year old woman from Bubi (Inyathi) district explained that

> the good thing about dealing with *ngozi* (avenging spirit) in our custom is that, once appeasement has been offered and cleansing rituals conducted, the spirit of the deceased finds rest and so does the community. Everyone gets peace and redress to the affected family comes from the livestock that is offered. (23/05/2016)

The peace that is referred to above is a state of social harmony whereby the spirit of both the "living living" and the "living dead" is not burdened. A burdened spirit presents challenges for the people because as one of the "living dead," such a spirit fails to guard and protect the "living living" as well as intercede to the Supreme Being on behalf of the living, any petitions and prayers they have. Consequently, the lives of the "living living" will be compromised because the one who is supposed to act as the intermediary is not able to perform the ancestral duties. What came out strongly among the research participants was the need to ensure that the justice rendered for the *Gukurahundi* genocide offers people both psychosocial and spiritual healing because social harmony is crucial to establishing an equilibrium between their physical and metaphysical worlds.

CONCLUSION

That *Gukurahundi* was a genocide has been established and is no longer an item for debate. The Dumbutshena and Chihambakwe commissions of inquiry, as well as the ONHRI, were a farce and amounted to no resultant accountability, hence they signified the death of statist transitional justice in

Zimbabwe. Even the NPRC has already created doubts among the local populace in terms of the reliability of state institutions in delivering redress for the past. In the absence of state-led processes of justice, the affected communities have resorted to indigenous practices of justice, among other practices, in order to cope with the effects of the genocide.

For now, it seems the indigenous justice practices have been offering relief to the affected parties given that it has taken the government more than three decades to address the Gukurahundi genocide. What remains pertinent for the research participants with regard to justice is being able to retain social harmony in their communities. This social harmony has best been offered by conducting reburials of remains of their loved ones in accordance with their customs of the day, as well as performing rituals and ceremonies to uphold the cosmological balance between the physical and metaphysical worlds that make their being.

NOTES

1. Ruth Murambadoro is a postdoctoral fellow at the Centre for Sexualities, Aids and Gender at the University of Pretoria, while Chenai Matshaka is a doctoral candidate in the Department of Political Sciences at the same university.

2. The Dumbutshena Commission of Inquiry was set up to investigate the violence that occurred at Entumbane in Bulawayo and other demobilisation camps across the country following the 1981 clashes between ex combatants of the Zimbabwe African National Liberation Army (ZANLA) and the Zimbabwe People's Revolutionary Army (ZIPRA). The Chihambakwe Commission of Inquiry was established to investigate the *Gukurahundi* massacres in the Midlands and Matabeleland regions (Mashingaidze 2009, 24).

3. "Predatory state" is a metaphor that describes a condition whereby those who control the apparatus of the state appear to flourish without any regard for the welfare of the whole populace (Musewe 2014).

4. Spirituality is used to refer to the belief in the powers of the universe and this universe is made up of a network of actors that exist in the physical and metaphysical realm who all embody a spiritual component that guides their relations as entities in the universe.

BIBLIOGRAPHY

Amstutz, Mark. 2006. "Restorative Justice, Political Forgiveness, and the Possibility of Political Reconciliation." In *The Politics of Past Evil: Religion, Reconciliation and the Dilemmas of Transitional Justice*, edited by Philpott, Daniel, 151–82. Notre Dame: University of Notre Dame Press.

Babbie, Earl, and Johann Mouton. 2001. *The Practice of Social Research*. Cape Town: Oxford University Press.

Benyera, Everisto. 2014a. *Debating the Efficacy Transitional Justice Mechanisms: The Case of National Healing in Zimbabwe*. PhD diss., University of South Africa.

Benyera, Everisto. 2014b. "Exploring Zimbabwe's Traditional Transitional Justice Mechanisms." *Journal of Social Sciences* 41 (3): 335–44.

Bosha, Sarah. 2014. *Addressing Past Injustices in a Wounded Zimbabwe: Gukurahundi*. www.beyondintractability.org/casestudy/addressing-injustice-zimbabwe. Accessed 15 June 2015.

Catholic Commission for Justice, Peace in Zimbabwe, and Legal Resources Foundation Zimbabwe. 1997. *Breaking the Silence, Building True Peace: A Report on the Disturbances in Matabeleland and the Midlands, 1980 to 1988*. Catholic Commission for Justice and Peace in Zimbabwe.

Chiromba, Fradereck. 2015. *Sunday Opinion: Peace Commission: Our right, Our Duty*. The Standard 20 December 2015. www.thestandard.co.zw/2015/12/20/peace-commission-our-right-our-duty/.

Ellis, Stephen, and Gerrie Ter Haar. 2004. *Worlds of Power: Religious thought and Political Practice in Africa*. London: Hurst & Company.

Eppel, Shari. 2003. "A Brief History of Violations of Human Rights in Zimbabwe since 1965 to Present." Paper for the International Centre for Transitional Justice, New York.

Eppel, Shari. 2006. "Healing the Dead: Exhumation and Reburials as Truth-telling and Peace-building Activities in Rural Zimbabwe." In *Telling the Truths: Truth Telling and Peace-building in Post- Conflict Societies*, edited by Tristan Anne Borer, 259–88. Notre Dame: University of Notre Dame Press.

Eppel, Shari. 2009. "A Tale of Three Dinner Plates: Truth and Challenges of Human Rights Research in Zimbabwe." *Journal of Southern African Studies* 35 (4): 967–76.

Eppel, Shari, and Brian Raftopoulos. 2008. *Political Crisis, Mediation and the Prospects for Transitional Justice in Zimbabwe*. Cape Town: IDASA.

Gelfand, Michael. 1973. *The Genuine Shona: Survival Values of an African Culture*. Gweru: Mambo Press.

Hayner, Priscilla. 1994. "Fifteen Truth Commissions—1974 TO 1994: A Comparative Study." *Human Rights Quarterly* 16: 597–655.

Heal Zimbabwe Trust & Zimbabwe Civic Education Trust. 2016. *Exploring Indigenous Transitional Justice Mechanisms in Zimbabwe*. Accessed 6 June 2016. www.veritaszim.net/.../Policy%20Brief%20on%20Transitional%20Justice.

Human Rights Watch. 2011. *Perpetual Fear: Impunity and Cycles of Violence in Zimbabwe*. New York: Human Rights Watch.

Johnstone, Gerry. 2013. *Restorative Justice: Ideas, Values, Debates*. Abingdon: Routledge.

Lan, David. 2006. *Guns & Rain: Guerrillas and Spirit Mediums in Zimbabwe*. London: J. Currey.

Machakanja, Pamela. 2010. *National Healing and Reconciliation in Zimbabwe: Challenges and Opportunities*. Cape Town: Institute for Justice and Reconciliation.

Mashingaidze, Terence. M. 2010. "Zimbabwe's Illusive National Healing and Reconciliation Processes: From Independence to the Inclusive Government 1980–2009." *Conflict Trends* 1: 19–27.

Mbire, Moreblessing. 2011. *Seeking Reconciliation and Healing in Zimbabwe: Case of the Organ on National Healing, Reconciliation & Integration (ONHRI)*. The Hague: International Institute of Social Studies.

Morreira, Shannon. 2014. *Exploring Transitional (and Other Kinds of) Justice in Zimbabwe*. http://pambazuka.org/en/category/features/93438. Accessed 12 January 2015.

Morrel, Penny, ed. 2003. *Declaration of the Johannesburg Symposium, August 2003, in Civil Society and Justice in Zimbabwe Summary of Proceedings held in Johannesburg 11–13 August 2003*. South Africa: Themba Lesizwe.

Msindo, Enocent. 2012. *Ethnicity in Zimbabwe: Transformations in Kalanga and Ndebele Societies, 1860–1990*. Rochester: University of Rochester Press.

Muchadehama, Aleck. 2018. NTJWG Welcomes the NPRC Act. www.newsday.co.zw/2018/01/ntjwg-welcomes-the-nprc-act/. Accessed: 29 September 2018.

Murambadoro, Ruth. 2015. "'We Cannot Reconcile Until the Past Has Been Acknowledged': Perspectives on Gukurahundi from Matabeleland, Zimbabwe." *African Journal on Conflict Resolution* 15 (1): 33–57.

Musewe, Vince. 2014. *Beware of Predatory Politics*. News Day 9 October 2014. www.newsday.co.zw/2014/10/09/beware-predatory-politics/.

Muzondidya, James, and Sabelo Ndlovu-Gatsheni. 2007. "Echoing Silences: Ethnicity in Post-colonial Zimbabwe, 1980–2007." *African Journal on Conflict Resolution* 7 (2): 275–97.

National Transitional Justice Working Group. 2016. "*NPRC Bill is Unconstitutional*". Accessed: 7 April 2016. www.ntjwg.org/article.php?id=161

Ndlovu-Gatsheni, Sabelo J. 2009. "Nation Building in Zimbabwe and the Challenges of Ndebele Particularism." *African Journal on Conflict Resolution* 8 (3): 27–56.

Ndlovu-Gatsheni, Sabelo J. 2012. "Rethinking Chimurenga and Gukurahundi in Zimbabwe: A Critique of Partisan National History." *African Studies Review* 55 (03): 1–26.

Nyathi, Pathisa. 2015. *Ngozi: An African Reality…Ensuring Social Justice and Fairness*. www.herald.co.zw/ngozi-an-african-reality-ensuring-social-justice-and-fairness/. Accessed 28 April 2018.

Sasa, Mabasa. 2015. *VP Mphoko Opens up on Gukurahundi*. Sunday Mail. 15 February 2015. www.sundaymail.co.zw/vp-mphoko-opens-up-on-gukurahundi/.

Setiloane, Gabriel M. 1978. "How the Traditional World-View Persists in the Christianity of the Sotho-Tswana." *Pula: Botswana Journal of African Studies* 1: 27–42.

The Standard 30 October 2011. *Chokuda Case: Avenging Spirits Exact Justice?* www.thestandard.co.zw/2011/10/30/chokuda-case-avenging-spirits-exact-justice/.

Van der Merwe, Hugo, Victoria Baxter, and Audrey R. Chapman. (eds.). 2009. *Assessing the Impact of Transitional Justice: Challenges for Empirical Research*. Washington, DC: United States Institute of Peace Press.

Zimbabwe Human Rights NGO Forum. 2016. '*NPRC Bill is Unconstitutional*'. Accessed: 7 April 2016. www.hrforumzim.org/news/nprc-bill-is-unconstitutional/.

Chapter 8

Grassroots Mechanisms for Justice, Peace-building, and Social Cohesion in Zimbabwe's "New" Farm Communities

Tom Tom and Clement Chipenda

INTRODUCTION

Zimbabwe witnessed a radical change of the rural landscape in the context of extensive redistributive land reform under the Fast Track Land Reform Programme (FTLRP). In an attempt to reverse racially skewed land tenure that was tilted against the black majority, the government of Zimbabwe (GoZ) embarked on three phases of land acquisition and resettlement—the first and second phases of land acquisition and rural resettlement, and the FTLRP (Bhatasara and Helliker 2016; Moyo 2013; Moyo 2011; Mkodzongi 2011). The land reforms created a new and diversified rural landscape through the fusion of people from various socioeconomic, political, and ethno-regional backgrounds (Chipenda 2018; Chibwana 2016; James 2015; Mkodzongi 2013; Murisa 2009; Moyo, Chambati, Murisa, Siziba, Dangwa and Nyoni 2009). The reconfiguration is more pronounced under the FTLRP, which led to the resettlement of 180,000 families (170,000 under A1 and 10,000 under A2 schemes) on 13 million hectares (Hanlon, Manjengwa and Smart 2014; Moyo and Chambati 2013; Scoones, Marongwe, Mavedzenge, Murimbarimba, Mahenehene and Sukume 2011). The focus of the chapter is particularly on the FTLRP, which according to Cliffe, Alexander, Cousins, and Gaidzanzwa (2011), is the most topical of all Zimbabwe's land reforms and has been dramatic and transformational. Among other outcomes, the FTLRP created fertile opportunities and challenges for social cohesion in relation to a variety of aspects including access to and control of prime land and appended natural resources, farm boundaries, farm infrastructure, and equipment, ethno-regional differences, and so on. Due to its fast-track nature, the programme was accompanied by lack of planning and provision of infrastructure, and systems for effective resettlement on various aspects. How grassroots mechanisms for justice, peace-building, and social cohesion played out in the new farm communities that are composed of a diversified "social texture" is important.

The breadth and nature of the FTLRP led to a major demographic reconfiguration of the former large-scale commercial farms (LSCFs) through a mixture of people's diverse backgrounds and aspirations (Chipenda 2018; Chibwana 2016; Hanlon, Manjengwa and Smart 2014; Moyo and Chambati 2013). The resettled families have wider diversity in terms of cultural, religious, ethnic, political, and economic values and practices, thereby creating opportunities, challenges, and problems for the achievement of the goals FTLRP. The expectation was that despite diversity, the people would put aside these differences, and live and work together amicably in the pursuit of the goals of land acquisition and resettlement. The field evidence shows diversity, conjecture, and disjuncture on these issues.

Despite lack of acknowledgment of land reforms as social policy instruments in mainstream social policy literature and low engagement with the social policy dimensions of the FTLRP in Zimbabwe's land reform literature, the chapter vigorously argues that the FTLRP and the other two land reforms are social policy instruments for enhancing the wellbeing of the majority of the population. The capability of a program to initiate, sustain, and enhance social cohesion is a vital dimension in social policy. Accordingly, the FTLRP can be evaluated on the bases of several social policy outcomes (production, redistribution, social protection, social reproduction, and social cohesion). These are the pillars of transformative social policy (Adesina 2011; Mkandawire 2007). In this chapter, social cohesion is prioritized and merged to local grassroots mechanisms for justice and peace-building in fast-tracked farm communities. Peculiarly evident in diverse literature on the FTLRP is scanty specific focus on transitional justice in the new farm communities of Zimbabwe. However, given a context of social fluidity, limited availability of critical farm infrastructure and equipment increased ethno-regional diversity and heightened occurrence of conflict, transitional justice in the form of traditional local grassroots beliefs and mechanisms for conflict resolution, the pursuit of justice and social cohesion is essential.

Grounded and nuanced grassroots mechanisms for justice, peace-building, and social cohesion in Zvimba district in Mashonaland West Province of Zimbabwe is informed by evidence from various former large-scale commercial farms including Dalkeith, Whynhill, St Lucia, and Lion Kopje. Particular focus is on the broader dimensions of social cohesion including consensus, existence of social conflict, the parties involved, conflict management, cohesive, and peace-building initiatives through local and traditional mechanisms. Access to and ownership of prime land as a key resource, natural resources appended to the land, farm boundaries, farm infrastructure and equipment, and farm labor are prioritized. However, ethno-regionalism, domestic disputes, personality differences, and so on are also explored. The interactions and contributions of traditional leadership, land beneficiaries, farm community households, Committee of Seven (Co7), Neighborhood Watch Committee (NWC), District Land Committees (DLCs), Zimbabwe Republic Police (ZRP), officials from the Ministry of Lands, Agriculture and Rural Resettlement and judiciary are at the crux of the chapter.[1] The principal argument is that effectiveness of the responses to injustice and negative conflict in the spirit of upholding healthy social organisztion and institutions in the farm community, and broadly goals of land reforms in addressing the social question are indispensable.

CONCEPTUALIZING SOCIAL COHESION AND CONFLICT

Focus on social cohesion has occupied various fields in the social sciences. However, credit is given to the sociologist Emile Durkheim for popularizing the concept by emphasizing on social forces, interdependence, and collective effervescence. The diversity of contributors and aspects included under social cohesion is evidence that the concept defies a uniform categorization. There are several other contributors to the conceptualization of social cohesion (Doreian and Fararo 2016; McPherson and Smith-Lovin 2002; Hogg 1992; Bettenhausen 1991; Levine and Mooreland 1990; Mudrack 1989; Carron 1982; Kellerman 1981; Evans and Jarvis 1980; Stein 1976; Lott and Lott 1965). Social cohesion refers to specific behaviors and attitudes which are shared and aimed at bringing about peace and consensus in the communities; and to contribute directly and indirectly toward nation building. Broadly, social cohesion is a quality of society that denotes individuals and groups as products of society who are bound together through the action of specific values, attitudes, behaviors, rules, and institutions which depend on consensus, not coercive actions (Green, Janmaat and Cheng 2011; Prasad, Hypher and Gerecke 2013).

Adesina (2007) arguing from a social policy perspective, reiterates the need for social policies to create and sustain social cohesion within and across communities. An expanded view of social cohesion at national-level benefits the whole country. For example, sound famers' relations and collaborative agricultural schemes may lead to high-farm productivity in Zvimba district. In addition to benefiting people within Zvimba, such high agricultural productivity may be redistributed to Zimbabwe at large. Overall, in the context of transformative social policy, social policies should achieve social cohesion; its absence (particularly stemming from unequal distribution of resources and income) implies the existence of conflict. In cases where the conflict over unequal distribution of income and resources is not managed, it may create a viable environment for degeneration into national political conflict that stalls national development (Mkandawire 2007). Social cohesion is a vital element of progressive societies due to its overall influence on institutions, governance, and policies. The FTLRP, at surface value, is in line with redistribution of resources and capital accumulation that paves the way for instilling a sense of belonging and citizenship among the people contributing directly and indirectly toward nation building.

Conflict and cohesion are central themes in the work of key sociologists such as Georg Simmel, Auguste Comte, Emile Durkheim, Karl Marx, Lewis Coser (1956), Randall Collins (1975), and Ralph Dahrendorf (1959). These sociologists vary in conceptualizing conflict and cohesion but a critical understanding that can be derived from their contributions is that conflict and cohesion are part of all societies and that they influence one another. For example, only those who interact (and possibly are bound by consensus) may experience conflict. In addition, after conflict, cohesion, peace, and stability set in. Social relations are therefore marked by both conflict and consensus.

Broadly defined, conflict is an expressed struggle between at least two interdependent parties who perceive incompatible goals, scarce resources, and interference from others in achieving their goals (Wilmot and Hocker 2011, 9). Conflict can also be understood as a communication process within which a problematic situation with certain characteristics arises (Abigail and Cahn 2011, 20). Conflicts fall in various categories—structural, relationship, interest, value and so on. Basically, conflict behaviors can be changed because such behaviors are not inborn. Similar arguments have been advanced by renowned scholars in search for cohesive societies (Wilmot and Hocker 2011, 9).

Several conflicts occur at various levels between and among those in the new farm communities of Zvimba district, therefore, this chapter is restricted to conflicts pertaining to access to and ownership of land, farm boundaries, farm infrastructure and equipment, natural resources, farm labor, and ethno-regionalism. Conflict in the farm communities is double-edged (both functional and dysfunctional) and should be managed effectively, prioritizing traditional grassroots mechanisms for peace-building and social cohesion.

TRANSITIONAL JUSTICE AS A DISPUTED CONCEPT

Justice and injustice are highly contested concepts. Despite the contestations, generally, justice can mean that which is right, fair, appropriate, and deserved (Pearce 2012, 161). According to Villa-Vicencio (2004, 33), there are several kinds of justice namely, retributive, deterrent, compensatory, rehabilitative, exonerative, and restorative. Not all these kinds of justice address the needs of victims, but all are useful depending on the issues and contexts.

Benyera (2014) reports that transitional justice is a growing field of study and practice in restoring peace and fostering reconciliation in postconflict countries. Accountability, truth recovery, reconciliation, institutional reform, and reparation are the five pillars of transitional justice. Benyera (2014) and Boraine (2000) focus on these pillars of transitional justice. Transitional justice is a wide range of mechanisms and institutions used in response to gross violations of human rights (Benyera 2014, 236). In essence, these could be judicial or non-judicial measures that are implemented by post-conflict communities to redress abuses. Transitional justice is concerned with the choices, mechanisms and the quality of justice implemented by states emerging from episodes of gross human rights abuses such as civil wars and totalitarian rule to respond to past oppression and injustice while constructing a new future based on democracy and rule of law (Benyera 2014).

Among the most common mechanisms for transitional justice are amnesties and pardons, criminal and non-criminal sanctions, commissions of inquiry and truth and reconciliation commissions (Braithwaite 2002, 2010; Braithwaite, Braithwaite, Cookson and Dunn 2010). However, these mechanisms do not cover customary institutions that are being used as transitional justice mechanisms to seek reconciliation and peace-building (Benyera 2014).

DEBATING TRADITIONAL LOCAL JUSTICE MECHANISMS AND SYSTEMS

Traditional local justice mechanisms are equally contested concepts. However, these are communal and collectivist methods of conflict resolution embedded in group rather than individual rights. In essence, traditional justice mechanisms are part of the broader indigenous African legal customs. They are accompanied by rituals and ceremonies inherent in customary institutions (Benyera 2014, 23). In such contexts, justice has to be achieved to the satisfaction of the community, which is made up of three groups namely the "living dead," the "living," and the "living unborn." In traditional justice mechanisms and systems, the ancestors (*midzimu*), spirit mediums (*masvikiro*) and traditional leaders (e.g., *madzishe*) form the hierarchy that leads to

God (*Mwari*). That hierarchy is used by the Shona people to seek and interpret traditional justice (Rutsate 2011, 1).

In relation to Africa, traditional transitional justice mechanisms concur with theoretical calls for the continent to reinvent its traditions to solve its transitional justice challenges. African philosophy informs African tradition. One essential philosophical value that should be incorporated into human rights is *hunhu/ubuntu* (Benyera 2014, 335). This value is central to realist transitional justice mechanisms that are marked by bottom-up, non-legal, victim-centered, broad-based, continuous redress mechanisms that heal and reconcile communities fragmented by gross human rights. *Hunhu/ubuntu* emphasizes that the self is defined by its relationship with other beings; and happiness and fulfillment are found in relations between individuals (Ndlovu-Gatsheni 2007; Nabudere 2011).

Benyera (2014, 336) reiterates that *hunhu/ubuntu* is based on reciprocity, limitation of power, respect for human rights, acknowledgment of wrong doing, communal solidarity, unity, humanity despite differences. These ideals of African philosophy are functional in most rural areas and can be widely tapped on for peace-building and development. In comparison to idealist transitional justice, realist transitional justice prioritizes humanity and communal solidarity. These values are pursued in ways that seek to balance restorative and retributive justice (Du Plessis and Ford 2008, 3).

The alternatives to formal transitional justice are confirmed by several authorities. The former United Nations secretary general Kofi Anan in her 2004 report on the rule of law and transitional justice in conflict societies urged that "due regard must be given to indigenous and informal traditions for administering justice or settling disputes to help them to continue their often vital role and to do so in conformity with both international and local tradition." To date, most analyses of transitional justice have focused on the orientations and behavior of political elites. Scant attention is paid to the preferences of ordinary citizens, their beliefs, and practices (Bratton 2011, 357). Zimbabwe has never had meaningful and comprehensive programs to provide justice in the many issues that cascade from conflict and violence in the nation. This incomplete decolonization provoked the violent Fast Track Land Reform Program (*Third Chimurenga/Hondo Yeminda/Jambanja*) that was formalized in 2000 (Ndlovu-Gatsheni and Benyera 2015, 13). True healing is important for the continued well-being of society (Ngwenya and Harris 2015) in support for social cohesion.

According to Von Heinegg and Epping (2007, 251), effective healing entails reconciliation, that is, the normalization of relations between the parties, victims, and offenders. Essentially, reconciliation is the beginning of cordial relations, trust, and willingness to talk to each other. This is accompanied by a mutual capacity to listen and readiness to take cautious risks. Reconciliation regards justice as an essential ingredient in any settlement while recognizing that there are different ways of achieving and understanding justice (Villa-Vicencio, Doxtader and Goldstone 2004, 4).

CONFLICT IN THE SELECTED FARM COMMUNITIES OF ZVIMBA DISTRICT

Most major conflicts worldwide have been and continue to be over the land and other key resources (Anseeuw and Alden 2010; Tom 2015, 89). Land conflicts feature prominently in the history of Zimbabwe as evidenced by the first, second, and third anti-colonial struggles (Moyo 2011; Moyo and Yeros 2007; Sachikonye 2005). Conflicts over the land and other natural resources are therefore universal issues (Tom 2015, 89).

Existence of Conflicts Pertaining to Land in Zvimba District

The existence of conflicts in the selected farms of Zvimba district, particularly those directly or indirectly linked to the land was very high. From the fieldwork done by the researchers, it was noted that 96 percent of the farmers in the study were aware of the existence of land conflicts in the farming communities of Zvimba district. However, 3 percent explained that there are no land conflicts in the farm communities while 1 percent was not sure of the existence of conflicts pertaining to land, natural resources, farm infrastructure and equipment and farm labor. Accordingly, the majority of land beneficiaries (those who were allocated land in both A1 and A2 schemes) were aware of such conflicts in the selected farms of the district. Furthermore, 85 percent have personally been involved in the conflicts.

Exploration of the existence of conflicts was extended to other residents in the farms, District Land Committees (DLCs), traditional leaders, former farm workers, "squatters," members of nearby communal areas, and the local agricultural technical and extension (AGRITEX) officers under the Ministry of Lands, Agriculture, and Rural Resettlement. Incidence of conflict pertaining to the key identified categories was confirmed to having been high particularly before formalization, participation of DLCs and farm-level committees. On the basis of the voices from the field, land conflicts are highly prevalent in the new farming communities of Zvimba district. Given the unplanned processes of the FTLRP and diversified texture of the rural social relationships brought by the reform, high prevalence of conflict, particularly those conflicts relating to the land and other key resources, are expected.

Conflicts and Social Cohesion: Factoring the Diversity of Actors and Experiences

The conflicts in the selected farm communities of Zvimba district are varied. The key players are formal land holders, other household members, traditional leaders, Neighborhood Watch Committees, war veterans, former workers of LSCF, "squatters," members of nearby communal areas, officials from the Ministry of Lands, Agriculture and Rural Resettlement as well as District Lands Committees. Varied involvement was emphasized. Moreover, some conflicts overlap and straddle the actors.

The sources of conflicts were directly or indirectly linked to land with farm infrastructure and equipment (particularly, that left by the white large scale commercial farmers) and natural resources (flora and minerals) appended to the land were the most common sources of conflict in the selected post FTLRP farms in Zvimba district. Farm labor, farm boundaries and land ownership (mostly within households) were identified by the lowest number of farmers with frequencies of 31, 10, and 5, respectively. Such context-based evidence shows significant changes in conflict trajectories. In earlier phases of the FTLRP, Moyo, Chambati, Murisa, Siziba, Dangwa, and Nyoni (2009), contributors to the African Institute for Agrarian Studies (AIAS) (now Sam Moyo African Institute for Agrarian Studies, SMAIAS) 2005/6 Baseline Survey, farm ownership and boundaries were the major sources of conflict. Such a state of affairs in the early 2000s was caused by absence of formal pegging by lands officers, unavailability of offer letters and multiple allocations.

Farm Infrastructure and Equipment

Tractors, ridgers, planters, irrigation equipment, tobacco barns, farm houses, green houses, roads, dams, fences, and recreational facilities are among the farm infrastructure and equipment at the core of conflict in the selected farms (Moyo et al. 2009). The FTLRP opened opportunities for the majority black population to raise claims for infrastructure and equipment. Common claim and ownership may not necessarily translate into equal or equitable use thereby creating a viable environment for conflict. Farm infrastructure and equipment are state property. The Government of Zimbabwe through the Ministry of Lands, Agriculture and Rural Resettlement has overall ownership while the farmers should merely have user rights of especially the major ones.

Some farm infrastructure and equipment left by large-scale commercial farmers are still functional at some farms while in others these were vandalized, have worn out, or collapsed due to use without maintenance and general lack of responsibility mainly resulting from common ownership. Conflicts emanating from use of farm infrastructure and equipment ranked highest, signaling its significance in farm production and in devising ways for improving social cohesion in new farms. Among the "ills" of common claim and ownership are monopolization, general unwillingness to share, delays in sharing and neglect leading to damage of the equipment or infrastructure result. These may lead to conflicts.

Use of irrigation equipment, tractors, and tobacco barns are topical. However, conflicts emanating from use of barns for curing tobacco have declined in recent years. Unlike the early 2000s when tobacco farmers were sharing barns left by the large scale white commercial farmers, most farmers have built minor barns. However, collective use of major barns is enduring due to their effectiveness. Usually, conflicts emerge when tobacco curing is done in turns and entails meeting electricity and maintenance costs jointly. Some farmers refuse to meet the costs while some may keep their tobacco longer than is agreed. In other cases, some farmers may not want to give other farmers a chance. Yet in other cases, relatives, and friends of "powerful" farmers in neighboring farms may bring their tobacco for curing while the immediate beneficiaries are waiting for their turn. This may be done to earn cash, vital commodities, and favors from the farmers they would have helped. Latent and manifest conflicts emerge in such instances, threatening cohesive farming and general social life. Failure of cooperative farming to deliver can partly be attributed to these problems.

Appended Natural Resources

The FTLRP broadened access to a variety of fauna and flora by the new farmers after the white farmers left. Wildlife and other natural resources were abundant in early years of occupation in 2000s (Mkodzongi 2013; James 2015). Wild animals such as impala and warthog are common although they have declined. Woodlands are exploited for timber and firewood (for curing tobacco and cooking). Wildlife is being exploited for household consumption and as an income generation activity. Fauna and flora are on major decline trend due to widespread (and in some cases unsustainable use). Conflicts erupt due to widening scarcity and common ownership and competition over natural resources in "no man's land" areas.

Competition for Farm Labor

Extra farm labor may be a source of contention among the households in the farm communities. In most A1 farms, the farmers mainly rely on household labor. Only when household labor is in short supply or in peak periods do these households hire additional labor. However, A2 farmers rely on hired labor. Their plots are bigger than those in the A1 scheme. Extra farm labor is hired within and between the schemes or from the communal areas. Competition for extra labor is rife between households or schemes and may spiral into open conflict. Chambati (2013) dwells on changing labor relations after Zimbabwe's land reform while Chibwana (2016) interrogates labor as a production constraint in the Kwekwe case study.

Farm Boundaries

Formal and informal contestations over farm boundaries threaten social cohesion. However, few farmers raised this issue as source of conflict. In most cases, such conflict involves neighboring households and poachers of natural resources such as forests, wild animals, and gold. In other cases, conflicts over farm boundaries emanate over fertile land or where there are vital appended resources to the piece of land.

The farms were demarcated and pegged by the officials from the then Ministry of Lands and Rural Resettlement (now Ministry of Lands, Agriculture and Rural Resettlement). In principle, every farmer knows the boundaries of his or her farm. However, some farmers may extend farming operations or resource extraction into their neighbors' pieces of land. In other cases, a farmer may deliberately shift the pegs, especially in areas where the land is fertile or where the appended natural resources are vast or even outweigh the benefits of farming. These deliberate actions of shifting pegs or extending into a neighbor's farm stimulate both latent and manifest conflict. These are unjust actions that strain harmonious relations and cohesive farming entities.

"No man's land" may also stimulate conflicts. Such land is for common exploitation and exists outside the demarcated individual plots, yet they are part of the overall farm. In some cases, a household nearest to this common land claims "ownership" of the land and its related natural resources. The use of such land is not formally prescribed. Informal "agreements" and "social rationality" are therefore applied.

A common practice across the A1 and A2 farms, which however, is more pronounced in the A1 farms is informal sub-divisions for the consanguineal and social dependents. Such boundaries may create conflicts, especially where there are 'unjustified' real and perceived inequalities in land allocation. The situation is worse when the formal land owner dies and the dependents may seek to reverse the informal allocations or contest for the household leadership role to have apex control of the land and related resources. Yet in other cases, the traditional head of the household stays in the urban areas while the other members stay and work on the farm. The members staying on the farm may take over the portion allocated to the urban dweller. The members staying on the farm may differ on boundary extension. Resolution of conflicts pertaining to farm boundaries is a turf for officials in the Ministry of Lands, Agriculture and Rural Resettlement. However, the police and traditional leaders may be called upon to assist in resolving the conflicts.

Land Ownership

Redistribution and equity in owning and using prime agricultural land and appended natural resources are key determinants in attaining justice and social cohesion. Land ownership was the least source of conflict in current post-FTLRP farms in Zvimba district. From the onset, it is important to note that land dispossession from black majority has been at the epicenter of Zimbabwe's liberation struggles and war veterans–led occupation of large-scale white-owned commercial farms (Sadomba 2013; Masuko 2013). In such struggles, the focus has been between the black majority versus the white minority. However, during and in the aftermath of the FTLRP, contestations are among the new black farmers. This fluidity of ownership was a source of conflict, leading to strained social organization.

In early phases of land reform, conflicts emerged between formal owners (those with offer letters) and informal occupiers (those who invaded land from the white farmers but had no offer letter). Both considered themselves as owners. On the other end are evicted large-scale commercial farmers who claimed ownership of the land on the basis that they had legal documents of ownership and inheritance and that they were not compensated for the land and farm infrastructure taken. Yet on the other end are former farm workers on who had found home in LSCF.

Conflict also arise in relation to absentee land holders versus neighboring farmers who take advantage of land underutilization without approval of the Ministry of Lands, Agriculture and Rural Resettlement; squatters among themselves or in relation to other groups (a squatter is any person who was not formally allocated land or is not informally acknowledged by the farmers as an "authorized" owner or user of the land); land allocation and inheritance issues within families (land is an essential resource worthy inheriting and conflicts arise in the redistribution of the estate, which obviously includes the farm); those who are nearest to unmarked land and natural resources also claim ownership of such land and appended natural resources (those who have used the land longer, claim ownership of the land); and members of the communal areas also claim ownership of the former large-scale commercial farms. Their argument is that that the quest for land acquisition from the whites and its redistribution was a black majority goal. Accordingly, its benefits should be enjoyed by all. This argument partly justifies why members of the communal areas do not regard unauthorized gold panning, tree cutting and hunting, brick molding, sand and gravel extraction as poaching.

Broadly, the conflicts over land ownership were higher in the early phases of the FTLRP due to double allocations, formal and informal settlement, multiple farm grabbing by the elite and the eviction of early black occupiers from the land. However, the Farm-Level Land Committees (FLLCs), District Land Committees (DLCs), Committee of Seven and Ministry of Lands, Agriculture and Rural Resettlement have significantly worked to reduce land ownership conflicts. The issues pertaining to land ownership (although this conflict source scored the least among the causes of conflicts) was a significant area to be considered in efforts to enhance social cohesion in the selected farming communities.

Other Conflicts: Personal, Domestic, and Ethno-Regionalism

The conflicts occurring in the selected new farms are not restricted to farm boundaries, access to and use of natural resources, farm infrastructure, and equipment and land ownership. Other conflicts are rooted in ethno-regionalism, domestic issues (gender and distribution of resources), and personality differences (Chibwana 2016; James 2015; Mkodzongi 2013; Moyo et al. 2009). Conflicts emerge from general personality differences. Naturally people are different and the differences in personality are potential sources of conflict because they determine values, likes and dislikes; and ultimately the nature of interaction among those living on the farms. Other conflicts pertain to domestic issues between spouses or spouses and their children or dependents. Such conflict may extend to domestic violence. Inter-household conflicts may also emerge. These may include stray livestock destroying fields and gardens of neighbors, fights among children, competition, use and payment of farm workers, marriage problems and divorces. Production time may be lost as people engage in unproductive conflicts.

Fusion of people from various regions, tribal and ethnic backgrounds created farm communities of varying cultural beliefs and practices. For instance, the people allocated land in the selected farms came from diverse areas within and outside Zvimba district. Masvingo, Zhombe, Harare, Chitungwiza, Guruve, Bubi, Banket, Bocha, Goromonzi, Mount Darwin, Murewa, Nyanga, Tsholotsho, and Chipinge are some of the areas from which the new farmers emerged from. These areas are diverse in terms of ethno-regional attributes. Such variety may be good for cultural sharing. However, diversity may create sour relations and antagonism. In simple terms, conflicts emerging from ethno-regionalism can be analyzed in their own right and can be linked to land conflicts for deeper understanding. For example, ethno-regionalism manifests in inclusion and exclusion of certain stereotyped groups, leading to differential access to and use of farm infrastructure and equipment, inputs and marketing networks. The households in the farm community, AGRITEX officers and DLCs indicated that conflicts emanating from ethno-regionalism are on a major decline trend as the households increasingly transformed from being "strangers" to neighbors and relatives who can be relied upon.

Situating the Conflicts in the Context of Local Traditional Grassroots and Formal Mechanisms for Justice, Conflict Resolution, and Enhanced Social Cohesion

Conflicts are prevalent in the selected farms and such prevalence was very high in early years of occupation. Individuals and social institutions in and outside the selected farm communities are managing conflicts in various ways and with varying levels of success. Traditional grassroots mechanisms in use are anchored on customary institutions (family and household elders and other members, village heads and chiefs; customary law, rituals and ceremonies; and nonviolence and limited use of force. Overall, traditional grassroots mechanisms for attaining justice are dominating in the resolution of conflict, reconciliation, and peace-building as compared to formal mechanisms through the District Administrator (DA), judiciary, officials from the Ministry of Lands, Agriculture and Rural Resettlement and other institutions who have power to mediate and arbitrate.

The farmers, respective families and household, traditional leadership system, and the farm-level committees are the most immediate local-level stakeholders that respond to conflicts in the selected farming areas. The other important social institutions that address conflicts exist in new farming communities include the Committee of Seven (Co7), District Lands Committees (DLCs), Neighborhood Watch Committee and Zimbabwe Republic Police (ZRP). These were put in place by the farmers and government to ensure a peaceful and productive environment. These institutions deal with different cases of conflict and in principle, they should do by endeavoring as much as possible to ensure the highest level of justice, transparency, fairness, and integrity. These institutions, particularly the family and household, headmen's traditional courts and the 'council' of elders, were reiterated by both the farmers and key informants as central and more effective in conflict mediation and resolution, and sustainable peace-building.

Intra and inter-household injustices and conflicts over land ownership, boundaries, infrastructure and equipment, and natural resources appended to the land, or purely domestic disputes are usually handled by the family or household members concerned. The family and household are central building block of the farm community (and the communal areas). The conflicting members can discuss and achieve a solution although this may not always work out. In addition, the elders of the conflicting families or households may take a leading position in reconciling the families.

It is important to note that family in the traditional African context is understood in relation to the whole community. When injustices and conflicts emerge, collective existence of the whole community is threatened; therefore, restoration of sound relations is prioritized. However, when the conflicts cannot be contained within or between the family or households, other elders from the community are incorporated. In most cases, conflicts are sustainably addressed at intra and inter family or household levels. In such cases, people in the farm communities will be applying locally and traditionally based justice mechanisms outside the formal legal machinery.

The intervention of traditional leaders, however, may be sought when the injustice and conflicts are not resolved at earlier levels. The institution of traditional leadership, which may comprise of village heads, council of elders and chiefs is central to social organization of the new farm communities (and that of communal areas). These may mediate or "impose" solutions non-violently or with minimum force. Consultation of both parties and maximizing continued sound relations are prioritized by traditional leadership. Fair compromise seeking, public forgiveness requests and payment for damages (*kuripa*) may be done. The traditional leadership institutions address various conflict issues from domestic to land issues. They even address pegging and farm boundary issues, a function that should in principle and formally be done by lands officers. In most cases they are effective because they understand the issues better and they strive for social reproduction of the farm community. These dimensions of grievance handling and conflict resolution are outside those set by the government, where injustices and conflicts are to be channeled through the formal judicial mechanisms.

The traditional leaders were hailed as central stakeholders in conflict resolution, particularly on the basis of the leadership position they hold in the farming communities and generally the whole country. They uphold customary law which is an essential attribute of traditional local mechanisms for justice. The traditional court (*dare/inkundla*) is a common feature of the farms (and the communal areas). Social disputes may be brought before the traditional leaders. Most social disputes are resolved at this level, especially if the traditional leaders do their work fairly and concentrate on issues that are within their scope of work. The traditional court imposes fines and may impose compensation to be given to the winning party. Varying levels of success are achieved. The parties involved in conflict may seek the services of higher traditional and legal courts if they are not satisfied by the local traditional court. Mkodzongi (2013) focuses on the reconfiguration of traditional leadership under the FTLRP.

Religious institutions are also important in addressing injustices and attaining social cohesion through bringing people together and sharing religious culture. Firstly, the shared existence encouraged and sustained by these institutions is important in the pursuit of the goals of the FTLRP. Secondly, these institutions may also mediate in conflicts that affect their members including those relating to land, farm infrastructure, boundaries, domestic disputes, personality clashes, and so on. Formally, for example, conflicts pertaining to the land conflicts should be addressed by the Farm-Level Land Committees and District Lands Committees. However, the centrality of religious and all other traditional leaders and intrusion into formal systems are widely reported, including their effectiveness in restoring or endeavoring for social cohesion.

Concerns were raised over traditional leadership. First, most traditional leaders act on the basis of tradition and therefore may not bring change to the conflict situation. Examples include resolution efforts on domestic violence and wrangles over ownership and land inheritance. Secondly, the traditional leaders may impose solutions on the basis of their positions. In such cases the root cause of conflict is not addressed, and the "solution" is not shared; therefore, is unsustainable. Thirdly, some traditional leaders may venture into conflicts that are beyond their scope of work of the Traditional Leadership Act (1998, consolidated 2001). For example, some traditional leaders are arbitrating on conflicts over land boundaries, yet this function falls within the jurisdiction of the Ministry of Lands and Rural Resettlement. Officials from this Ministry should work with the traditional leaders in resolving boundary conflicts. Fourthly, traditional leaders' arbitration on land conflicts is not legally binding because it is not supported by law. However, the traditional leaders' civil court is important in addressing civil cases that fall within the formal jurisdiction of traditional leaders. Where imposition is done or where respect for the traditional leaders is prioritized at the expense of justice, conflict is "resolved" manifestly yet is rife latently. Such conflicts endure and may explode later.

Farmers associations, credit associations, and women's groups are pivotal in social cohesion. They do so with the view of maintaining families, households, and communities; and improving the productive capacity of members. Shared vision, common values, aims, and objectives among the farmers are shaped by these institutions. These encourage co-operative existence among their members, and are playing preventive, reconciliation, and mediation roles at farm level. Members may turn to these institutions in times of conflict or when they need mediation. Generally, members and non-members are socialized to be "good" citizens—loving and helping one another. These qualities of the farmers' associations, credit associations and women's groups are necessary for social cohesion. However, they may not address the underlying structural bases of inequality and conflict thereby leading to its perpetuation. Patriarchy and domestic violence (against both men and women) are cases in point.

The Committee of Seven also solves disputes, especially land disputes, and they may refer unresolved cases to the District Administrator or the DLC. The Committee of Seven works on disagreements and open conflicts over farm boundaries, infrastructure, equipment, and other farm resources. Ideally, the Committee of Seven should be found on each farm because these are farm-level institutions that should be responsible for running and providing leadership on particular farms, which were subdivided by the FTLRP. This committee uses farm-grown, local and traditional means, often based on custom and nonviolence in resolving conflicts.

The Committee of Seven is usually expected to be composed of a Chairperson and six members. These members should be holding various portfolios in the Committee. This committee is usually in office for a minimum of a year. The farmers elect the Chairperson and other members. The committee members are part of the farm community and should not be imposed from outside. When conflicts arise, the Committee of Seven is usually the first port of call in resolving farm conflicts. The Committee is recognized by the government and as such has been given significant authority to address conflicts. Having accumulated legitimacy, power and authority, the Committee is a well-respected institution, hence, its significant acceptance in conflict resolution at farm level.

The committee members are familiar with the farm boundaries and the subdivisions; therefore, they are essential in addressing the conflicts emerging from boundaries. Usually, all or some of the members of the committee actively participated in the pegging of farms or were present when the pegging was done by the responsible government departments. The implication is that the Committee of Seven has considerable knowledge of the farm and its boundaries (both the main with other farms and internal boundaries for plot holders). Bearing in mind that farm boundaries may be a major cause of conflict, the committee is essential in identifying boundary (peg) shifts and their restoration.

The role of the Committee of Seven extends to conflicts emerging from environmental exploitation and protection. This role entails the incorporation of traditional leaders, Environmental Management Agency (EMA) (also composed of farm committees), ZRP and Neighborhood Watch Committee (NWC). Conflicts pertaining to natural resources exploitation are high in the selected farms and their occurrence and outcomes may justify the intervention of the ZRP and NWC. These two institutions deal with criminal and security issues such as theft and related disputes. ZRP and EMA are formal institutions established by the government. However, they work in collaboration with traditional leaders and farmers whose social cohesion is paramount. However, some land conflicts may not be effectively addressed through traditional ways and lower-level formal institutions.

The Committee of Seven may fail to resolve all conflicts due to the diverse scope of conflicts in the farms and jurisdictional limitations. Such conflicts are then referred to the District Lands Committee (DLC), which is chaired by the District Administrator (DA). This committee has greater power and usually provides a final decision at district level on farm conflicts and is composed of several government departments who have different but related mandates. The implication is that issues and conflicts dealt with by the DLC are complex and that the legal authority, technical expertise, and manpower at that level are higher. Rarely does the DLC fail to solve the conflicts tabled before them. However, case evidence shows that local traditional mechanisms that are based on *hunhu/ubuntu* may determine how the Committee of Seven and the DLCs operate. First, they only take over the case when they are fully satisfied that the family and local traditional have exhausted all their options. Secondly, they consult the family members and traditional leaders. Thirdly, they execute their duties in the spirit of preserving the community of farmers in terms of collective conscience and effervescence.

Government departments and ministries, the courts and political parties (formal machinery) are also instrumental in social cohesion, which is an essential ingredient for development and nation building. Ideally, the government departments and ministries cater for the socioeconomic needs of all the residents of the farms while the political parties and other membership organizations usually cater for the needs of their members only. In addition to these institutions, sporting, and recreational clubs and activities are contributing variedly to social cohesion. However, these institutions can also stimulate conflicts; especially the political parties. They may be out of touch with realities of the farm community and emphasize formal legal mechanisms which may prolong, deepen or start new conflicts. A key dimension that gives credit to the local traditional mechanisms over the formal structures and mechanisms for conflict resolution and peace-building is that the former is "within" the people and enshrined in their culture while the later are alien and often imposed on the people. The local traditional mechanisms are part of their philosophy/worldview and mode of life while the formal institutions are imported and unsustainable.

Despite the high incidents of conflict in the district, there is overwhelming evidence that the new farmers cooperate and work together, which is evidence of social cohesion. Farming tasks like tillage, planting and cultivation; meeting operating expenses such as water and electricity costs for irrigation purposes; environmental maintenance and protection to safeguard their properties and ensure the sustainability of natural resources; collective efforts through farmer's co-operatives to acquire cheaper agricultural inputs; sharing knowledge and technical expertise to enhance agricultural activities and farm life are all examples of areas of co-operation. This diversity of farmer co-operation is essential for social cohesion.

CONCLUSION

Importance of grassroots mechanisms for justice and peace-building in building cohesive "new" farm communities in Zimbabwe, with particular emphasis on Zvimba district in Mashonaland Central is the thrust of the chapter. The FTLRP led to major reconfiguration and diversification of the rural landscape through the resettlement of 170,000 black families on 7.6 million hectares of prime agricultural land, which is approximately 20 percent of the total land area of the country. Such prime agricultural land was previously owned by white large scale commercial farmers. The black majority was relegated from mainstream development through colonialism. The fast tracked land reform was not planned by the government therefore, no advance infrastructural, financial, equipment, technical, research, and extension support was provided. The new farmers had to rely on farm infrastructure and equipment left by the large scale commercial farmers. The resettled families are diverse in terms of ethno-regional, social, religious, political, and economic attributes. Conflicts over land and its appended natural resources, farm boundaries, farm labor, farm infrastructure and equipment were explored. Such conflicts emanate from real or perceived injustice.

Conflict like cohesion, is part of social organization and relations of the new farm communities. Significant evidence shows that the new farm communities are cohesive regardless of the existence of conflict. Social cohesion can be noted on farming tasks like tillage, planting, and cultivation; meeting operating expenses such as water and electricity costs for irrigation purposes; environmental maintenance and protection to safeguard their properties and for the sustainability of natural resources; collective efforts through farmer's co-operatives to acquire cheaper agricultural inputs; sharing knowledge and technical expertise to enhance agricultural activities and farm life. This diversity of farmer co-operation is essential for social cohesion. Social cohesion is an essential condition for the effective achievement of the goals of the FTLRP, and broadly in addressing the social question.

Conflicts are a problem in the fast tracked farm communities. As opposed to the prominence of formal systems for conflict resolution and justice, the chapter shows that local traditional mechanisms for traditional justice are popular and more effective in resolving most conflicts and building peace in the new farm communities. These include customary institutions, customary law, rituals and ceremonies. Their effectiveness stems from emphasis on reconciliation, unity, communal solidarity and nonviolence, and limited use of force. However, not all injustices are effectively addressed through local traditional mechanisms. Formal judicial mechanisms may be essential.

NOTE

1. The research which has informed this chapter was undertaken ethically in line with the rules and regulations of the University of South Africa (UNISA), as contained in the Ethical Clearance Certificate issued by the institution for the study. Measures have been put in place to protect the identity of all respondents who were informed that their contributions would be used in this book chapter.

BIBLIOGRAPHY

Abigail, Ruth Anna, and Cahn, Dudley. 2011. *Managing Conflict Through Communication*, 5th ed. Boston: Pearson.

Adesina, Jimi. 2007. *Social Policy in sub-Saharan African Context: In Search of Inclusive Development.* Basingstoke: Palgrave.

Adesina, Jimi. 2010. *Rethinking the Social Protection Paradigm: Social Policy in Africa's Development.* Background paper for European Report on Development. Paper presented at the 'Promoting Resilience through Social Protection in Sub-Saharan Africa' conference, organized by the European Report on Development, Dakar, Senegal, 28–30 June.

Anseeuw, Ward, and Chris Alden. (eds.). 2010. *The Struggle Over Land in Africa—Conflicts, Politics and Change.* Cape Town, HSRC Press.

Benyera, Everisto. 2014. "Exploring Zimbabwe's Traditional Transitional Justice Mechanisms." *Journal of Social Sciences* 41 (3): 335–44.

Benyera, Everisto. 2015. "Debating the Efficacy of Transitional Justice Mechanisms: The Case of National Healing in Zimbabwe, 1980–2011." PhD diss., University of South Africa.

Bettenhausen, Kenneth.1991. "Five Years of Groups Research: What We Have Learned and What Needs to be Addressed." *Journal of Management 17 (2):* 345–81.

Bhatasara, Sandra, and Kirk Helliker. 2016. "The Party-state in the Land Occupations of Zimbabwe: The Case of Shamva District." *Journal of Asian and Peasant Studies* 53 (1): 18–97.

Boraine, Alex. 2000. *A Country Unmasked: Inside South Africa's Truth and Reconciliation Commission.* Oxford: Oxford University Press.

Braithwaite, John. 2002. *Restorative Justice and Responsive Regulation.* New York: Oxford University Press.

Braithwaite, John. 2010. *Reconciliation and Architectures of Commitment: Sequencing Peace in Bougainville.* Canberra: ANU E Press.

Braithwaite, John, Valerie Braithwaite, Michael Cookson, and Leah Dunn. 2010. *Anomie and Violence: Non-truth and Reconciliation in Indonesian Peacebuilding.* Canberra: ANU E-Press.

Bratton, Michael. 2011. "Violence, Partisanship and Transitional Justice in Zimbabwe." *The Journal of Modern African Studies* 49 (3): 353–80.

Carron, Albert. 1982. "Cohesiveness in Sport Groups: Interpretations and Considerations." *Journal of Sport Psychology* 4 (2): 123–38.

Chambati, Walter. 2013. Changing agrarian labour relations after land reform in Zimbabwe. In *Land and Agrarian Reform in Zimbabwe: Beyond White-Settle Capitalism*, 157–194.

Chibwana, Musavengana Winston Theodore. 2016. "Social Policy Outcomes of Zimbabwe's Fast Track Land Reform Programme (FTLRP): A Case of Kwekwe District." PhD diss., University of South Africa.

Chipenda, Clement. 2018. "After Land Reform: What About the Youth?" Conference Presentation Delivered at the International Conference on Authoritarian Populism and the Rural World organized by the Emancipatory Rural Politics Initiative (ERPI), International Institute of Social Studies (ISS), The Hague, Netherlands, 17–18 March 2018.

Cliffe, Lionel, Jocelyn Alexander, Ben Cousins, and Rudo Gaidzanwa. 2011. "An Overview of the Fast Track Land Reform in Zimbabwe: Editorial Introduction." *Journal of Peasant Studies* 38 (5): 907–38.

Collins, Randall. 1975. *Conflict Sociology: Toward an Explanatory Science.* New York: Academic Press.

Coser, Louis. 1956. *The Functions of Social Conflict.* Glencoe, IL: Free Press.

Dahrendorf, Ralph. 1959. *Class and Class Conflict in Industrial Society.* Stanford: Stanford University Press.

Doreian, Patrick, and Thomas Fararo. 2016. *The Problem of Solidarity: Theories and Models.* London: Routledge.

Du Plessis, Max, and Jolyon Ford. 2008. *Justice and peace in a new Zimbabwe: transitional justice options.* Institute for Security Studies Paper, No. 164. Pretoria: Institute for Security Studies.

Evans, Nancy, and Paul Jarvis. 1980. *Group Cohesion: A Review and Reevaluation.* London: Sage.

Hanlon, Joseph, Jeanette Manjengwa, and Teresa Smart. 2014. *Zimbabwe Takes Back Its Land.* Sterling: Kumarian Press.

Hogg, Michael. 1992. *The Social Psychology of Group Cohesiveness: From Attraction to Social Identity.* New York New York University Press.

James, Gareth. 2015. "Transforming rural livelihoods in Zimbabwe: Experiences of Fast Track Land Reform, 2000–2012." PhD diss., The University of Edinburgh.

Kellerman, Henry. 1981. *Group Cohesion.* London: Grune and Stratton Incorporated.

Levine, John, and Richard Mooreland. 1990. "Progress in Small Group Research." *Annual Review of Psychology* 41 (1): 581–634.

Lott, Albert, and Bernice Lott. 1965. "Group Cohesiveness as Interpersonal Attraction: A Review of Relationships with Antecedent and Consequent Variables." *Psychological Bulletin* 64 (1): 259–309.

Masuko, Louis. 2013. "Nyabira-Mazowe War Veterans Association: A Microcosm of the Land Occupation Movement." In *Land and Agrarian Reform in Zimbabwe: Beyond White-Settler Capitalism*, edited by Sam Moyo and Walter Chambati, 123–56. Dakar: CODESRIA, pp. 123–155.

McPherson, Miller, and Lynn Smith-Lovin. 2002. "Cohesion and Membership Duration: Linking in Group Processes." *Advances in Group Processes* 19 (1): 1–36.

Mkandawire, Thandika. 2007. "Transformative Social Policy and Innovation in Developing Countries." *The European Journal of Development Research* 19 (1): 13–29.

Mkodzongi, Grasian. 2011. *Land Occupations and The Quest for Livelihoods in Mhondoro Ngezi Area, Zimbabwe*. Huntingdon: Mimeo.

Mkodzongi, Grasian. 2013. "Fast Tracking Land Reform and Rural Livelihoods in Mashonaland West Province of Zimbabwe: Opportunities and Constraints. 2000–2013." PhD diss., The University of Edinburgh.

Mkodzongi, Grasian. 2013. "New People, New Land and New Livelihoods: A Micro-study of Zimbabwe's Fast-track Land Reform." *Agrarian South Journal of Political Economy* 2 (3): 345–66.

Moyo, Sam. 2011. "Three decades of agrarian reform in Zimbabwe". *Journal of Peasant Studies* 38, no 3: 493–531.

Moyo, Sam. 2013. "Land Reform and Redistribution in Zimbabwe since 1980." In *Land and Agrarian Reform in Zimbabwe: Beyond White-Settler Capitalism*, edited by Sam Moyo and Walter Chambati, 29–78. Dakar: CODESRIA.

Moyo, Sam, and Paris Yeros. 2007. "The Radicalised State: Zimbabwe's Interrupted Revolution." *Review of African Political Economy* 34 (111): 103–21.

Moyo, Sam, and Walter Chambati. 2013. "Introduction: Roots of Fast Track Land Reform." In Land *and Agrarian Reform in Zimbabwe: Beyond White-Settler Capitalism*, edited by Sam Moyo and Walter Chambati, 1–28. Dakar: CODESRIA.

Moyo, Sam, Walter Chambati, Tendai Murisa, Dumisani Siziba, Charity Dangwa, and Ndabezinhle Nyoni. 2009. *Fast Track Land Reform Baseline Survey in Zimbabwe: Trends and Tendencies, 2005/06*. Harare: Africa Institute for Agrarian Studies.

Mudrack, Peter. 1989. "Defining Group Cohesiveness: A Legacy of Confusion?" *Small Group Behaviour* 20 (1): 37–49.

Murisa, Tendai. 2009. "An Analysis of Emerging Forms of Social Organisation and Agency in the Aftermath of 'Fast Track' Land Reform in Zimbabwe." PhD diss., Rhodes University.

Nabudere, Dani Wadada. 2011. *Archie Mafeje: Scholar, Activist and Thinker*. Pretoria: African Institute of South Africa.

Ndlovu-Gatsheni, Sabelo. 2007. "In Search of Common Ground: Oral History, Human Rights and the United Nations (UN) Council on Human Rights." Keynote presentation delivered at the International Conference on Human Rights and Social Justice: Setting the agenda for United Nations Human Rights Council, organized by the University of Winnipeg (Global College) as part of Human Action Week, 23–25 February.

Ndlovu-Gatsheni, Sabelo, and Everisto Benyera. 2015. "Towards a Framework for Resolving the Justice and Reconciliation Question in Zimbabwe." *African Journal on Conflict Resolution* 15 (2): 9–34.

Ngwenya, Dumisani, and Geoff Harris. 2015. "The Consequences of Not Healing: Evidence from the Gukurahundi Violence in Zimbabwe". *African Journal on Conflict Resolution* 15 (2): 35–56.

Pearce, Charles. 2012. *Kirsty: A Father's Fight for Justice*. Bloomington: iUniverse.

Sachikonye, L. M. 2005. "The Land is the Economy: Revisiting the Land Question". *African Security Review* 14 (3): 31–44.

Sadomba, Zvakanyorwa Wilbert. 2013. "A Decade of Zimbabwe's Land Revolution: The Politics of War Veteran Vanguard." In *Land and Agrarian Reform in Zimbabwe: Beyond White-Settler Capitalism*, edited by Sam Moyo and Walter Chambati, 79–122. Dakar: CODESRIA.

Scoones, Ian, Nelson Marongwe, Blasio Mavedzenge, Felix Murimbarimba, Jacob Mahenehene, and Chrispen Sukume. 2011. *Zimbabwe's Land Reform: A Summary of Findings*. Brighton: Institute of Development Studies.

Scoones, Ian, Nelson Marongwe, Blasio Mavedzenge, Felix Murimbarimba, Jacob Mahenehene, and Chrispen Sukume. 2012. "Livelihoods after the Land Reform in Zimbabwe: Understanding Processes of Rural Differentiation." *Journal of Agrarian Change* 12 (4): 503–27.

Stein, Arthur. 1976. *Conflict and Cohesion: A Review of the Literature*. New Haven: Yale University.

Tom, Tom. 2015. Social Services in the Aftermath of the Fast Track Land Reform Programme (FTLRP): The Case of Mupfurudzi Farm (Shamva District, Zimbabwe). *IOSR Journal Of Humanities And Social Science*, 20 (10): 62–66.

United Nations Security Council. 2004. *Report of the Secretary-General on the Rule of Law and Transitional Justice in Conflict and Post-conflict Societies (S/2004/616)*. Accessed March 20, 2018. http://daccessdds.un.org/doc/UNDOC/GEN/N04/395/29/PDF/N0439529.pdfOpenElemen.

Villa-Vicencio, Charles. 2004. "Restorative Justice." In *Pieces of the Puzzle: Keywords on Reconciliation and Transitional Justice*, edited by Charles Villa-Vicencio, and Erik, Doxtader, 33–38. Cape Town: Institute for Justice and Reconciliation.

Villa-Vicencio, Charles, Erik Doxtader, and Richard Goldstone. 2004. *Pieces of The Puzzle: Key Words on Reconciliation and Transitional Justice*. Cape Town: Institute of Justice and Reconciliation.

von Heinegg, Heintschel, and V. Epping. 2007. *International Humanitarian Law Facing New Challenges: Symposium in Honour of Knut Ipsen*. Frankfurt: Springer.

Wilmot, William, and Joyce Hocker. 2011. *Interpersonal Conflict*. New York: McGraw-Hill.

Chapter 9

Young Women in Peace-building and Development in Zimbabwe

The Case of Zimbabwe Young Women's Network for Peace-building in Mutoko

Patience Thauzeni and Torque Mude

INTRODUCTION

In this chapter we explore the role played by women in general and young women in specific in peace-building and development in Zimbabwe's rural areas. Since more women than men reside in rural areas in Zimbabwe, the premise of this chapter is to examine the contribution of young women to peace-building and development in Mutoko[1] with a view to illuminate the invisible role of young women in rural development. There are several other programs and interventions in rural areas including Mutoko that focus on men or women, while others may focus on youth or disabled people. This is an exploratory case study of Zimbabwe Young Women's Network for Peacebuilding which has peace-building and development projects operational in Mutoko district located in Zimbabwe's Mashonaland East Province. The central argument for this chapter is the depiction of young women not as passive citizenry, but as a section of the population which increasingly is using its agency to claim its humanity and to seek redress for past atrocities and subsequent development.

It suffices to indicate that this chapter is concerned with young women's peace-building and development initiatives in the aftermath of the politically motivated violence that occurred after the 2008 disputed elections. The chapter responds to the question: How are the young women in Mutoko seeking redress for past atrocities for sustainable peace and development and what mechanisms are they using to achieve this goal?

CONCEPTUALIZING PEACE-BUILDING AND DEVELOPMENT

Peace-building as a sui generis notion must have local perspectives, definitions, and conceptualizations which are based on local realities. The absence of a local definition of peace-building not only in Mutoko district but generally in Zimbabwe is partly because the notion of peace-building is an imported one, so is the nature and extent of violence which necessitates peace-building. Like peace-building, the term development lacks a local definition largely because the concept is broad, lacks a universally accepted definition and is of Western origins. If not qualified, the term development is implicitly intended to denote something positive and desirable (Bellu 2011). In this chapter and in the context of Mutoko, the concept is employed to imply positive change.

On the universal plane, peace-building is defined differently by different groups, organizations, and institutions. Barnett, Kim, O'Donell and Sitea (2007, 37) conceptualizes peace-building as external interventions intended to reduce the risk that a state will erupt or return to war in the aftermath of violent conflict. According to Schirch (2008, 7), "peace-building seeks to prevent, reduce, transform and help people recover from violence in all forms, even structural violence that has not yet led to massive civil unrest." Hence, peace-building requires the reconciliation of structural, relational, and socio-economic differences, truth-telling, apology, and forgiveness of past wrongs as well as establishment of a cooperative relationship between groups, replacing the adversarial or competitive relationship that used to exist.

Okot (2011) conceptualizes peace-building as a term used to describe peaceful interventions and initiatives designed to prevent the occurrence and recurrence of conflict by creating lasting peace with Burton (1996) adding that peace-building initiatives create constructive relationships between people and society they live in. It is therefore collective role of a series of different actors including individuals, religious organizations, civil society, traditional leaders, government, and other structures. From the above, it can be argued that peace-building takes place at different levels of society, community, government, villages and towns, and schools and business. Hence, Ghali (1992) states that peace-building involves multiple actors. ZYWNP fits within these actors and levels as it is part of community efforts to foster sustainable development through peace-building by young women.

Furthermore, peace-building should include all individuals regardless of age and gender and all institutions regardless of their social status or positions. Peace-building also includes full participation of young women, access to information and on-going processes and capacities which resolve conflict by peaceful means. These conditions create a sustainable environment for peace and development.

AN OVERVIEW OF PEACEBUILDING IN ZIMBABWE

Present-day Zimbabwe has experienced violent conflict since the wars conquest in the nineteenth century, war of liberation from 1964 to 1979 and the post-independence epoch that featured the occurrence of political violence. These violent conflicts which prevailed during these periods were characterized by different challenges which at different levels have emanated into violent conflict, fragmenting societies and infrastructure and hindering development in all aspects including economic, political, and human development among others. The government and the people of Zimbabwe, NGOs, and government institutions have throughout these phases worked together or separately to build peace. In addition to being a signatory to treaties, conventions, declarations, and protocols that seek to maintain regional and international peace, Zimbabwe has also made it a mandate to include as one of its national objectives in the (Zimbabwean Constitution 2013, 12) Chapter 2, under Article 10 on National unity, peace and stability: "the state and every person, including juristic persons, and every institution and agency of government at every level, must promote national unity, peace and stability." It is within the ambit of this provision that young women in Mutoko through ZYWNP have taken upon themselves to drive development through building peace in the community to prevent the recurrence and occurrence of violence.

At the national level, Zimbabwe has endeavored to include young women in government institutions through constitutional regulations such as the reversed seat quotas within parliament and other affirmative action requirements. Efforts to have young women participate in peacebuilding and development activities have been made throughout the world. However, these have not yielded the desired results, particularly in Zimbabwe and specifically in Mutoko and other rural areas.

The first peacebuilding efforts in Zimbabwe were seen at the Geneva conference of December 14, 1976, through diplomacy. The objectives of the conference were to put an end to the Rhodesian war between the Rhodesian government led by Ian Smith and guerrilla fighters led by Mugabe and Nkomo as well as create conditions for lasting peace and development in the country. It is important to note that there were no young women present—yet they were also fighting in the Rhodesian bush war. This conference inaugurated diplomatic negotiations which were held at the Lancaster House Agreement of December 21, 1979, which was the final step to political independence for Rhodesia following the Unilateral Declaration of Independence. The purpose was to find common ground whereby the Rhodesian government and all parties represented could declare a ceasefire and reach an agreement pertaining issues of a new constitution and land reform (Gann 1981).

Just like at the Geneva conference, not a single young woman was present at the Lancaster House Conference. These were all formal peacebuilding processes aimed at creating a peaceful coexistence between the Rhodesian government and citizens. From the definitions stated above peacebuilding should avert the resumption of violent conflict and should include everyone. However, this is not true for Zimbabwe since violence has continued to occur over time and peacebuilding has mostly involved women and men in positions of power to the detriment of young women.

Immediately after independence, Zimbabwe was plunged into another phase of violent conflict during Gukurahundi. Gukurahundi saw the death of many people in Matabeleland and the Midlands. In an effort to get past this devastating event and build peace ZAPU, represented by Joshua Nkomo and ZANU represented by Robert Mugabe, respectively, signed the Unity Accord on December 22, 1987 (Zimbabwe Mirror 2012). The Unity Accord set the stage for unifying the two parties represented into one: ZANU PF, as a way of bringing the Shona and Ndebele together as Zimbabweans. The Unity Accord was another formal peace process in Zimbabwe which seems to have not yielded much as there still seems to be the latent conflict with the Ndebele people group feeling inferior vis-a-vis the majority Shona people. In order for peacebuilding to strive in Zimbabwe, such issues should be addressed, or the country will risk another wave of violent conflict. According to Dube and Makwere (2012), the Unity Accord was considered as a missed opportunity that was supposed to reconcile Shona-Ndebele relations.

In continuation from the above, Zimbabwe has been mostly engaged in formal peacebuilding processes that encompass the conclusion of peace agreements between the government and other governments and between the political parties in the country. One such formal peacebuilding process was the Global Political Agreement that was signed between the two MDC formations and ZANU PF following the 2008 harmonized elections which were marked by a wave of political violence and human rights violations. According to Mutisi (2011), the Global Political Agreement made it possible for the political parties in Zimbabwe to resolve to work together in consolidated efforts to achieve peace and development in the country.

The Global Political Agreement culminated in the formation of the Government of National Unity (GNU) to implement notable reforms to foster economic development, peace, and good governance. It united hostile political parties and temporarily ended political violence in the country. To address the issue of governance, commissions were established, such as the Zimbabwe Human Rights Commission (ZHRC), Zimbabwe Electoral Commission (ZEC) and Zimbabwe Media Commission (ZMC). However, according to Dube and Makwere (2012), peacebuilding in Zimbabwe tends to be politicized and as such loses significance and does not yield positive results in society due to its state-centric foundations.

To further consolidate peacebuilding efforts, Zimbabwean government established the Organ of National Healing, Reconciliation and Integration (ONHRI) in 2009. Its mandate was to facilitate national healing and reconciliation against the background of violence, torture, murder and many other human rights violations during the 2008 in the country. According to Chemhuru (2014), ONHRI's attempts at national healing and reconciliation were futile with many challenges. Indeed, ONHRI was not visible enough to facilitate healing because it was largely politicized. Dube and Makwere (2012) argue that the organ has remained purely political in approach and design.

Apart from being political, the other problem with the formal peacebuilding processes in Zimbabwe is that none of them include young women. This gap has led to young women's organizations such as the Zimbabwe Young Women's Network for Peacebuilding and other women organizations to come together and demand through different initiatives to be included in peacebuilding processes which drive development. Although Zimbabwe is one African country whose government and government institutions have taken steps to include women in positions of leadership, such as the swearing-in of Joyce Mujuru as the first women vice president of Zimbabwe on December 6, 2004, women both young and old are still more marginalized in nation building processes.

Yet peacebuilding and development initiatives require the ability to create constructive relationships and opportunities for all peoples. Hence, the greatest concern with peacebuilding in Zimbabwe has been the desire to increase the number of young women involved in the peacebuilding process of the country. As argued by the liberal pluralist theory, women have a right to equal representation; any peacebuilding and postconflict reconstruction processes that do not include them are therefore regarded as unsustainable. More so, since young men contribute to development the same way or even more than young men in rural settings, their participations should accelerated.

Nevertheless, young women remain alienated from the peacebuilding processes, both formally and informally. According to the Women's Coalition of Zimbabwe (2013), the political atmosphere in Zimbabwe has limited the ability of young women to participate for fear of being intimidated, sexually abused, and being forced out of their homes. There is a considerable need to include young women in the peacebuilding processes in Zimbabwe. Young women's role in peacebuilding in Zimbabwe has been limited to the community level and when they do engage in formal peace processes, their efforts are disregarded or have largely been swept under the carpet. Dube and Makwere (2012, 303) state the need for Zimbabwe to take a multistage process to peacebuilding where issues are addressed at different levels of society and every voice is heard. Zimbabwe needs to move from a country of violence to one characterized by positive peace.

The situation in Zimbabwe as mentioned in the article by the International Coalition for the Responsibility to Protect attracted both international and regional attention and concern. This led to the signing of the Global Political Agreement in September 2008 and the formation of the government of national unity. Young women and young women's organizations were engaged in community dialogues and were advocating for a peaceful Zimbabwe. Campaigns and workshops were held across the country until the drafting of the new constitution. The constitution-making process saw many young women also actively involved in the consultative meetings and outreach programs. Young women also sought accreditation from COPAC, the Constitution Select Committee to participate during the constitutional awareness campaign before the referendum. They were also at the forefront of mobilizing and encouraging other young women to go out and vote in peace for the new constitution.

Young women constitute the majority of the Zimbabwean youth population and have a significant role to play in peacebuilding. According to Gondo (2012), the youth constitute 67 percent of the total population in Zimbabwe and their role is to define the pace of the nation and to build Zimbabwe. Empowering the youth is not only a priority but also a panacea of peace in Zimbabwe. Young women should be empowered to make decisions on matters that affect them by empowering them with free space, free participation, and freedom of choice. According to Piazza (2011), the youth present the biggest threat to peace consolidation. However, they also offer a major opportunity with their energy, innovative mind-set, and natural optimism. There is no doubt that peace begins with the respect of every man and woman, developed through their rights and the fulfillment of their aspirations. Peace also signals a dedication to a better future based on shared values, through dialogue, tolerance, respect, and understanding.

The underlying assumption in view of Okot (2011) is that if young women are included and recognized in peacebuilding processes they will help in designing a sustainable peace that is advantageous to the empowerment, inclusion, and protection of women. As such, young women should be included in all areas of peacebuilding. They should not only rely on gender-based roles to participate in the peace process but should be empowered to hold more public and official positions at the center of mainstream decision-making.

Ernest (2010) argues that despite various drawbacks women face in peacebuilding activities, community peacebuilding initiatives led by women have created an aiding environment for peacebuilding and nonviolent conflict management. Young women, especially those in Zimbabwe's less privileged and most rural communities like Mutoko, have been the link to their community's development through their memberships in varying non-governmental organizations, either focusing on human rights, peacebuilding or entrepreneurship. This has helped strengthen family and society structures through the implementation of community development projects and access to information; hence creating peaceful coexistence among societies once fragmented by conflict and violence.

In Zimbabwe's rural areas young women have faced criticism against any newfound freedoms and they have always been forced back into the kitchen and fields. Yet they have an important role to play during and after conflict and subsequent postconflict development processes which follow. Young women have persistently called for recognition as active agents in the reconstruction of social structures, prevention of war, and rehabilitation of victims. Zimbabwe has endeavored to include young women in government institutions through constitutional regulations such as the reserved seat quotas within parliament and other affirmative action requirements.

Isike and Okeke (2012, 33) have maintained that women have been at the epicenter of peace processes across different precolonial African societies. However, young women in neo-colonial African states appear to have lost this status that once surrounded their social existence in precolonial Africa. This is mainly because apart from being social, economically and politically marginalized, young women have become victims of male violence. Be that as it may, this does take away the contribution of young women to not only peacebuilding, but development that comes after reconstruction. This is the case in Mutoko with the facilitation of ZYWNP.

YOUNG WOMEN AS A DEVELOPMENT MILESTONE IN MUTOKO

Against the background that young women in Zimbabwe have a limited understanding of peacebuilding and development, ZYWNP has taken it upon itself to link the Mutoko community with government institutions such as Mutoko Rural District Council (RDC) in implementing livelihood projects that unite families, create employment, and minimize economic hardships. The organization is committed to ensuring that young women, especially those at the grassroots level, understand and are actively involved in peacebuilding and development. ZYWNP also desires to see as many young women as possible occupy positions of decision making and governance.

In Mutoko, platforms for facilitating engagement processes between policy makers, public service providers, young women and the community at large were established through ZYWNP. This has been done to through community dialogue, access to information campaigns, young women cafe, storytelling, and other activities. Through these platforms, young women have been able to contribute to decision making concerning the development of their communities. For instance, in Ward 9 in Chimoyo C Block, young women came together to mold bricks for the construction of an early childhood development block after the Mutoko RDC and Ministry of Education has failed to do so. This illustrates the effort and ability of young women to decide and organize themselves to drive community development.

YOUNG WOMEN AND CONFLICT RESOLUTION IN MUREWA

Young women have also played critical roles in conflict resolution in Mutoko. As argued by Mapuranga (2013), the participation of young women in Zimbabwean politics has been criticized amid concerns that very few young women are participating in peacebuilding processes and are taking up positions of power, yet they account for the bulk of the population. However, young women in Mutoko faced a difficult time during the political violence that followed the 2008 harmonized elections. Some of them participated and were involved in the conflict as instigators of violence; however, the majority of these young women experienced abductions, torture and gang rape.

The severity of these women rights abuses made it difficult for the community to accept them as real. Yet, the government did not give young women the opportunity to be involved and participate in conditions that could promote sustainable peace. According to Ernest (2010), despite various shortcomings young women face in peacebuilding activities, young women's informal conflict resolution initiatives have employed methods that have created an aiding atmosphere for peacebuilding and nonviolent conflict management at all levels.

Ernest's (2010) argument holds water even though at national level young women's role is invisible and compromised in conflict times with much of their role in peacebuilding is largely ignored and played down by a traditionally male-dominated society (Bangalie 2011, 46). Nonetheless, through ZYWNP, young women in Mutoko have been crucial educating and sensitizing the community on issues of governance, peace, and conflict resolution. According to the Zimbabwe Young Women's Network for Peace Building Report (2012), young women in Musanhi village in Mutoko engaged in community dialogue sessions and formed peace circles in order to deal with the effects of political violence following the 2008 harmonized elections. This was after the village was left in a quagmire with property destroyed, families dispersed, communities divided, and brother turning against brother. In such a tense environment, there was an immediate need for peacebuilding and conflict resolution. It was the young women working together with ZYWNP who took the first steps towards conflict resolution and peacebuilding in this community through peace and healing campaigns and meetings.

Young women's quest for peace through equal representation to partake healing processes in Mutoko reached its peak during the formulation of the new constitution in the country in 2013. Young women participated in community outreach and consultative meetings; they also made sure that others in the community were aware of the draft provisions of the draft constitution through pamphlets compiled by the Women's Coalition of Zimbabwe (WCOZ). During the period, they aired their views on the need to have the government augment their healing and unity campaigns in Mutoko. Even though the government did little to listen to the voices of the young women in Mutoko, the latter continued with peacebuilding efforts.

Young women from Mutoko have not confined themselves to peacebuilding activities in their community only but have also been actively engaged and participated in peacebuilding activities held on a national level. The Zimbabwe Young Women's Network for Peacebuilding Report (2012) highlight that following a series of police brutality instigated on civilians, especial women, through unlawful arrests and rape, young women felt the need to air their concerns against such harsh treatment by the law enforcement agents. It was then that a peaceful march was held in December of 2012 under Katswe Sistahood at the African Unity Square in Harare, bringing together young and elderly women from different parts of Zimbabwe. The peace march attracted a lot of publicity, though most of it negative, with some journalist referring to it as an attempt by loose, immoral feminists to get society to accept and conform to their distractive and immoral behaviors. In reality, the peace march was aimed at bringing Zimbabweans together and advocating for law enforcement to treat the citizens with respect and to protect and not harm and constrain their freedoms. Despite the bad publicity, the objectives of the campaign were fulfilled.

Young women from Musanhi village were also represented at the Great Zimbabwe Scenarios project which was held in Bulawayo in 2013. It comprised a dialogue session between young people from the community, young people organizations, Crisis Coalition in Zimbabwe, the Ministry of Youth, political parties, and church leaders. The dialogue session allowed for an assessment of where Zimbabwe is and where it should be in terms of peacebuilding and development. Zimbabwe has been lagging behind in terms of peacebuilding and development because of an inability to engage all parties and institutions at all levels of society in peacebuilding and development processes. The Great Zimbabwe Scenarios project was implemented in 2012 in the absence of young women and has not generated the desired outcome. However, with the inclusion of youths including young women, some of the project's goals where achieved. Therefore, peacebuilding can be achieved if and only when all levels of society including young women are involved.

On another occasion, young women from Mutoko, Musanhi village were engaged in an interface with Senator Rorata and Senator Femayi at the Crisis Coalition in Zimbabwe boardroom (ZYWNP Report 2012). The purpose of the interface was to encourage leaders to ensure that young women can participate in the presidential elections without fear of harassment or intimidation. Young women aired their voices but much of what was discussed and the results of that formal peace process remained behind closed doors, with the only recognition of the noble act remaining in the reports compiled by the Zimbabwe Young Women's Network for Peacebuilding (ZYWNP Report 2012).

Young women from Musanhi organized themselves and implemented community peacebuilding projects such as Mukando, an idea which soon spread from the rural areas to urban cities like Harare. They also started community gardens where they cultivated vegetables for consumption and for selling. The profits were used to reconstruct houses and buy livestock, mostly goats. Musanhi area is still far from being developed but it has certainly risen from where it was in the aftermath of the political violence that took Zimbabwe by storm in 2008.

According to the MA Youth Newsletter (2012, 12), young people are not only a resource for development but key agents for change. The irony, however, is that the presence of youths, in particular, young women, in key strategic fora and platforms is still largely ceremonial and often an afterthought. It cannot be doubted that young women have played an important role in moving the country to its first democratic constitution, which made it possible to hold peaceful elections in fulfillment of the Global Political Agreement. All these efforts by young women presented opportunities for peace and confirmed the success of young women in peacebuilding processes.

Young women from Mutoko also contributed toward the maintenance of the law and order through community monitoring by engaging with community policy and traditional leaders and NGOs focusing on the law, such as Zimbabwe Lawyers for Human Rights (ZLHR). This created awareness and allowed the community to be educated on their human, constitutional, and legal rights to make them aware of their rights and those of others and how to defend them. Young women from Musanhi also provided care for the underprivileged in the community. Young women worked and continue to work with the necessary authorities to ensure peace at all levels of society

Apart from national and community levels, young women in Mutoko have also participated in peacebuilding and development processes at the family level. "Peace begins at home" is a common phrase that has reinforced the role of young women in peacebuilding in their homes. According to Messina-Dysert (2013), women are the fabric of our society, holding families and communities together. Young women in Mutoko, Musanhi village served as feminists peace educators not only in their community but in the home and at family level as they shape the moral and values of children and instill a sense of responsibility by creating positive human relationships in both family and community. Young women also provide for their families' basic needs through income generated from community projects, thus ensuring happy and peaceful homes. Peacebuilding also entails exhibiting an urge to meet the needs of the population. Young women in Mutoko, Musanhi village began a path of peace and development by exhibiting behavior intended for the innovatively challenging social injustice that they face on a daily basis at home, community and as a nation.

CONCLUSION

The chapter illuminates on the role of young women in peacebuilding and development in Zimbabwe. The chapter sought to identify the role of young women in peacebuilding and development, to identify how best young women can be supported in their participation in peace and development processes.

Young women's role in peacebuilding and development became more noticeable with their participation in national processes such as the constitution-making process, referendum and elections. Although facing many challenges, young women ceased to remain mere victims of violence and conflict and became agents of peacebuilding. Young women ensured their survival and maintained their freedoms; this was made possible with interventions by prominent young women's organizations and women's movements within Zimbabwe.

The chapter pointed to the role of young women in peacebuilding and Mutoko Zimbabwe Young Women's Network for Peace Building peacebuilding and development projects. The research, however, also highlighted the weakness of the government to offer more assistance and support and provide a platform to include young women in formal peacebuilding processes. Young women still face challenges in their endeavor to increase their involvement in both formal and informal peacebuilding and development processes, yet despite all obstacles and opposition young women continue with their quest for peacebuilding and development.

NOTE

1. Mutoko is a 4,740 km² granite rock district located north of Harare in Mashonaland East Province. It is one of the ruling party, Zimbabwe African National

Union-Patriotic Front (ZANU PF), strongholds. With a growing young population the main opposition, the Movement for Democratic Change, has made steady inroads into the district, eroding ZANU PF's hegemony. This set the district on a violent warpath mainly pitting young loyalists against each other.

BIBLIOGRAPHY

Bangalie, Folerence, N. 2011. *An Examination of the Role of Women in Conflict Management: Sierra Leone A Case Study.* London: Oxford University Press.

Barnett, M., H. Kim, M. O'Donell, and L. Sitea. 2007. "Peacebuilding: What Is In a Name?" *Global Governance* 12 (2): 156–81.

Bellu, Lorenzo Giovanni. 2011. *Development and Development Paradigm: A Review of Prevailing Vision.* Rome: FAO.

Burton, John. W. 1996. *Conflict Resolution: Its Language and Process.* Lanham: Scarecrow.

Chemhuru, Noleen. 2014. *Reconciliation, Integration and National Healing: Possibility and Challenges in Zimbabwe.* "Crisis Group Africa Report" No 173, 2014. Available at: www.ejournals.library.ualberta.ca/../15158. Accessed 5 March 2014.

Dube, Donwell, and David Makwere. 2012. "Zimbabwe towards a Comprehensive Peace Infrastructure." *International Journal of Humanities and Social Science* 2 (2),: 1–23.

Ernest, John. 2010. *Best Practice in Peacebuilding and Non-Violent Conflict Resolution.* Zurich: ATAR Roto Press.

Gann, Lewis. H. 1981. *The Struggle for Zimbabwe.* New York: Praeger Publishers.

Ghali, Boutros. B. 1992. *An Agenda for Peace.* New York: United Nations Department Public Information.

Gondo, Misheck. 2012. *Push Forward: Women and Youth in Peacebuilding.* "Youth Official Ilizwi Association of Youth Organizations Newsletter", Zimbabwe. Harare: NAYO Publication.

Isike, Christopher, and Ufo Uzodike Okeke. 2010. *Moral Imagination, Ubuntu and African Women: Towards Feminizing Politics and Peacebuilding in KwaZulu Natal.* South Africa: Gandhi Marg.

"MA Youth Newsletter". 2012. *Discussing the SADC Gender Protocol Barometer on Zimbabwe.* Available at: www.mayouthnewsletter/news/africa. Accessed 23 May 2014.

Mapuranga, Donald. 2013. *Soccer Helps Bury Political Hatchet.* "The Zimbabwean", 9 April 2013.

Messina-Dysert, Gina. 2013. *Mothers for Peacebuilding* [Online]. Available at: http://ginamessinadysert.com/mothersandpeacebuilding. Accessed 1 April 2014.

Mutisi, Martha. 2011. *Beyond the Signature*: "Appraisal of the Zimbabwe Global Political Agreement (GPA) and implications for interventions. Policy and Practice Brief, Knowledge for Durable Peace". The African Centre for the Constructive Resolution of Disputes Policy & Practice Brief: Knowledge for Durable Peace, No. 4 March. Durban: The African Centre for the Constructive Resolution of Disputes.

Okot, Maureen. 2011. *Women and Peace in Africa*. New York: McGraw Hill.

Piazza, Gregory. 2011. *Contemporary Sociological Theory and Its Classical Roots*. New York: McGraw-Hill.

Schirch, Lisa. 2008. "Strategic Peacebuilding: State of the Field." *Southern Asian Journal of Peacebuilding* 1 (1): 109–23.

Women's Coalition of Zimbabwe. 2013. *Increasing Women's Participation in the Zimbabwe Peacebuilding Process* [Online]. Available at: www.womankind.org.uk/where-we-work/zimbabwe/womankind-projects/wcoz-project/. Accessed 6 March 2014.

Zimbabwe Young Women's Network for Peace. 2012. *Zimbabwe Young Women's Network for Peace Report*. Retrieved from: https://www.peaceinsight.org/conflicts/zimbabwe/ (Assessed on 2 June 2018).

Chapter 10

Stains on the Wall

Struggle to Survive Post-Genocide Violence by Nama-Herero Communities in Namibia

Tafirenyika Madziyauswa

INTRODUCTION

"Nothing can be about us, yet without us; anything about us, but without us is necessarily against us!"

(Ovaherero-Nama Declaratory statement)

It is against the foregoing statement, that the first part of this chapter gives a brief outline of the 1904–1908 German-Herero-Nama War which, not without contestation, has come to constitute an act of genocide perpetrated by the Germans on the Namas and Hereros of the German South West Africa (henceforth GSWA), now Namibia. The consequences of this war are now regarded by the United Nations as acts that constitute crimes against humanity that include, genocide, war crimes, crimes against humanity, and the crime of aggression. This chapter discusses the efforts of the three organizations that were tasked with dealing with the aftermath of the over a century-old war. The discussion centres on the role they played to find social justice for the victims. The three organizations whose efforts are the central subject of this chapter are: Genocide Reparations Technical Committee, The Nama Genocide Technical Committee, and lastly Ovaherero/Ovambanderu Genocide Technical Committee. Focus will be placed on the strategies that were used by the descendants of the victims of the genocide to survive and cope with the mass violence perpetrated upon their ancestors by the Germans. In conclusion, this chapter explores some important pointers to theoretical contributions than can be drawn from this case study.

GENOCIDE OR ATROCITIES? THE 1904–1908 WAR

The Imperial German war on the Nama and Herero took place between 1904 and 1907. Gewald (2003, 279) stated the war which broke out in Okahandja on January 11, 1904, when the Ovaherero rebelled against colonial rule by the Germans. The Ovaherero were later joined by the Namas in late 1904. The main grievance involved land which the Germans expropriated from the Ovaherero and Namas as well as the livestock that were confiscated by the Germans. When the war ended an estimated 60,000 to 80,000 Ovaherero perished at the hands of the colonial troops of Germany (*Schutztruppe*) (Drechsler 1980, 214). In fact, at the end of the war "no fewer than 80% of the Herero and at least 50% of the Nama had lost their lives." This implies that the Germans killed more than 80 percent of the Herero and 50 percent of the Nama.

Most of the Herero who remained, primarily women and children, survived in concentration camps as forced labourers employed on state, military, and civilian (Gewald 2003). The intent to exterminate Ovaherero was even crueller: they were either killed in direct confrontation with German troops or died due to starvation and dehydration after fleeing into the Omaheke (Kalahari) Desert to evade the German troops. In addition, those that survived the battle and the harsh desert conditions died due to the brutality and the inhumane conditions they were subjected to in German concentration camps known in German as *Konzentrationslagern* (Drechsler 1980).

According to Gewald "[i]n keeping with Von Moltke's principles of separate deployment and encirclement, Von Trotha sent out his armies to annihilate the Herero at the Waterberg" (Gewald 2003, 282–283). Lieutenant-General Lothar von Trotha, the German Imperial Army commander in the then German South West Africa, was intent on decisively crushing and exterminating the Hereros since even those that managed to escape were pursued and killed even if they were not armed. Since the war turned into an act of extermination, the Germans wanted ownership of the land and livestock as the spoils of war especially if all the owners were to perish in the war. All the escape routes from the lands formerly occupied by the Hereros were sealed off by von Trotha's troops thereby leaving only the Kalahari Desert (known as the *Omaheke* to Ovaherero) as the only option for the Ovaherero to escape to with a relative safer then British Bechuanaland, now Botswana laying across the desert. The German troops acting under the Extermination Order employed the scorched earth policy where they poisoned water and water points in their pursuit of the Herero groups culminating many of the Hereros dying of dehydration or from drinking poisoned water (Gewald 2003, 283). Drechsler posits that many of those who were not killed or captured by troops died of dehydration and exhaustion and with only 1,000 managing to get as far as Bechuanaland (Drechsler 1980, 166).

On October 1, 1904, General Lothar von Trotha, who was actively taking part in the pursuit, and his retinue reached the Osombo-Windimbe waterhole (Gewald 2003). The following day, General Lothar von Trotha read out what was an Extermination Order Proclamation (*Vernichtungsbefehl*) issued by the German Kaiser Wilhelm 11 in Otjiherero at Waterberg, stating that

> the Herero people must . . . leave the land. If the populace does not do this, I will force them with the *Groot Rohr* [Cannon]. Within the German borders every Herero, with or without a gun, with or without cattle, will be shot. I will no longer accept women and children, I will drive them back to their people or I will let them be shot at. These are my words to the Herero people. The great General of the mighty German Kaiser. (Gewald 2003, 281)

By the end of 1904, social and political pressure in Germany coerced Kaiser to accept the surrender of the Ovaherero (Gewald 2003). However, Kaiser ordered those who surrendered to be incarcerated in five concentration camps that were constructed for that purpose (Gewald 2003). These people were to act as a source of forced labour to meet military and settler demands in the colony. Not only were the conditions in the concentration camps appalling with mortality rate high, medical experiments were also conducted on those perished in these camps (Gewald 2003). Added to that, the Germans shipped a number of Herero skulls and preserved bodies to Germany in order to conduct research on the racial inferiority of the African (Gewald 2003, 189). It was only in 1908 that these camps finally shut down name the camps or use their location. The 1904–1908 events drastically transformed the precolonial Ovaherero society as they lost tracts of land and almost all of their livestock especially cattle. Gewald argues that "the war and its aftermath were characterized by acts of excessive violence and cruelty on the part of German soldiers and settlers" (Gewald 2003, 282). The next section discusses the work of the three organizations involved in non-state transitional justice in Namibia starting with the Genocide Reparation Technical Committee.

GENOCIDE REPARATION TECHNICAL COMMITTEE (GRTC)

Despite the lingering historical injustices that were committed by the Germany troops and the overt intentions to exterminate the Hereros and later the Namas as language groupings, at independence the Namibian government did nothing to address this traumatic historical memory of some of its citizenry. Instead, the government seemed concerned with its bilateral trade agreements with its erstwhile colonial power. The benefits of cordial relationship with

Germany translated in billions of financial aid pouring into Namibia, hence it was insensible to rock the boat by bringing up historical injustices. This resonates with the notion of coloniality of power wherein the former colonial masters continue to have influence over former colonies. Initially, the Namibian government was reluctant to engage the Germany government on the subject of genocide. This position was manifest in the actions of the Namibian ambassador to Germany, Andreas Guibeb who chastised German parties in the Bundestag to either withdraw or reject any motion calling Germany to apologize and pay reparations for the genocide committed in Namibia. He took this decision in order to lend weight to the government discussions on bilateral relations between Germany and Namibia. Both governments were content with leaving the historical memory of genocide in the past and purportedly co-operate on developmental issues. Significantly, both governments had a change of heart on issue as they agreed to appoint envoys to deal with the issue at governmental level. In articulating this new position, Krug asserts that the German Special Envoy for Namibian German Relations stated that

> In cooperation with the Namibian side we would like to find a common language for dealing with a very dark chapter of the German colonial period . . . . We would like to find a formula that expresses the regret of the German side. Ultimately, it is also important to us that Namibia is able to accept an apology from the German side. Then, on that basis, we would like to develop and maintain a common culture of remembrance. (Krug 2016, 1)

For its part, the Namibian government announced that it had decided to work with those calling for reparations to be paid by the German government "by driving a N$400 billion lawsuit against the German government" (Immanuel and Kahiurika 2017, 1). The Namibian government had always steered clear of demanding reparations from the German government. However, the court case was abandoned in favour of negotiations between the two governments which manifested in the appointment of special envoys by both countries to spearhead the discussions on their shared past. As such the Genocide Reparations Technical Committee (GRTC) was convened to help the Namibian special envoy in negotiating a settlement with the German government on behalf of the Namibian government. According to the special envoy, Dr. Zed Ngavirue GRTC's strategy of negotiation was based on three principles, namely, German government must take responsibility for the genocide, unconditionally apologize, and pay reparations. In terms of all three principles of negotiation, Germany has flatly repudiated the discourse that is being used to define the colonial war against the then German South West Africa. As will be discussed in subsequent sections, the German government objects to the use of the words "reparations" and "genocide" as much as they are not prepared to publicly apologize for historical injustices perpetrated against the Hereros and the Namas. It is to this end, that the obstacles that are being encountered by the GRTC demonstrate the failure of the statist transitional justice to resolve historical injustices in Namibia which will bring closure to the descendants of the victims of genocide. It is due to the failure of statist transitional justice in Namibia that paves the way for an alternative form of justice which seeks to bring not only justice, but reconciliation, forgiveness, and closure between the perpetrators and the victims. It is through the use of the Indigenous. Traditional and non-state justice mechanisms in Namibia that the painful historical chapter might finally be closed.

Indigenous, traditional, and non-state mechanisms create a bottom-up inclusive judicial system where the state cannot or does not want to provide justice. As with the Herero-Nama case, neither the Namibian nor the German government had the legal instruments which they could use to resolve a case of the magnitude of a genocide crime especially since this crime against the humanity of the Ovaherero and Namas was committed over a century ago. The case is further complicated by the absence of direct perpetrators or direct victims. In the absence of statist legal framework or due to the inadequacies of such systems in dealing with over century-old social injustices, indigenous, traditional and non-state transitional justice mechanisms prove not only to be viable but also that these mechanisms are not a substitute or compliment to their statist counterparts but the only available mechanisms. In the case of the Herero-Nama Genocide these mechanisms are indeed the main source of transitional justice. Of importance is that the Namibian and German governments have agreed to find ways to resolve a historical injustice outside the framework provided by state-centric legal systems which leaves indigenous justice mechanisms as the preferred form of social justice. It is in this context that the activities and initiatives of the GRTC must be framed and comprehended. There is need at this point to critically interrogate the three principles that Ngavirue alluded earlier on, in the context of indigenous, traditional and non-statist justice mechanisms.

First and foremost is the principle of the German government taking full responsibility for the mass violence by the German colonial troops which now constitutes acts of genocide. The troops were acting under orders of an Army General who represented the German government which makes the entire situation a collective German colonial expedition. Unlike South Africa, there was no truth commission in Namibia to deal with this issue. The Truth and Reconciliation Commission (TRC) of post-apartheid South Africa borrowed heavily from the indigenous institution of *ubuntu* to allow the perpetrators time and space to publicly take responsibility for the crimes they committed by sharing their truths with their and victims and admit the full extent of their wrongdoings (Malan 2008, 136–9). Similarly, the Germans should assume responsibility for the genocide by admitting to the affected communities the magnitude of the crimes that grossly and crudely impacted the humanity of the Hereros and Namas. This will ease the burden of the intragenerational trauma of the historical memory of mass killings, rapes, forced labour, loss of cattle, and land to the German colonizers suffered by the descendants. Murithi (2008) argues that in complex conflicts, community organs, and elders also take a mediating role. In this case the Namibian special envoy plays the role of chief negotiator due to the complexity of the conflict and the stakeholders involved thereof. Though initially refusing to assume full responsibility of the actions of the German Imperial troops, the Germany government now admits that the actions of the troops were extremely brutal without admitting that such actions constitute an act of genocide. The German government now acknowledges the massacres of the Hereros and the Namas did take place but falls short of defining such acts as the "first genocide" or a "genocide" at all. It is in this light that the issue of the court cases that are being filled against Germany have resulted in increased caution on the German side not to give any apology or mention the genocide, since that could be seen as a basis for accepting their responsibility to give reparations (Hinz 2010, 397).

Secondly, Ngavirue states that the German government must unconditionally apologize for the heinous crime of genocide infiltrated on the ancestors of the present-day Hereros and Namas. The emphasis of many traditional methods is on forgiveness, healing, reconciliation, and restorative justice on rebuilding social trust (Murithi 2008, 16–17). In this case there is need to restore the affected communities to their dignity by making Germany admit to the crime of genocide. To this end the transformative justice mechanisms tends to offer social justice to the affected groups who are in transition from conflict to peace. The German government is not agreeable to the use of the term "genocide" to describe the actions of the German Imperial force between 1904 and 1907. The preferred term within the German government is the word "atrocities" which resonates with the brutalities of the soldiers in a war situation. To admit that the war of 1904 and 1907 constitutes an act of genocide would set a precedent that is likely to haunt the German colonial policy (and of other colonial powers like Britain, France, Belgium, and Portugal) creating a ripple effect in the process. Thus, Germany government is reluctant to admit to the crime of genocide. The use of the term "genocide" is argued to be anachronistically applying a term to describe an act which was not known as such in the period it occurred.

Lastly, according to Ngavirue, the German government must pay reparations to atone for the crimes against humanity committed between 1904 and 1908 which constitutes retributive justice. This resonates with the Rwandan traditional Gacaca courts adopted to deal with the post-genocide of 1994. An ideal *Gacaca* court hearing would be where defendants confess their crimes, express remorse, ask for forgiveness, provide restitution, and then offer food and drink to all parties as a symbol of reconciliation (Vandeginste 1999). Such a non-statist and indigenous conflict resolution mechanism as contested by Drumbl (2002) bears a close correspondence to the principles of restorative justice. The paying reparations which is a form of restitution is aimed at reconciling the defendant (Germans) with the victims (Namas and Hereros). Like with the issue of the use of the term "genocide," the Germans object to the use of the term "reparations." The German government prefers the use of the politically correct term "developmental aid" to describe the financial aid that is being given to the Namibian government. The payment of reparations to the affected communities is regarded as being "out of the question."

Without overtly expressing their reasons for their preference to adopt non-statist judicial forms, the Namibian government convened the GRTC to act on their behalf and that of the affected communities. According to an interview with *The New Era*, the Namibian special envoy alluded to the fact that

> one of the committees is already part of our committee. They have representatives on the technical committee; they have representatives on the negotiation team, and whether we meet here or in Germany they are part of the team. But you know that there are those that stayed out and they have been unwilling to cooperate because they feel the whole thing has to be changed. (Tjitemisa 2017, 3)

The GRTC is made up of representatives from the technical committees of the affected groups as well as representatives of the chief associations; however, this position has been challenged by the groups representing the affected communities. These "[r]epresentatives of the respective committees on genocide and reparations were invited to participate in the structures set up for the negotiations" (Tjitemisa 2017, 3). It is in this light that the principles that form part of the strategy adopted by GRTC to deal with the German government constitute the hallmarks of the indigenous, traditional and non-state justice systems or mechanisms. As such Namibia's special envoy was negotiating with the German special envoy in order to reach a favourable settlement for the affected groups.

THE NAMA TRADITIONAL LEADERS ASSOCIATION

Desmond Tutu, the Chairperson of the TRC contends that:

> The past, far from disappearing or lying down and being quiet, has an embarrassing and persistent way of returning and haunting us unless it has in face been dealt with adequately. Unless we look the beast in the eye we find it has an uncanny habit of returning to hold us hostage. (Tutu 1999, 28)

It is important to begin the discussion in this section by citing Tutu who made interesting observations about the links between the past and the present (and possibly, the future). Social injustices from the past have a tendency to haunt the present and the future if not addressed in a way that engenders full closure. This closure is only attainable if "we look the beast in the eye [because it has] a habit of returning to hold us hostage" (Tutu 1999, 28). It is in this context that a discussion of the activities and the initiatives that are currently being pursued and engaged by the Nama Traditional Leaders Association through their committee, Nama Genocide Technical Committee, needs to be comprehended. In a number of ways, the activities and initiatives that this group employs to survive and cope with a past of mass violence share similarities with those of the Ovaherero and Ovambanderu affected communities as will be discussed later. It should be underscored that the affected communities find themselves in a situation where it is difficult to match specific forms of punishment to the severity of the historical crime against humanity visited upon their ancestors by German colonial troops in GSWA. We argue that such a situation is best suited to an approach that combines restorative and retributive forms of justice, but always allowing predominance of the former on the latter. As Malan contends, the main focus of indigenous forms of justice still remains on a transition from past wrongs to a shared future (Malan 2008).

It is in this context that indigenous, traditional, and non-state transitional justice mechanisms have proved not only to be viable but also that these mechanisms are not a substitute or compliment to the state-centric forms of justice. As this case study seeks to demonstrate, indigenous, traditional, and non-state transitional justice mechanisms are indeed the main source of transitional justice for the Herero and Nama in Namibia. Thus, the Namibian genocide is to be framed within the indigenous, traditional, and non-state transitional justice mechanisms which are not just complimentary to statist and other formal transitional justice but that they are in most cases the main and only mechanisms available (Wielenga 2012).

NAMA COPING MECHANISMS ACROSS GENERATIONS

The activities and initiatives used by the Namas to survive the intragenerational trauma of genocide show evidence that are both restorative and retributive in nature, that is, they seek reparations, admittance to the crime committed by the German troops, a public apology and reconciliation. Whilst reparations are mainly retributive, reparators take responsibility for the crime, offer an apology, and often lead to reconciliation which connote restorative justice. This stance resembles with the *Gacaca* justice which is a Rwandan version of indigenous justice system that combines both restorative and retributive justice. Nyseth Brehm et al. puts succinctly that "the *gacaca* were heralded as a new form of transitional justice that uniquely combined mechanisms of punitive and restorative justice" (Nyseth Brehm et al. 2014, 337).

As a society that is undergoing transition from a historical social injustice, the Nama communities seek to make sense of their past as they forge a future in a post-conflict environment by appealing to an approach that can address the crime of genocide. Since the main feature of indigenous, traditional, and non-state justice mechanisms is morality—rather than prosperity—as both the means and condition for justice is well suited in a transition (Albert 2008). The Namas as the affected community have decried their exclusion from the Namibian-German negotiation initiatives yet the Namibian special envoy has maintained they chose not to be part of the government genocide justice.

One such recourse to restorative justice as a way to attain social justice was publicly expressed in a meeting between the Nama, Ovaherero, and Ovambanderu[1] Traditional Authorities and the members of German *Bundestag* in Okahandja on May 25, 2016. Historically, Okahandja is the town where the war between the Ovaherero and the Germans broke out on January 11 or 12, 1904, and it is the same place where Paramount Chief Kahimemua Nguvauva and Nicodemus Kavikunua were executed on June 12, 1896. In the address reference is made to Germany's to use developmental aid to Namibia "to obstruct demands for restorative justice" thereby imploring the members of the German Bundestag to engage the communities in the direct dialogue:

> The Government of the Federal Republic of Germany is guilty of a crime of genocide against the Herero and Nama people. And we, the Herero and Nama Leaders have no other business to discuss with German leaders, but and only the Official Recognition of the Crime of Genocides, the Rendering of an Official Apology to the Herero and Nama people of Namibia, South Africa, Botswana and elsewhere in the diaspora. This is the cornerstone that will reshape our historic ties and further truly build our friendship and lasting bilateral relations among the nations of the world. (Rukoro et al. 2016, 3)

From the foregoing, it is particularly clear that restorative justice is not only attractive approach to find justice but is the only viable option that can help close a painful chapter of the past and move on to the future with an unburdened collective conscience. This can be achieved if German is held accountable for the colonial mass violence against the ancestors of the affected groups. These groups insist that German should pay reparation because "there shall be no lasting solution negotiated about us without us. All such negotiations on genocide, apology and reparation payments without our direct participation shall be rendered futile and waste of resources" (Rukoro et al. 2016, 4). Thus, approaches to transitional justice in Africa can be either restorative or retributive. Whilst restorative justice stresses inclusionary and rehabilitative and compensatory tendencies, retributive justice on the other hand, highlights issues of punishment and prosecution as a means of resolving social injustice.

INTERGENERATIONAL TRAUMA

Because the emphasis of restorative justice is on morality, the Nama together with the Herero communities can heal from the wounds inflicted on their individual and collective memories. These initiatives and activities that engage public space through open discussions about the painful past, permit the affected communities offer a viable outlet to victims therapeutically talk about their experiences. This helps in creating a public record of events and actors involved, and to improve present social relations through shared discussions (Morgan 2010). Namas also embark on programmes like annual genocide reparations walks where speeches that involve around genocide and its repercussions on the present-day Namas are delivered at the end of the walk. The Namibian government is usually represented by low ranking officials. On the other hand, the German government snub such genocide walks as a way to avoid being seen as admitting to acts of genocide. These annual walks take place in towns where the Hereros and the Namas suffered from the violence of the war against German. Such walks involve walking in the chosen town or city as a way to remember and commemorate the fallen heroes/heroines of 1904–1908. The walks usually end at a historical site where traditional leaders and invited guests deliver speeches. For instance, the 10th annual was held in Swakopmund in 2017 with the theme "It cannot be about us without us" (Hartman 2017). The walk ended at Swakopmund cemetery where the fallen heroes were remembered with speeches and rituals for the dead.

In order to cope with a past of mass violence, the Namas, like the Ovaherero and Ovambanderu, are involved in activities that have brought the first genocide to the attention of the German government and the international community. One way has been to coalesce with the other group in effecting a class action or suit in United States of America (USA) against the German government due the precedent set by the Alien Tort Claims. In other words, the USA legal system makes it feasible for cases against non-state perpetrators even when events took place outside of the United States to be heard in a US court (Sarkin-Hughes 2009). The former chairperson of the Nama Genocide Technical Committee, Ida Hoffman had this to say on the issue:

> Yes, I am totally aware that the Nama and Ovaherero brought a case against the German government. The German government remains in total disregard about

the justice principle of the case. They disregard our demands. They still refuse to have direct talks with us the descendants and activists, and we the victims. We the activists and descendants demand to be included in all the negotiations. Genocide is about us, it's about the government. (*The New Era*, 11 January 2017)

Key points that ensue from the above statement centre on negotiation, exclusionary politics, and the role of the activists, victims, and descendants of the genocide in conflict resolution. The demands that Ida Hoffman highlights here form part of restorative justice which seeks to restore the humanity and dignity of the victims, in this case that of the descendants of the victims of genocide. This is one of the hallmarks of indigenous, traditional and non-state justice mechanisms. It is noteworthy that in the most of cases, conflict settlement in Africa takes the form of mediation or third-party-supported negotiation on the basis of agreed principles (Zartman 1999). For instance, an authoritative or powerful figure such as the chief or elders normally heads the process of mediation and resolution, the verdict that is arrived at is on morality and shared values. The overall idea is to reconcile the two conflicting parties in a face to face negotiation or mediation. However, as it stands there are claims that the activists, victims and descendants of the genocide are excluded from the direct talks. McWilliam asserts that traditional, customary, and indigenous transitional justice implicate the use of shared patterns of dispute resolution, conciliatory dialogue, the admission of guilt or wrongdoing, and "compensatory concessions and a ritual commensality where food exchanges symbolise the end of animosities and the harmonious re-engagement of the flow of social life" (McWilliam 2007, 88). Both the Namas and the Hereros have appealed to restorative justice by seeking an official apology and reparations from the Germans so as to restore the humanity of both parties.

CULTURAL PRACTICES, SITES, AND ARTIFACTS DESTROYED AND LOST

For the Namas, the healing process involves both individual and collective memory on the events that led to the brutal massacres of their ancestors to the point of extinction by the Germany colonial troops. One of the mechanisms used by the Namas to attain healing is storytelling where stories around how the genocide occurred are retold and in the process the narrative is passed across generations. In other words, collective memory forms part of a shared culture that emanates from a historical event that binds a people together. While individual memory involves the stories that the Namas pass on from one generation to the next about the history of genocide, collective memory is staged publicly through memorials that are annually held to commemorate their fallen heroes and heroines with visitations to the graves of Chief Hendrina Afrikaner and Kaptein Jonker Afrikaner as well as Kaptein Hendrik Witbooi who was killed in 1905 in battle against the Germans. This is in line with Hunt's view that "[c]ollective memory is information about society that is accumulated over the years and develops into a kind of 'social fund' and is drawn upon in the development of social discourses and individual narratives" (Hunt 2010, 5). At these annual visitations to the graves of the fallen Namas, rituals are performed to honour the dead for the sacrifices they made. It is in this context that these graves now form part of cultural sites which were destroyed or lost due to the genocide war. The perspective of personal and collective narratives form part of the broader narrative through which we make sense of the world (Wielenga 2012). The individual/family and collective memorialization interlink in trying to remember and build a shared past based on historical events that are told within successive family generations and those told as part of a larger grouping.

In addition, there is also cultural education which happens in Nama and Herero dominated schools. These play an important role as a strategy with which to cope with the historical injustice that the Namas and the Herero as a people have endured. As such cultural resilience is pivotal in healing the wounds of the genocide and in finding closure. By re-living the memory of the war, Namas empathize with the actual victims of the war thereby coming to terms with an act of violence suffered by their ancestors. This is attained through demonstrating the resilience and perseverance of the Nama and Herero as victims of German genocide. Instead of the war of extermination breaking the Namas and the Hereros, it bred resilience among the victimized groups. Thus, cultural resilience becomes an act of actual dealing and confronting the dark past in order to chart the way forward through group and personal healing and closure.

There is an elaborate dress especially for women that symbolize the cultural identity of the group. Maintaining an identity against a situation that almost led to the extinction of the entire Nama communities is crucial in surviving the brutal extension of their forebears. Besides, the cultural dresses, the Namas have traditional food which includes Nama bread. Added to that is the Nama Step (Stap), though bearing some colonial influences, is regarded by the Namas as performance relics that constitute the group's identity. It is a dance defined by movement signature evident in the use of drawn out hands and moving forward and backward within a given space. The dance forms part of the Nama cultural artifacts like mud ovens, Nama bread, and round huts and is performed during social gatherings. Nama Step dance is performed at one significant rite of passage of female puberty marked by the young woman's first menstrual cycle and the ceremony is led by post-menopausal old women. In short, the Nama Step dance is characterized by shuffling of feet, holding of hands and gliding. Such a dance illustrates the way the Namas have chosen to deal with the trauma of genocide through forging group and individual identities.

Furthermore, the re-enactments of the battles of 1904–1908 are done to dramatize the violence that the Namas and the Hereros endured during the war against Germany. These are meant to serve as recollections of a shared past whose effects are still felt in the present. It is the effects of the war that the Namas seek justice through an appeal to traditional justice due to the failure of statist form of justice to close the sad chapter of history. As well be detailed in the sections to follow, the return of the Nama (and Herero) skulls from Germany and public discussions of the genocide are used as some of the numerous ways of how to remember the past so as to find closure.

THE OVAHERERO TRADITIONAL LEADERS

The Destruction of the Herero Nation with Some Herero Now Staying in Botswana

In the absence of active governmental involvement in the resolving a lingering social, economic, and cultural reproductive injustices, the Ovaherero adopted a number of initiatives and activities meant to find closure to collective memory of mass violence and move on with their lives as a group. For the Ovaherero the events that transpired between 1904 and 1907 in the then Germany South West Africa were "disturbing and devastating" and a root cause of their present-day socioeconomic suffering. In this regard, Hinz (2010, 402) asserts that "the events in and after 1904 eventually resulted in the almost total extinction of the Ovaherero as a nation: physically, socially, politically, culturally and spiritually." The intragenerational trauma of the genocide still haunts and negatively impacts welfare of the descendants of the victims of genocide. Through oral history, even the younger generations have come to understand the trauma their ancestors endured in the forgettable war. The historical injustices such loss of land and cattle, Ovaherero people continue to suffer due to the effects and after effects of the genocide. The genocide forms part of their historical memory and lived experiences of the war. In addition, present-day economic hardships experienced by the Hereros are linked to losses of land, cattle, and cultural heritage are a result of the colonial war.

In order to deal with the historical social injustices in the absence of state-centric mechanism such as the truth commission, the Ovaherero adopted a number of initiatives to help heal the wounds of the war and its intragenerational trauma. Since independence in 1990 the Ovaherero sought ways to address the effects of the genocide through engaging the German government as the perpetrator of the genocide on the Hereros. Namibian Independence in 1990 brought with it calls for Germany to treat and view that 1904–1908 German-Herero and Nama War as constituting an act of genocide. The late Chief Kuaimo Riruako who was the Paramount Chief of Ovaherero and Ovambanderu as well as the leader of an opposition political party, National Unity Democratic Organization (NUDO) as its representative in Parliament, tabled a motion in Parliament on this historical injustice. It is under the leadership of Riruako and his group that the events of the 1904–1908 grabbed international limelight through a lawsuit against the German government that the group lodged in a court in United States of America (USA) under the Alien Tort Claims.

Though the group subsequently lost its court case against the German government they had managed to internationalize a historical social injustice which later culminated in the war being described as the "first genocide." Of importance here is that the loss of the court case hinted at the failure of the statist transitional justice in Namibia to resolve a historical injustice. The rationale of the group's initiatives required the use of alternative forms of justice system in form of traditional, customary, and other non-state transitional justice mechanisms. The appeals which are better understood when contextualized within the African indigenous justice systems (AIJS), included calling Germany to acknowledge the war as constituting an act of genocide, to take responsibility of its consequences, offer a public apology to the affected communities and pay reparations as a way to reconcile with the affected people. It is clear that the overall aim was to pay reparations and to arrive at point of reconciliation between the perpetrator and the victims. Both reparations and reconciliation constitute restorative justice since the idea is to return to some kind of a status quo which the 1904–1908 war violated. It is hoped that human dignity of the aggrieved communities which was violated through loss of land and livestock will be restored through some form of compensation such as reparations.

As argued by Tutu, restorative justice is deeply entrenched in African culture and jurisprudence, hence:

> [For restorative justice] the central concern is not retribution or punishment but, in the spirit of *ubuntu*, the healing of breaches, the redressing of imbalances, the restoration of broken relationships. This kind of justice seeks to rehabilitate both the victim and the perpetrator, who should be given the opportunity to be reintegrated into the community he or she has injured by his or her offence. This is a far more personal approach, which sees the offence as something that has happened to people and whose consequence is a rupture in relationships. Thus, we should claim that justice, restorative justice, is being served when efforts are being made to work for healing, for forgiveness and for reconciliation. (Tutu 1999, 51)

It is against this framing of restorative justice that in a situation like the Ovaherero case, restorative justice becomes not a complimentary or alternative form of justice, but the only form of justice that can address an act of historical impunity like the said genocide with resounding success. In situations like this, restorative justice becomes an avenue that promises to the Ovaherero a way that will heal and reconcile them to the Germans. The strength of restorative justice lies in that it seeks to deal with both the conflict and the resultant effects in order to redeem such unjust situation. An apology from the Germans and the forgiveness from the affected groups allow for an opportunity to find closure to a crime against humanity which dehumanizes both the victim and the victimizer. By accepting an apology and forgiving the perpetrator, in this case the Germans, the victimized communities help the perpetrator to heal and recover lost humanity. The strength of restorative justice lies in its attempts to restore the humanity of both the victims and the perpetrators of a crime like genocide who, like slavery, were dehumanized. Though, restorative justice has been treated as an appendage or an alternative form of justice, case-studying the Ovaherero in Namibia proves otherwise. It is restorative aspect of indigenous, traditional, and non-statist justice system that the Ovaherero can find a resolution to enduring social injustice in form of crimes against humanity visited upon their ancestors.

Stolen Wealth in the Form of Cattle Resulting in their Current Poverty

It would be a misrepresentation of the realities of what is happening in the Ovaherero if we were to focus attention on the restorative justice at the expense of other initiatives that have and continue to be used to forge a future against the canvas of genocide. The aftermath of the saw the Hereros being forbidden to own any form of livestock especially cattle which was their symbol of wealth. The effects of these are seen in the current state of poverty among these victimized groups. In order to come to terms with crimes against humanity, Ovaherero use individual and collective memory to define a future beyond post-mass violence. Collective memories about the past are vital in coming to terms with a past that where a people suffered mass violence, where subjected to rape, forced labour, and lost livestock and land which served as a means of survival. This forms the collective and personal memories of the descendants of the Ovaherero. In defining memory, Wielenga posits:

> Memories are first and foremost stories that we tell ourselves and each other about the past. As human beings, we are constantly in the process of writing and rewriting the stories of our lives, in order to make sense of the world around us. Our memories become part of this story and part of our sense-making efforts. (Wielenga 2012, 3)

For the Hereros, memories as stories that pass from one generation to another orient around the issue of violence (physical, social, political, and economic) that the Herero ancestors suffered at the hands of the German Imperial troops. The losses incurred at the hands of the Germans are constantly invoked as the cause of a century of political and economic marginalization. Such a situation is blamed on land, cattle, and cultural heritage dispossession. For some Hereros, there is a sentiment that the trauma suffered by their ancestors, especially rape, evident in their own present-day stigmatization among Ovaherero.

THE RETURN OF THE SKULLS

One lingering issue of in the crimes against humanity which the Germans committed include the translocation of the human remains of the Hereros and the Namas to Germany ostensibly for scientific studies. What this means is that some of genocide victims were never property buried and the remains of others are yet to be identified. Through the efforts of the Ovaherero traditional leaders and nongovernmental activist organizations in Germany such as the NGO (Nongovernmental) Alliance No Amnesty on Genocide, the issue of the repatriation of the skulls from Germany is still an on-going issue. As recently as August 29, 2018, skulls were to be returned to Namibia[2] where a delegation led by the Minister of Education Katrina Hanse-Himarwa was attend the ceremony before the return of the skulls to Namibia (Kahiurika 2018, 3).

The process to return of the skulls to Namibia started in 2011 with the return of 20 skulls which were housed at the Charite University Hospital Berlin. This was followed by the 2014 repatriation of further 34 skulls from the same university and 2 skeletons came from Freiburg and Berlin. There are certainly many more human remains stored in collections found in a number of German cities besides Berlin and Freiburg. Ceremonies are performed both in Germany and in Namibia where rituals that relate to the dead are performed through songs. The first repatriation of October 2011 was an elaborate event in Namibia that saw a huge crowd attending the welcoming ceremony Hosea Kutako International Airport in Namibia. On October 4, 2011, the human remains were taken to the Parliament Gardens where they were displaced for all to see. On the following day, the memorial event was held at the Heroes' Acre. The memorial event was attended by representatives in government positions, Members of Parliament, the Diplomatic Corps and Traditional Leaders and community members. The speeches were delivered accompanied by a parade of the Namibia Defence Force, as well as traditional performances (Sasman 2011). The subsequent repatriation in 2014 was a low-key event which resonates with the 2018 event with markedly small delegations sent to Germany. The skulls are being kept in national museums.

However, the process of determining the origins of anthropological collections is difficult owing to the scatteredness of the collections some which are likely to be individual collections. Of importance, is that no DNA tests were undertaken to link the human remains with the present-day Hereros and Namas. It becomes difficult to determine the true origins of those remains in the absence of DNA or any other scientific tests to establish links between the skulls and the people who are said to be their descendants. It would be difficult to depend on basic documentation compiled at the time of repatriation to determine origin of individual human remains for such remains to be returned to Namibia for suitable burial.

Thus, collective and personal memories are examples of local resources that were employed by the Herero to make sense of the enduring atrocities of the past. These are buttressed physical aspects of a past that comes through human remains. As "stories" that the affected communities tell each other from generation to generation, memory has been and continues to be used by the Ovaherero to forge a future after mass violence. Centenary celebrations or the 100th anniversary held in Swakopmund[3] in 2004 to remember between 60,000 and 80,000 Ovaherero who died in the 1904–1908 war, served as collective memory available to the descendants, not only to come to terms with their past, but to forge a future after acts of mass violence.

PUBLIC PERFORMANCE OF MEMORY

Besides the centenary celebrations, other forms of collective memories of the Ovaherero included the reenactment of the battles that took place in the colonial war dramatized with some Hereros on horsebacks representing the Germans in mock battles with the Herero foot warriors. In addition, the making of memory can happen through "memorials, ceremonies, monuments, education the media and social discourse" (Wielenga 2012, 1). Such public displays of collective memory become a vehicle that the Ovaherero use to reconcile their past within Namibia as well as between Namibia and Germany.

Public rehearsal of memory is a significant component that of the healing and reconciliation process that the Ovaherero have employed to make sense of the past in the absence of statist interventions. It is in this context that Wielenga contends that "how we remember is more important than what we remember if the process of remembering is to contribute positively to the post-conflict recovery process" (Wielenga 2012, 1).

Since the advent of Namibia's independence, a series of public events have been used to collectively recall Germany's colonialization of the then GSWA. On the Namibia government, such actions are merely tokenism due to its siding with the perpetrator government of Germany to block the prosecution of the Germans state by the victims and their families. However, it is not these events that singularly matter but, as Wielenga (2012) cautions, arguing alongside Miroslav Volf, that it is the "how" not the "what" of the remembered past that has a bearing on the post-conflict recovery [healing and reconciliation] process. A new dimension to the collective memory of the Ovaherero is how these memories being nationalized and internationalized to the governments Namibian and Germany and globally, respectively, through the activities of the Ovaherero and Ovambanderu Genocide Committees. These committees were trying to move beyond the coping mechanisms of individuals as they seek to make sense of the past as they also seek to have rights to land that they lost due to the genocide war. Such a situation would mitigate the state of poverty that is attributed to loss of land.

The Ovaherero and Ovambanderu Traditional Authorities promote their own approach and interests by engaging their cultural resources in form of the dress code. The Herero women have cultural identity that manifests itself in the way they dress in long and flared dresses with petticoats to exaggerate their appearance so as to look huge and bulky. The long dresses are worn together with a characteristic cow-horn-shaped headgear with two horns protruding from either side to symbolize their respect for cattle. Normally, the dress symbolizes a progression into womanhood which is accompanied by rituals that center on rites of passage. On the other hand, men wear cavalry khaki shorts or trousers and shirts and khaki cardboard hats similar to the uniforms worn by the German Schutztruppe especially during traditional or cultural ceremonies. The clothes adorned by men symbolizes the violence perpetrated by the German Imperial troops or the German Schutztruppe. The men also carry ceremonial insignia especially during cultural memorials to commemorate their fallen ancestors. These help them to cope with the history of rape, brutality, loss of cattle and land. The dress code serves as a galvanising and cultural rallying point or cultural identity that unites the group. This allows the group to forge a future built on the past as exemplified by the cultural dress.

The Ovaherero women are distinguished by the long cultural dresses (*otjikaiva*) with a headdress (*ekori*) with an imitation of two cow horns protruding from both sides. These dresses make the women look big and bulky. Such a dress "highlights female procreative powers and the positive association of women with cattle" (Hendrickson 1994, 26). The dress which is linked to the Victorian dress, was adopted and modified to suit the Ovaherero women and today serves as a form of identity (Hendrickson 1994). On the other hand, men wear khakis and helmets especially during ceremonies such as the commemorative annual genocide walks. These walks revoke the memories of the brutalities and violence visited upon their ancestors. Besides, Hereros have specific traditional food that they eat like the Hereros bread which is made of flour and roasted over an open fire.

THEORETICAL INFERENCES

Case studying the Herero-Nama genocide complicates and enriches the perspective or theory of indigenous, traditional, and non-state transitional justice systems in an interesting way. What emerges from this study is the exemplification of how the indigenous, traditional, and non-state justice mechanisms are forms of transitional justice that are more capable than state-centric transitional justice systems. Not only are such forms of transitional justice financially cheap to administer, they can be efficacious in situations where social, cultural reproductive Cultural practises, sites, and artifacts destroyed and lost and economic injustices as well as other human-related have lingered over time without been resolved to arrive at closure and healing or recovery. However, there are inherent challenges within these traditional, community, or indigenous transitional justice systems. These forms of transitional justice tend oversimplify the raptured status quo especially in cases where there was peaceful coexistence between the victim and the perpetrator. Prior to the outbreak of the 1904 war between the Germans and the Hereros, the latter had increasingly become covetous of the land and the cattle that the latter owned. It took a series of misunderstandings due to German settler paranoia to spark the [disastrous] war (Gewald 1999, 141–191). If the status quo ante was restored between the two groups, it certainly would not be of peaceful coexistence between the two groups.

Of significance is the definition of terms that tend to immobilize even attempts at using traditional, community, or indigenous transitional justice systems to resolve conflicts especially those that go way back into the past like the 1904–1908 colonial war. Prior to post–World War II, the term "genocide" was no used to delineate a series of acts of mass violence or mass killings as constituting a genocide even though traits of what constitutes a genocide today were present. Germany has repeatedly refuted the use of the term "genocide" to describe the action of von Trotha and his troops in GSWA preferring the word "atrocities" instead. Germany refuse culpability of the 1904–1908 colonial war as this admission will mean they are responsible for the crimes against humanity committed by the German colonial force. This would imply that as a nation, Germany is morally liable and obligated to paying reparations to the aggrieved communities in Namibia to atone for the violence of the war. The reasons also include the Germany's contention that this was a war fought in another era, hence there is no justification to suffer the sins of their forefathers.

In addition, the German government objected to "reparations" in place of developmental aid that characterize the bilateral relations between the two governments. Germans want to conflate developmental aid with reparations without publicly acknowledging that the two are synonymous. To say developmental aid amounts to reparations will be an act of accepting culpability of the war and its aftermath, hence the Germans are bent of playing a semantic game over "developmental aid" and "reparations." In essence, developmental aid is far removed from reparations as this is aid that is distributed to the entire country indiscriminately. There is no separation between those that are descendants of the genocide and those who are not; hence, such cannot be viewed as reparations especially as argued by the traditional leaders of the two victimized communities. Instead, developmental aid constitutes coloniality of power as evidenced by the relationship between the former colonizer (Germany) and the former colonized (Namibia). Germany as the former colonizer remains ranked superior above its former colony of Namibia. Germany continues to dominate its relations with Namibia and will determine the success or lack of the two countries' engagements over the issue of genocide. As such the words "genocide/atrocities" and "reparations/developmental aid" have a bearing on the theorization endeavours because such terms are being used retrospectively to describe a historical event which appeals to traditional, community or indigenous transitional justice systems.

ON THE MARGINALIZATION OF THE HERERO-NAMA VICTIMS BY THE STATE IN NAMIBIA

Colonization greatly affected the structure and the operations of traditional transitional justice systems as exemplified by this case study. In the Namibian case, the processes of negotiation and mediation were hijacked by the nation-state to the exclusion of the affected communities that are seeking justice to the lingering and unsolved historical crimes of genocide. Instead of the Namibian government playing a mediator's role between the affected communities and the German government, it has, through its special envoy, Dr Zed Ngavirue, assumed the role of a chief negotiator. The special envoy works with the Genocide Technical Committee made up of technocrats in the art of international relations. However, three points are worth noting here: First, the two chiefs' associations were side-stepped as they are not part of the actual negotiation process: instead, it is the two special envoys (Zed Ngavirue for Namibia and Ruprecht Polenz for Germany) who are tasked with this process.

Secondly, in the absence of the Ovaherero and Ovambanderu Genocide Committees and the Nama Technical Genocide Committee from the actual talks, it means that mediation was sacrificed. The aspect of restorative justice where victims and perpetrators are supposed to meet face to face in order to reconcile the two and find closure to a painful past, was omitted. This omission was a deliberate act meant to keep the issue as a bilateral matter between two governments. Through, such an arrangement, the German government would be spared other similar cases being brought before them. This is despite the fact that the face-to-face interaction between the victim and the perpetrator is vital because "[r]estorative justice demands that the accountability of perpetrators be extended to making a contribution to the restoration of the well-being of their victims" (TRC Report 1998, 125).

Thirdly, in the case study, the African Indigenous Justice Systems have been called to deal with two unequal sides, a government and associations of traditional chiefs. The German government categorically refused to negotiate with associations of chiefs[4] yet African Indigenous Justice Systems are hinged on two pillars: negotiation and mediation because the overall outcome is based on restoration than on retribution. Without overtly stating their disregard of the African chiefs as leaders of their lands, the German government prefers engagements that are between governments as an extension of the principles of international relations. This is albeit the fact that same government had historical engagements with Jewish organizations and not necessarily the State of Israel. This seemingly double standard of dealing with almost two similar cases of genocide, perhaps is offshoot of how skewed the international relations are since the international community actively supported victimized Jewish case and never did anything for the victimized Namas and Hereros.[5] It is not far-fetched, therefore, that other former colonial powers like Britain, France, Portugal, and Belgium are keen on avoiding a ripple effect that the Namibian genocide may pose for their own historical colonial projects especially in Africa which are not far from being acts of genocide. This certainly explains the tepid reception of the Namibian genocide on the international diplomatic scene. In light of such double standards, Rukoro's et al. (2016, 4) pose a pertinent question: "How on earth can the perpetrator of such heinous crimes against humanity dictate such oppressive terms of negotiation against us Africans when it accommodated the Jewish Victim Groups along-side the State of Israel?"

The exclusion of the victimized Namas and Hereros from directly engaging with the Germany government is in sharp contrast with the traditional justice system. This system of justice stipulates that negotiation involves the victims and the perpetrators around a negotiation forum which is what the Ovaherero and Ovambanderu and the Nama Traditional Leaders Associations are now contesting through a lawsuit in USA. The lawsuit is meant to oblige the Germany government to allow the traditional leadership to be present during the process of negotiation. In the absence of negotiation, mediation by a third party was the other available alternative, this was not adopted to the conflict between the affected communities in Namibia and the German government with the Namibian government coming in as a mediator. Naturally, this complicates the indigenous, traditional and non-state justice mechanism as a form of justice that can operate as a standalone system in the tapestry of modern-day international relations.

Though, indigenous justice systems across the continent have continued to function during periods of transition and meet people's justice needs, the challenges that confront them arises from the context that originates them. Indigenous justice systems mainly use endogenous approaches when resolving a conflict. It is in this context that Karbo and Mutisi contend that approaches to conflict resolution are endogenous when such methods:

> are rooted in the culture and tradition of a community [...] [and these] mechanisms of conflict resolution emerge from a complex set of knowledge and technologies that were developed around specific conditions effecting particular populations and communities indigenous to a particular geographic area. (Karbo and Mutisi 2008, 5)

What it means is that conflict situations are the ones like the Rwandan 1994 Genocide, South African apartheid crimes against humanity, the Zimbabwean genocide in parts of Midlands and Matabeleland Provinces or those events in the civil wars of Liberia, Angola, Democratic Republic of Congo (DRC), and Sierra Leonne, can be resolved through the traditional, indigenous justice systems. This because "[e]ndogenous conflict resolution methods are unique, informal, communal, restorative, spiritual, context-specific and diverse, apart from being integrated into life experiences" (Karbo and Mutisi 2008, 4). Of importance is that such methods are specific to a particular geographic area. This implies that conflict has to be between or among people who share a specific geographical area defined by the same culture. In leaner terms, this means the conflict is between people of the same country. In cases when the conflict is between people from other geographies as is evident in the Namibian-German situation, traditional justice systems have serious limitations. However, since the two parties were dehumanized by a war that brutalized both sides, there is then need to restore social relations that makes it possible for humans to relate and close a sad chapter.

In fact, Zartman (2000, 7) asserts that conflict resolution mechanisms in Africa, can only be regarded as endogenous if "they have been practiced for an extended period and have evolved within African societies rather than being the product of external importation." Further to that traditional justice mechanisms are premised on restoring the status quo of social interaction between conflicting groups. If such a status quo did not exist, what are restored are the social relations that make people related as human being, that is, humanity or humane dignity. Restoration is achieved through the interaction between the conflicting groups where the offender admits culpability and renders apology to the aggrieved part who are then obliged to accept the apology and forgive the offender. At times, this process is accompanied by some form of compensation as an admittance to wrong-doing. Forgiving and being forgiven is therapeutic as it helps both parties to help and find closure. Thus, a significant facet of traditional justice systems is to deal with the conflict and its effects as a way to restore or form new social relations that assert the humanity of all parties to a conflict.

This, therefore, limits the applicability of indigenous justice systems to the case of the Herero and Namas in Namibia. The genocide was perpetrated against specific communities in Namibia mainly the Hereros and the Namas and not every other community within the borders of the then GSWA. The perpetrators were troops acting under orders from an imperial commander acting on behalf of the interests of a sovereign nation-state which makes it (the nation-state) culpable for the actions of its colonial troops. Since the indigenous justice systems were not developed to respond to this unique situation such as the Nama-Herero genocide, it brings questions of whether it would it possible for affected groups of people to negotiate on equal terms with a foreign national government outside the statist legal justice mechanisms. Whilst the appeals of the Namas and Ovaherero/Ovambanderu, for instance, bear some markings of indigenous justice systems especially the aspect of restorative justice in form of reparations and reconciliation, this is as far as it goes. This explains why the Namibian government established a Genocide Reparation Technical Committee (GRTC) which acts as an equal party to the German party so as to level the playing field (as discussed earlier).

In a modern-day society, the nation-states play the symbolic role of the affected parties in a conflict situation, hence the Namibian government negotiates with the Germany government as an aggrieved party (Hereros and the Namas) seeking social justice. In other words, the government represents the interests of its people. Since the main aim of indigenous systems of justice is to solve disputes or conflicts in order to reestablish peace and harmony within a particular area, it can be argued that the Namibian government is playing that role as it engages restorative justice to right a wrong. This echoes Kariuki's et al. (2016) contention that in instances of conflicts amongst African communities, parties often resort to negotiations and, in other instances, to the institution of council of elders or elderly men and women who act as third parties in the resolution of conflicts. The Namas and Ovaherero/Ovambanderu can neither negotiate with the German government in an open space like that of the *Gacaca* system of Rwanda nor can they have access to third-party mediation because the special envoy is doing just that.

The Rwandan *Gacaca* system was reintroduced as a pathway to transitional justice and reconciliation in Rwanda as it had to deal with cases of the 1994 genocide in a way that meant to result in restoration of peace and harmony. This was a form of traditional court system revived through the legal instruments coupled with the training of those who were to be the judges. Because the Namibian entered into the historical conflict between the Hereros and the Namas after a series of fall-starts, no attempts were made to revive and re-establish indigenous justice mechanisms to help conflict resolution efforts. Relying on the concept of Parliamentary representation, the government through its special envoys negotiates with Germany for a settlement on behalf of its affected communities. Thus, the challenge to the indigenous, traditional and non-state justice mechanisms is that there are no clear-cut separation of modern-day statist legal systems and non-statist ones especially in instances where there is disequilibrium in power politics between the victims and the perpetrators in the absence of those directly involved either as victims or the perpetrators.

However, the Namibian case study proves that unresolved, lingering and enduring historical injustices cannot be resolved through the statist legal frameworks even though the affected communities announced [that they had decided] to bring their claims before the International Tribunal in The Hague (Beukes 2016). It is the indigenous, traditional and non-state justice mechanisms that allow the victims of historical and social injustices to make sense of a painful past and heal from such wounds in a way that permits them to move on with their lives in a post-conflict and post-mass violence society. As such the practise has been to regard the indigenous, traditional and non-state justice mechanisms as complimentary forms of justice or appendages to state-centric justice systems. Instead, the indigenous, traditional and non-state justice mechanisms can operate as standalone entities with commendable success ratio.

However, another misconception would be regarding the indigenous, traditional, and non-state justice mechanisms as static forms that are warped in time: they change as cultures that brought them undergo ramifications. This illustrated by the Rwandan and South African models. The adoption and adaptation of the *Gacaca* in post-genocide Rwanda with its indigenous, traditional and non-state justice mechanism used to resolve historical and social injustices, shows how effective such systems can be in conflict resolution that aims to at restoration than at the retribution of statist justice.

CHALLENGES OF THE INDIGENOUS, TRADITIONAL, AND NON-STATE JUSTICE MECHANISMS

Indeed, like any other perspective, the indigenous, traditional, and non-state justice mechanisms are not without defects of their own especially as the case study of the genocide on the Herero and Namas amply demonstrates. As intimated already, in cases where the conflicting groups emanate from different geographies, traditional justice systems show serious fault lines.

The predicaments and the obstacles that seem to waylay the Hereros and the Namas in their attempts to engage the Germans can be partly explained by a consideration of the distance that separates them. Traditional justice system is a localized system that works effectively when the groups in conflict are geographical situated in each other's vicinity or within the same geographical space. As contested by Avruch (1998) a conflict is a feature of all human societies and, potentially, an aspect of all social relationships. One such feature is the tensions between the Herero-Nama and other Namibia peoples such as the Ovambo who are believed by the Herero Nama to be siding with the Germans. Of importance is the fact that contesting versions of the past exist within each community especially on the issue of genocide and the perceived monetary windfall that might come should Germany chose to assume responsibility of the genocide by way of paying reparations. This, then, weakens state building in Namibia as it undermines social cohesion especially as it relates to the remembrance of the past commemorated differently by different groups in Namibia.

CONCLUSION

The objective of this chapter was to explore how alternative forms of justice like the traditional, indigenous non-statist justice mechanisms can be used to resolve lingering historical injustices through case-studying the Nama-Herero genocide. The question lie in exploring how effective these non-statist systems of justice are in resolving conflicts that allow both the victimized and the perpetrator to find closure to a historical injustice. Through the case study of the genocide visited upon the Nama-Hereros by the German colonial troops, the concept of non-statist justice mechanism was contextualized. In the case study restorative justice was employed as a form of indigenous and non-state transitional justice with the aim of restoring the humanity and humane dignity of both the victimized groups and the victimizer. The statist forms of justice failed to heal the wounds caused by the atrocities committed by the Germans on the Nama-Herero groupings as witnessed by court failures lodged by the victimized groups. Even the court filled with the USA courts under the Alien Torts claims is unlikely to resolve the historical injustices of the Nama and the Hereros.

Interesting issues that emerged from the case study of the Nama-Hereros genocide that tended to complicate and enrich the theories that claim the viability of indigenous, traditional and non-state justice mechanisms. The relation between the Germany government and the Namas and Hereros is not spared such conflicts, but the media reports from Namibia indicated the tensions among stakeholder groups. The internal tensions resonate observation that conflict occurs individual, groups, or communities find between torn apart by irreconcilable differences or rivalries over ownership and control of natural resources. Of importance is that the tension has a bearing on the viability of indigenous justice mechanisms especially if such systems of justice are to be weaned from their statist counterparts. The case study showed that traditional justice systems are not without their won limitations. It is difficult to apply this system of justice where two conflicting sides are located in different and far-flung geographical spaces and in cases of inequalities between the victim (communities) and victimizer (nation-state). Groups representing the affected communities wanted to be directly involved in the negotiation process with German something which both governments dismissed as unpalatable. The point is that the Nama and the Ovaherero-Ovambanderu Traditional leaders were excluded from the negotiating team on the insistence of Germany. These are some of the challenges that confront indigenous justice mechanisms as the only viable mechanism in cases such as the Nama-Herero genocide. In the words of the chairman of the Nama leaders' association and Topnaar chief Seth Kooitjie, reparations' negotiations were still selective, deceptive and undemocratic. The struggle to survive genocide especially of women who were raped and the resultant children and the problematique of their identity, serve as stark reminders of the violence suffered by the Namas and the Hereros. As long as the issue of genocide is not fully resolved, it will remain as "stains of the walls" that need scrubbing to remove them.

NOTES

1. This is a subgroup of the Hereros. In fact, the Ovaherero consists of three separate groups and identities as a result of historical migrations and environmental factors. These include the Ovaherero, the Ovambanderu, and the Ovahimba.

2. The report is not specific on the number of skulls to be repatriated from German, the occasion of the hand-over was said to have barred entry by NGOs to the skull's ceremony in Germany.

3. Public activities of this nature include the welcoming ceremony to mark the return of the skulls of Herero and Nama ancestors which had been shipped to Germany for scientific studies, as way to find closure to a painful chapter in their history.

4. According to Rukoro et al (2016) Germany allowed both the State of Israel and the groups representing the victims to the negotiation and this would be an example of double standard motivated by racial overtones.

5. The only thing that the international community did was to recognize the German Colonial War in Namibia as the first act of "genocide," but did not go any further to insist on the direct involvement of the descendants of the victims in finding a negotiated settlement.

BIBLIOGRAPHY

Albert, Isaac. O. 2008. "Understanding Peace in Africa." In *Peace and Conflict in Africa*, edited by D. J. Francis, 31–45. London: Zed Books.

Avruch, Kevin. 1998. *Culture & Conflict Resolution*. Washington, DC: United States Institute of Peace Press.

Beukes, Jemima. 2016. "Genocide Gains Ground." *Namibian Sun*. www.namibiansun .com/localnews/genocide-gains-ground. Accessed on March 25, 2018.

Drechsler, Horst. 1980. *Let us Die Fighting: The Struggle of the Herero and Nama against German Imperialism (1884–1915)*. London: Zed Books.

Drumbl, Mark. A. 2002. "Restorative Justice and Collective Responsibility: Lessons for and from the Rwandan Genocide." *Contemporary Justice Review* 5: 5–22.

Gewald, Jan-Bart. 1999. *Herero heroes: Asocio-political history of the Herero of Namibia, 1890–1923*. Ohio: Ohio State University Press.

Gewald, Jan-Bart. 2003. "Herero Genocide in the Twentieth Century: Politics and Memory." In *Rethinking Resistance: Revolt and Violence in African History*, edited by J. Abbink, M. de Bruijn, and K. van Walraven, 281. Boston: Brill.

Hartman, Adam. "Herero, Nama Call for Inclusiveness in Reparation Talks." *The Namibian* March 27, 2017.

Hendrickson, Hildi. 1994. "The 'Long' Dress and the Construction of Herero Identities in Southern Africa." *African Studies*: 53 (2): 25–52.

Hinz, Manfred O. 2010. "'In View of the Difficult Legal Questions, I Beg You to Understand...': Political Ethics and the Herero-German War One Hundred Years Later." In *In Search of Justice and Peace. Traditional and Informal Justice Systems in Africa*, edited by Manfred O. Hinz and Clever Mapaune, 395–441. Windhoek: Namibia Scientific Society/Legal Research and Development Trust of Namibia. www.namibian.com.na/Skulls-received-by-Government/86407/archive-read. Accessed on 24 August 2018.

Hunt, N. 2010. *Memory, War and Trauma*. Cambridge: Cambridge University Press.

Immanuel, Shinovene, and Ndanki Kahiurika. 2017. "Government makes U-turn on Genocide." *The Namibian*, March 3, 2017.

Kahiurika, Ndanki. 2008. "Nam Bars Entry to Skulls Ceremony in Germany." *The Namibian*, August 24, 2008.

Karbo, Tony, and Martha Mutisi. 2008. "Psychological Aspects of Post-Conflict Reconstruction: Transforming Mindsets: The Case of the *Gacaca* in Rwanda". UNDP/BCPR paper prepared for the Ad Hoc Expert Group Meeting on Lessons Learned in Post-Conflict State Capacity: Reconstructing Governance and Public Administration Capacities in Post-Conflict Societies, Accra, Ghana, 2–4 October. Retrieved from: http://unpan1.un.org/intradoc/groups/public/documents/UN/UNPAN032152.pdf (Accessed on 25 July 2019).

Kariuki, Francis, Smith Ouma, and Raphel Ng'etich. 2016. *Property Law*. Nairobi: Strathmore University Press.

Krug, Clara. 2016. "Special Envoy for German-Namibian Relations on Namibian Colonial History." *German Information Center Africa*. Accessed March 23, 2018.

Malan, Jannie. 2008. "Understanding Transitional Justice in Africa." In *Peace and Conflict in Africa*, edited by David J. Francis, 133–47. London: Zed Books.

McWilliam, Andrew. 2007. "Meto Disputes and Peace-making: Cultural Notes on Conflict and Its Resolution in West Timor." *The Asia Pacific Journal of Anthropology* 8: 75–91.

Morgan, Karie L. ""To Heal the Wounds": Namibian Ovaherero's Contests Over Coming to Terms with the German Colonial Past." PhD Thesis, University of North Carolina, 2010.

Murithi, Timothy. 2008. "'African Indigenous and Endogenous Approaches to Peace and Conflict Resolution.'" In *Peace and Conflict in Africa*, edited by D. J. Francis, 16–30. London: Zed Books.

Nyseth Brehm, Hollie, Christopher Uggen, and Jean-Damascène Gasanabo. 2014. "Genocide, Justice, and Rwanda's Gacaca Courts." *Journal of Contemporary Criminal Justice* 30 (3): 333–52.

Rukoro, Vekuii, David Frederick, and Aletha Nguvauva. 2016. *The Dichotomy of Historic Responsibility and the Quest for Restorative Justice*. A Presentation by the Forum for the Nama Traditional Authorities Association and the Council of Traditional Leaders on Genocide and Reparations of the various Herero Traditional Authorities. Genocide, Apology and Reparation. Meeting with German Members of Parliament, Okahandja, Republic of Namibia. Accessed on March 20, 2018.

Sarkin-Hughes, Jeremy. 2009. *Colonial Genocide and Reparations Claims in the 21st Century: The Socio- Legal Context of Claims Under International Law by the Herero Against Germany for Genocide in Namibia, 1904–1908*. Westport, CO: Praeger Security International.

Sasman, Catherine. 2011. "Skulls Received by Government." *The Namibian*, June 10, 2011. *The New Era*, 'Genocide justice is about us, not government-Hoffmann.' January 11, 2017.

Tjitemisa, Kuzeeko. 2017. "Ngavirue gives Latest on Genocide Talks." *The New Era*, January 11, 2017.

Truth and Reconciliation Commission of South Africa Report. 1998. *Truth and Reconciliation Commission of South Africa Vol. 1–5*. Cape Town: Juta.

Tutu, Desmond. 1999. *No Future without Forgiveness*. London: Rider.

Vandeginste, Setef. 1999. *Justice, Genocide, and Reparation after Genocide and Crimes Against Humanity: The Proposed Establishment of Population Gacaca Tribunals in Rwanda*. Paper delivered to the All-Africa Conference on African Principles of Conflict Resolution and Reconciliation, United Nations Conference Center, Addis Ababa, Ethiopia, November 8–12, 1999.

Wielenga, Cori. 2012. Remembering together in Rwanda and South Africa Remembering together in Rwanda and South Africa. Paper presented at a Conference, January 2012.

Zartman, William. I. 1999. "Conclusions: Changes in the New Order and the Place for the Old." In *Traditional Cures for Modern Conflicts. African Conflict "Medicine"*, edited by W. I. Zartman, 219–30. Boulder, CO: Lynne Rienner Publishers.

Zartman, William. I. 2000. "Introduction: African Traditional Conflict Medicine." In *Traditional Cures for Modern Conflicts, African Conflict "Medicine"*, edited by W. I Zartman, 1–11. Boulder, CO: Lynne Reinner Publishers.

Chapter 11

Uncharted Waters

Reparations through Indigenous Forms of Transitional Justice for Namibian Victims of a Colonial Genocide

Christian Harris

A BRIEF HISTORY OF THE HERERO/NAMA GENOCIDE

It has been dubbed as the first genocide of the twentieth century and its legacy is still being felt in contemporary Namibia. Germans first reached the arid shores of southwestern Africa in the mid-1800s. Travelers had been stopping along the coast for centuries, but this was the start of an unprecedented wave of European intervention in Africa. This period is often described by many historians as the Scramble for Africa (Gross 2015).

In 1884, German chancellor Otto von Bismarck convened a meeting of European powers known as the Berlin Conference. Though the conference determined the future of an entire continent, not a single black African was invited to participate. Bismarck declared South-West Africa a German colony suitable not only for trade but for European settlement. Belgium's king Leopold, meanwhile seized the Congo, and France claimed control of West Africa (Gross 2015).

The German flag soon became a beacon for thousands of colonists in southern Africa and a symbol of fear for local inhabitants, who had lived there for millennia. Missionaries were followed by merchants, who were followed by soldiers. The settlers asserted their control by seizing watering holes, which were crucial in the parched desert. As colonists trickled inland, local wealth in the form of minerals, cattle, and agriculture trickled out back to the colonies (Gross 2015).

Angered by the theft of their land, the death of their cattle in a series of epidemics, and their treatment at the hands of settlers and colonial officials, the united clans of the Herero rose up to overthrow German rule (Harris 2013).

Contemporary estimates numbered the Herero at between sixty and a hundred thousand people (Harris 2013). According to Hull (2005) between 6 and 8,000 warriors targeted adult German male settlers, sparing German women and children, German missionaries, and non-German Europeans. The Herero killed about 125 German male soldiers. White missionaries, women, and children were spared because they had cultivated a good working relationship with the natives.

Following the uprising of Herero and Nama against German settlers, the German settlers, the German Schutztruppe (colonial troops) chased the Herero into the Omaheke Desert, forcing thousands of women and children to die of thirst while others were shot on sight (Cooper 2006). The beginning of the genocide came in the form of a chilling order from the German military commander, of German South West Africa Lothar von Trotha on October 2, 1904. The order read as follows:

> I, the great general of the German troops, send this letter to the Herero People. Hereros are no longer German subjects. They have murdered, stolen, they have cut off the noses, ears, and other bodily parts of wounded soldiers and now, because of cowardice, they will fight no more. [. . .] All the Hereros must leave the land. If the people do not do this, then I will force them to do it with the great guns. Any Herero found within the German borders with or without a gun, with or without cattle, will be shot. I shall no longer receive any women or children; I will drive them back to their people or I will shoot them. This is my decision for the Herero people. (Cooper 2006)

The above *Vernichtungsbefehl* ("extermination order") only made public a policy that was already in full effect—the genocide of the Herero. Stone (2001) argues that the order was no toothless document. Von Trotha justified it according to racist logic, and he fully intended for the Herero to die (Stone 2011). Neither was his order an emergency document, borne out of mere circumstance. Genocide was the colonial force's calculated goal to wipe out the tribes. Furthermore, von Trotha's colleagues and contemporaries understood the implications of the order, and argued with his judgment or agreed with it accordingly (Dyck 2014).

Those who were "fortunate" to escape certain death were sent to concentration camps, or coerced into working on German commercial farms, where many died from inhumane conditions (Dyck 2014).

AN OVERVIEW OF WHAT CONSTITUTES TRANSITIONAL JUSTICE

Transitional justice has been defined as "a field of activity and inquiry focused on how societies address legacies of past human rights abuses" in an effort to combat impunity and advance reconciliation during a period of definitive change in the political landscape (Bosire 2006). Transitional justice consists of both judicial and non-judicial mechanisms, including prosecution initiatives, reparations, truth-seeking, institutional reform, and a combination thereof. It has been argued that whatever combination is chosen must be in conformity with international legal standards and obligations (United Nations Human Rights Office for Human Rights, Rule of Law and Transitional Justice 2005).

Sooka (2006) states that over the past decade truth commissions have become the most common instrument chosen during the negotiated settlement to deal with issues of transitional justice. However, he cautions that we should be careful to ensure that truth commissions do not become the new panacea to address all the ills of the past.

Ownership of a transitional justice process is also a huge factor in countries ravaged by conflicts. In a number of African countries, specific approaches have been accepted because the peace process was influenced by external actors who helped to bring about the cessation of hostilities and who, therefore, were able to influence the instruments and institutions that go into the peace agreement. This can translate into a latent hostility by those in government who now have to implement the agreement. In these circumstances, the government may be indifferent to whether these institutions are established and properly funded. It may also result in the appointment of commissioners who have deference to the ruling party or faction and who are not committed to the work of the truth commission. This can have devastating consequences for such a commission (Sooka 2006, 313–314).

REPARATIONS AND TRANSITIONAL JUSTICE: INDIGENOUS AFRICAN HUMAN RIGHTS PHILOSOPHY

Contrary to popular Western narratives, Africa has its own indigenous approaches to transitional justice and human rights which do not fit the western model of transitional justice. These methods range broadly, from "participatory" criminal trials in Rwanda, highly localized cleansing ceremonies in Mozambique, healing customs for reconciliation in northern Uganda, and national truth-seeking testimony in South Africa. Notwithstanding the fact that these approaches vary widely, they all rely on "indigenous" as opposed to Western-centric practices of dispute resolution and employ identity politics as an important justification for their use (Jorstad 2015).

Moreover, many activists and some scholars believe that traditional justice is not just an alternative or possible supplement to more established processes. Rather, they take the view that it is better, or at least that a fully integrated approach is the best option; one in which conventional legal processes are not privileged, and "multiple pathways to justice" can be "interwoven, sequenced and accommodated" (Roht-Arriaza 2006, 8).

This view is premised on an acceptance that not only formal trials but also truth commissions are insufficiently attentive to social integration and reconstruction. The latter have often been portrayed as somehow more culturally embedded, but critics have argued that they can be equally remote from local realities. As Priscilla Hayner notes, "indigenous national characteristics may make truth-seeking unnecessary and undesirable, such as unofficial community based mechanisms that respond to recent violence or a culture that eschews confronting reality directly" (Hayner 2001, 186).

According to Asante (2004), there is a common belief among whites that philosophy originates with the Greeks. The idea is so common that almost all of the books on philosophy start with the Greeks as if the Greeks predated all other people when it came to discussion of concepts of beauty, art, numbers, sculpture, medicine of social organization. In fact, this dogma occupies the principal position in the academies of the Western world, including the universities and academies of Africa. It goes something like this:

> Philosophy is the highest discipline. All other disciplines are derived from philosophy. Philosophy is the creation of the Greeks. The Greeks are white; therefore, whites are the creators of philosophy. (Asante 2014)

In the view of this dogma, other people and cultures may contribute thoughts, like the Chinese, Confucius, but thoughts are not philosophy; only the Greeks can contribute philosophy. The African people may have religion and myths, but not philosophy, according to this reasoning. Thus, this notion privileges the Greeks as the originators of philosophy, the highest of the sciences (Asante 2004, 1).

Similarly, Wiredu (1998) argues that it is probably clear without further argument that the exorcising of the colonial mentality in African philosophy is going to involve conceptually critical studies of African traditional philosophies.

Africans do not espouse a philosophy of human dignity that is derived from natural rights and individualistic framework. African societies function within communal structures whereby a person's dignity and honour flow from his or her transcendental role as a cultural being . . . we should pose the problem in this light, rather than assuming an inevitable progression on non-Westerners toward Western lifestyle (Cobbah 1987, 331).

Fernyhough, who argues that human rights existed in precolonial Africa and that such events like the American or French revolutions might not have occurred in Africa and thereby did not aid the development of human rights in the region as it did in the American and European continents, but that there were distinctive African cultural milieus that facilitated the evolution of human rights in the continent (Fernyhough 1993, 40–41).

The reality is that just like An-Na'im and Deng argued, the failure of the Western scholars to grasp the concept of human rights in Africa could be as a result of the different ways in which the concept is observed and incorporated into the lives of people in different societies (An-na 'im A and Deng 1990, 159).

Those like Howard extend this argument further by suggesting that the concept of human rights in Africa is being confused with the idea of human dignity, and he posits that

> the African concept of human rights is actually a concept of human dignity, or what defines the inner (moral) nature and worth of a human person and his or her proper (political) relation with the society. Despite the twining of human rights and human dignity in the preamble of the universal declaration of human rights and elsewhere, dignity can be protected in a society not based on rights. The notion of African communalism, which stress the dignity of membership in, and fulfilment of one's prescribed social role in a group (family, kinship group, tribe), still represent how accurately how many Africans appear to view their personal relationship to society. (Howard 1990, 165–66)

THE LEGACY OF THE GENOCIDE

Economic

According to the Namibian Statistics Agency, households where the main language spoken is German, English, or Afrikaans reported the highest income per capita of N$ 150 730, N$ 74 952, and N$ 48 879, respectively. Households where German is the main language spoken has an income per capita of about 26 times higher than that of other black groups including the Hereros. The majority of white Namibians, and a small but growing black middle class, enjoy one of the world's highest standards of living, while the majority of black Namibians live in abject poverty, making Namibia one of the most unequal societies in the world (Publication by the National Planning of the Republic of Namibia.). It has been argued this inequality is rooted in the fact that the majority of Namibia's black population lacks secure tenure to land. This also contributes to Namibia being one of the most unequal countries in the world (Harris 2013).

Cultural Genocide

Cultural genocide extends beyond attacks upon the physical and/or biological elements of a group and seeks to eliminate its wider institutions. This is done in a variety of ways, and often includes the abolition of a group's language, restrictions upon its traditional practices and ways, the destruction of religious institutions and objects, the persecution of clergy members, and attacks on academics and intellectuals. Elements of cultural genocide are manifested when artistic, literary, and cultural activities are restricted or outlawed and when national treasures, libraries, archives, museums, artifacts, and art galleries are destroyed or confiscated (Nserssian 2005).

As a consequence of the genocide of tens of thousands of Hereros and Namas were displaced from their lands, many found themselves living among other communities or tribes, some were hostile to them, others were sympathetic and welcomed them. This led to forced assimilation of this fleeing Hereros into the cultures of their hosts.

Moreover the introduction of German culture also changed many aspects of life in Namibia.

Secret police and militia were not the only Germans coming to Namibia, as many settlers looked to Namibia to start a new life. German-speaking communities arose in Namibia, and German immigration became fairly common. This created: distinctions between cultures, a racial hierarchy and racism in the lower levels of society. Immigrants would arrive from Germany with a sense of adventure, excited about exploring a new continent. German was quickly established as the national language, and many immigrants felt comfortable hearing their native tongue in a foreign country (Armbruster 2008).

It has been argued that to make it in the then German-led Namibia, blacks had to learn to read and write German, and the few who did were able to make it up to higher-class positions of serving the wealthiest Germans. The German culture imposed was one that not only set up whites as the superior race, but also one that set up men as the superior gender. German culture is traditionally male-based and traces ancestry through the man, unlike many Namibian tribes who were matrilineal and traditionally gave power to women (Armbruster 2008, 620).

Population Displacement: The Hereros in Botswana

Besides forming a significant minority in Namibia, they are still OvaHerero speaking "Namibians" residing in Botswana. Their "Namibianness" and or "Tswananess" is open to debate. The prevailing viewpoint is that despite their generational residence in Botswana they still consider themselves Namibians. A number of OvaHerero, fleeing the German war of extermination in 1904, crossed from the then German South West Africa (Namibia) into the Bechuanaland Protectorate and settled in Ngamiland. These OvaHerero came under Tswana overlordship, but retained their cultural identity and even a large degree of their political structures. Initially destitute and unfamiliar with Bechuanaland conditions, they became richer over time (Manase 1991, 1).

Once the Germans were thrown out of the then territory of South West Africa, the surviving Hereros in Botswana had applied to the British for permission to return to Namibia. The British tried to delay it, as there was no realistic prospect of the South African authorities allowing them to settle. However with or without British approval, several Herero groups decided to cross the border into South West Africa but were stopped by South African police, and 108 of their cattle were shot. The migrants returned to Ngamiland, but did not give up the hope of returning to Namibia. They again applied for permission to go, and the British approached the authorities in Namibia but to no avail (Alnaes 1981).

The Hereros in Botswana seek to also play a pivotal role in the reparations claims negotiations with both the Namibian and German governments. To this end, the OvaHerero and Nama in Botswana have formed the Botswana Genocide Foundation, which will be tasked with among others, demanding reparations from the German government for the OvaHerero/Nama genocide (Kavahematui 2017).

After the country's independence, several groups of Hereros who have been residents of Botswana began a long process of reclaiming their Namibianness. The government policy of repatriating Hereros from Botswana has at times been attacked as being too cumbersome and discriminatory by some senior OvaHerero-speaking government officials. This demonstrates the failure of state-centric transitional justice. More, so given that the South African, Namibia, and Botswana government have not collectively sought to help the Hereros return to their land. In my view, this calls for some form of non-state transitional justice but not the fatal forceful and "illegal" attempted return by the Herero from Botswana back to Namibia.

NAMIBIA'S COMPLEX LAND ISSUE AND THE 1904–1907 GENOCIDE

One of the most contentious issues in post-independence Namibia is the land issue. There is a direct link between the 1904–1907 Namaqua genocide and the current land predicament affecting the majority of the OvaHerero and Nama communities. There are real fears that the affected communities might take the law into their own hands and forcefully seize white owned farms like in neighboring Zimbabwe.

Hereros and Namas being indigenous to the modern territory of Namibia have rights to their ancestral lands. Holley (1997) asserts that Indigenous peoples are increasingly recognized as having an inherent claim to traditionally occupied land, which they should be able to assert against further invasion by settler societies (i.e., groups which have colonized lands in the last 500 years). The development of the notion that indigenous peoples possess a customary right to their traditional lands has been especially evident in the Americas, where more and more indigenous communities with international support are resisting developers and claiming rights over resources in areas which formerly would have been legally considered "unoccupied."

White Namibians of mostly Dutch and German descent make up about 6 percent of Namibia's population of 2.4 million people, other non-black groups (mostly mixed race) make up less than 8 percent, and the rest (about 76%) are black Africans. However, whites control nearly 90 percent of the land in what is the world's 34th largest country by area. In addition, around 50 percent of the arable land is in the hands of just about 4,000 white commercial farmers (Sasa 2013, 38).

Referring to the 2001 *Draft Articles on Responsibility of States for Internationally Wrongful Acts*, Shelton (2004) argues that there might be some possibility of seemingly retroactive application of laws against slavery and other historical wrongs, if it were possible to show its continuous effects.

> Any rule which relates to the licit or illicit nature of a legal act shall apply while the rule is in force, but any rule which relates to the continuous effects of a legal act shall apply to effects produced while the rule is in force, even if the act has been performed prior to the entry into force of the rule. (Shelton 2004)

Furthermore, Thompson (2002) posits that injustice can cast a long shadow. It harms not only its immediate victims. Descendants of these victims are likely to lack resources or opportunities that they would have had if the injustice had not been committed, or to have been adversely affected in other ways by the suffering of their parents or grandparents or by other more indirect social ramifications of the wrong.

Thus, advocates for reparations might argue that the OvaHerero and the Namas present poverty and lack of land are an on-going effect of the genocide and dispossession, so that current laws about effects of past actions—even if the actions were not considered crimes at the time—should be applied at all.

TRANSITIONAL JUSTICE AMONG THE HEREROS IN NAMIBIA

The physical, social, and psychological impact of the genocide is still being felt today by the descendants of the victims. To cope with this historical cum collective trauma, the Hereros have resorted to various symbols, customs, and religious rites as forms of transitional justice.

GRAVEYARDS AS SYMBOLS AND SITES OF REMEMBRANCE

Förster (2005) posits that the memory of the graves of deceased members of the community turns the area into ancestral land. The graves of one's ancestors are regarded as a particularly spiritual place. Graves are visited to initiate communication with one's ancestors and thereby ensure the well-being of one's community, family, or household.

This custom continues to the present day: the graves of historical figures and well-known individuals serve as venues for celebrations that Herero community, for example, in Okahandja, where influential chiefs and politicians of the nineteenth and twentieth centuries like Samuel Maharero or Hosea Kutako were laid to rest. In addition, many Herero-speaking Namibians describe an emotional bond with the place where their ancestors are buried (Förster 2005). Arriving at the graves, permission is asked from the ancestors, whereafter the participants are led past the various graves. New comers are introduced individually to the ancestors (Gewald 1988).

OTJISERANDU

Otjiserandu or Herero Red Flag day is a very special day for OvaHereros and is celebrated universally by almost all the Herero clans in the country. Government officials have supported this ceremony and often sent high-level officials to represent the state at this event.

The Red Flag commemoration is a three-day annual community gathering to reaffirm and celebrate Herero culture, history, traditions, and fallen heroes. The commemoration is an imaginative genuflection and ventriloquizing of the memory of Samuel Maherero who led the resistance and frames him as a symbol and surrogate of the Herero war against German occupation. It is a symbolic sainthood of Maherero and other fallen forbearers who are cast as martyrs (Maedza 2018, 39)

The Red Flag Day as a commemoration is effective because the Herero condense and focus the remembrance of events and processes that occurred in the past over a single three-day-weekend-defined timeframe (Podeh 2011, 16). Maedza (2018) further posits that to better grasp the Red Flag Day effectiveness as a mnemonic device it is essential to appreciate the commemorations' form or dramaturgy alongside the content. The fiesta kicks off on Friday and on Saturday with guests and participant arrivals while the main ceremony is held on Sunday. On the first day and through the second day the pilgrims set up tents, caravans, and other temporary shelters and stables for the horses around the Kommando centre. These tents can be erected up to a week before the commemorations, as some people arrive early from different places using different modes of transportation. The tents and mass gathering do much more than provide accommodation. It is an act of land occupation, albeit temporarily, that uses history and memory to lay claim to space and community.

However, not all Hereros are represented by the red flag. According to Gewald (1988) in the period from 1990 to 1997, there were three main flags, each of them with its own colors and different sites of commemoration. The red flag (*erapi rotjiserandu*) has the largest following amongst Hereros from different clans that make up this ethnic group. In its intents and purposes, the red flag represents the Herero of central Namibia and commemorates the royal house of Tjamuaha, centered on the town of Okahandja. Another flag which represents other Herero clans is the green flag *(erapi rotjigreeni)*. The green flag centers on ceremonial sites in Okahandja, Okaseta, and Botswana and is generally associated with the followers of the Kahimemua royal house. The third flag is the black and white flag *(erapi rotjizemba)* which is centered on the town of Omaruru in western Namibia and represents the followers of the royal house of Zeraua. In recent years, the Herero day commemoration has expanded to include the remembrance of the 1904–07 genocide (Gewald 1988).

OHAMAKARI MEMORIAL

Steinmetz (2005) narrates that on January 12, 1904, anxious Germans opened fire on OvaHerero at Okahandja. This town was not only the center of "Hereroland" with its most powerful headmen but also the site of one of the earliest missionary churches in Central Namibia. It had a sizable number of German settlers and a colonial military station. In the next stage of the war, 126 Europeans settlers, almost all adult men, were killed by OvaHerero. Military hostilities then dragged on until June 11, when General Lothar von Trotha arrived in the colony from Germany to take over the direction of the campaign from the colonial governor, Theodor Leutwein. By early August, the majority of the OvaHerero nation was gathered with their cattle at the Waterberg (Hamakari). The decisive battle occurred on August 11, 1904, when 5,000 to 6,000 poorly armed OvaHerero warriors were encircled by 1,488 German troops and 96 officers armed with modern rifles, machine guns, and cannons. The Ovaherero were defeated and forced to flee, mainly in the direction of the waterless Omaheke desert to the east.

Today, the battle of Hamakari is commemorated by the descendants of the genocide victims and it is among the most important OvaHerero ceremonies which attract thousands of people each year. The Ohamakari commemorations are used by Hereros to overcome their collective and historical trauma brought upon by the genocide perpetrated by German imperialist forces.

HOLY FIRE

Like any precolonial African society, Hereros had their own indigenous forms of religions. The prominent one revolved and still revolves around the so-called holy fire.

The Herero believe in a supreme being whom they call Ndjambi Karunga, an omnipresent God who lives in Heaven, from where he protects and blesses his people with benevolence. The most striking characteristic of Ndjambi is kindness, and the Herero invoke his name only in thanksgiving after some unexpected luck, while for the rest, the utterance of his name is not allowed, a concept that has probably been introduced by the teaching and influence of European missionaries.

The place of worship is a sacred shrine, called Okuruo, standing prominently inside the village and can only be accessed by the priest who performs religious rituals. As for the Himba religion, the Okuruo contains the "holy fire" that symbolizes life, prosperity, and fertility.

When praying their God, the Herero invoke messengers, that is, their ancestors, to bring their prayers to Ndjambi and interact with God for help and protection. (Exploring Africa: Herero's rituals and religious beliefs.)

In the aftermath of the war, the Herero were enmeshed in a series of laws which sought to transform the survivors of Germany's colonial wars in Namibia into a single amorphous black working class (Bley 1971). Gewald (1998) notes that the Hereros were deported from their former areas of residence and allocated to those settlers and businesses demanding labor. Ancestor worship and the maintenance of Okuruo (holy fire) were prohibited.

SLAUGHTERING DOMESTIC ANIMALS
VIS-À-VIS ANIMAL SACRIFICE

In Herero culture, animals are often slaughtered not only for food but for ritualistic purposes. There are specific occasions in Herero culture on which animals are slaughtered, for example, funerals, marriages, and births. Whenever there is a funeral, they will slaughter some livestock. This is not only done so that meat can be served to the bereaved but also for ending the death ritual or wailing period of the bereaved. When they slaughter a cow, they sprinkle the entrails of the slaughtered animal into the wailing hut and at the sacred shrine *(okuruuo)* to end the funeral. Then the bereaved can start eating the meat that was set aside for the wailing period. The entrails *(tjadja)* of the slaughtered animal are prohibited food. This ritual releases the bereaved from their sorrow and gives them serenity (Kgatla and Park 2015).

CONCLUSION

The Herero/Nama claims for reparations against the German government will continue to feature in the politics and social arena of Namibia for many years to come. The descendants of the Herero genocides are determined to ensure that Germany pays its dues.

With the Namibian government's reluctance to entertain a South African–style truth and reconciliation program for victims of both the Herero/Nama genocide and the liberation war against South Africa from 1966 to 1990, I argue that only indigenous methods of transitional justice will bring closure to the victims and descendants of the atrocities committed by the said colonial powers.

Reparations aside, this chapter was aimed at interrogating various methods of transitional justice used by the OvaHerero in dealing with the legacy of the 1904–07 genocidal way. The rituals and commemorative ceremonies elucidated above dismiss the whole notion often advanced by Western scholars that Africa has no indigenous transitional methods of transitional justice.

Indigenous African belief systems as espoused by the Hereros illustrate the importance of traditional forms of transitional justice. It is through these belief systems that the Herero "nation" continues to promote peace and stability within its own community. The Holy fire ritual is so sacred and it is at the heart of Herero religious and cultural identity. Despite pressure from German authorities and missionaries after the genocidal war, the holy fire continues to be practiced by almost all Herero clans in the country. As alluded to above, the Holy fire connects the living with their ancestors.

The OvaHerero healing process revolves around the famed African concept of Ubuntu. As posited by various scholars, this important African concept has been described as a philosophy of life, which in its most fundamental sense represents personhood, humanity, humaneness, and morality; a metaphor that describes group solidarity where such group solidarity is central to the survival of communities with a scarcity of resources, where the fundamental belief is that *motho ke motho ba batho ba bangwe/umuntu ngumuntu ngabantu* which, literally translated, means a person can only be a person through others (Mbigi and Maree 1995). Communalism is an important feature among the Hereros. The interests of the community at large take precedent over those of an individual. This is crucial as many of the Hereros claim to suffer from what is referred to as "collective trauma" and the concept of individualism is thus shunned.

BIBLIOGRAPHY

Alnaes, K. 1981. "Oral Tradition and Identity, the Herero in Botswana." In *Collected Seminar Papers. Institute of Commonwealth Studies* 27: 15–23. London: Institute of Commonwealth Studies.

An-Naim, A. A., and F. M. Deng. (Eds.). 2010. *Human Rights in Africa: Cross-cultural Perspectives*. New York: Brookings Institution Press.

Armbruster, H. 2008. "'With Hard Work and Determination You Can Make it Here': Narratives of Identity Among German Immigrants in Post-Colonial Namibia." *Journal of Southern African Studies* 34 (3): 611–628, pg. 618.

Asante, M.K. 2004. An African Origin of Philosophy: Myth or Reality? Available online at: www.asante.net/articles/26/afrocentricity/.

Bley, H. 1971. *South West Africa under German Rule, 1894–1914*. London: Heinemann.

Bosire, L. 2006. Overpromised, Under Delivered: Transitional Justice in Sub-Saharan Africa. Available online at: https://ictj.org/sites/default/files/ICTJ-Africa-Overpromised-Underdelivered-2006-English_0.pdf.

Cobbah, J. 1987. "African Values and the Human Rights Debate: An African Perspective." *Human Rights Quarterly* 9: 309–331.

Cooper, A.D. 2006. *Reparations for the Herero Genocide: Defining the limits of International Litigation*. African Affairs: Oxford University Press.

Dyck, K. 2014. Situating the Herero Genocide and the Holocaust among European Colonial Genocides. available online at: www.iz.poznan.pl/plik,pobierz,921,39ff75735dbab2a13c53d6c2d9886a08/41-10-KIRSTEN-DYCK.pdf.

Fernyhough, T. 1993. 'Human Rights and Pre-colonial Africa." In *Human Rights and Governance in Africa*, edited by R. Cohen et al. Gainesville: University Press of Florida, pp. 40–41.

Förster, L. 2005. *Land and Landscape in Herero oral Culture: Cultural and Social Aspects of the Land Question in Namibia*. Windhoek: Konrad-Adenauer-Stiftung and the Namibia Institute for Democracy.

Gewald, J.B. 1988. "Herero Annual Parades: Commemorating to Create." In *Afrikaner schreiben zurück : Texte und Bilder afrikanischer Ethnographen* (Africans write back: Texts and pictures of African ethnographers), edited by H. Behrend and T. Geider, 131–51. Koln: Koppe.

Gross, D.A. 2015. A Brutal Genocide in Colonial Africa Finally Gets its Deserved Recognition, 28 October. www.smithsonianmag.com/history/brutal-genocide-colonial-africa-finally-gets-its-deserved-recognition-180957073/.

Harris, C. 2013. *Reparations under International Law: A Case Study of the Herero/Nama Claims for Reparations for Genocide Committed by the German Government*. MA Thesis, Faculty of Law, Windhoek: University of Namibia.

Hayner, Priscilla. 2010. *Unspeakable Truths: Transitional Justice and the Challenge of Truth Commissions*, 2nd edition. New York and London: Routledge.

Holley, M. 1997. "Recognizing the Rights of Indigenous People to Their Traditional Lands: A Case Study of an Internally-Displaced Community in Guatemala." *Berkely Journal of International Law* 15 (1): 8. Available online at: http://scholarship.law.berkeley.edu/cgi/viewcontent.cgi?article=1160&context=bjil.

Howard, R. 1990. "Group Versus Individual Identity in the African Debate on Human Rights." In *Human Rights in Africa: Cross-cultural Perspectives*, edited by A. An-na 'im and F. Deng, 165–66. New York: Brookings Institution Press.

Hull, V.I. 2005. "The Measure of Atrocity: The German War against the Hereros: The Military Campaign in German Southwest Africa, 1904–1907." Available online at: www.ghi-dc.org/fileadmin/user_upload/GHI_Washington/Publications/Bulletin37/6hull.pdf.

Kgatla, S. T., and J. Park. 2015. "Healing in Herero Culture and Namibian African Independent Churches." *HTS Theological Studies* 71 (3): 01–09.

Maedza, P. 2018. "Chains of Memory in the Postcolony: Performing and Remembering the Namibian Genocide." Thesis submitted for the degree of Doctor of Philosophy Centre for Theatre, Dance and Performance Studies University of Cape Town. South Africa.

Manase, G. U. 1999. "The Politics of Separation: The Case of the OvaHerero of Ngamiland." *Pula: Botswana Journal of African Studies* 13 (1 and 2): 3–13.

Nerserssian, D. 2005. "Rethinking Cultural Genocide Under International Law." *Human Rights Dialogue: "Cultural Rights"* 2 (12) 7–8.

Podeh, E. 2011. *The Politics of National Celebrations in the Arab Middle East*. Cambridge and New York: Cambridge University Press.

Sasa, Mabasa. 2013. "Landless in the Land of the Brave." *New African Magazine*, p. 38, February.

Stone, D. 2001. "White Men with Low Moral Standards? German Anthropology and the Herero Genocide." *Patterns of Prejudice* 35 (2): 33–45.

Sooka, Y. 2006. "Dealing with the Past and Transitional Justice: Building Peace through Accountability." *International Review of the Red Cross* 88 (862): 311–325.

Thompson, J. 2002. *Taking Responsibility for the Past: Reparation and Historical Justice*. Cambridge. UK: Polity Press.

United Nations Development Programme. 2005. *Human Development Report, United Nations Human Rights Office for Human Rights- Rule of Law - Transitional Justice*. Available online at: www.ohchr.org/EN/Issues/RuleOfLaw/Pages/TransitionalJustice.aspx.

Wiredu, K. 1998. "Toward Decolonizing African Philosophy and Religion." *African Studies Quarterly* 1 (4): 17–46.

Index

absence, 3, 10, 12, 23, 38, 39, 118, 137, 144, 148, 164, 171, 181, 189, 193, 196, 197, 200
abuses, 1–3, 11, 20, 23, 24, 38, 49, 52, 53, 76, 77, 86, 110–12, 145, 170, 206
accountability, 1, 9, 10, 18, 23, 39, 56, 61, 74, 75, 81, 107, 109, 111, 129, 132, 136, 145
accountable, 4, 35, 93, 128, 185
activists, 28, 111, 112, 187, 207
Africa, 2, 4–6, 9, 20–24, 27, 29, 33, 35, 36, 39, 42, 43, 49–65, 72, 73, 76–78, 82, 87, 89–91, 93, 97, 132, 146, 169, 177, 178, 180, 181, 185, 187, 189, 197, 198, 205–11, 215, 216
African, 3–5, 13, 17, 19, 20, 27, 28, 33, 35, 38, 39, 43, 50–64, 72, 75, 83, 108, 110, 126, 127, 131, 132, 134, 145, 146, 148, 154, 167, 169, 171, 179, 190, 197–200, 205, 207–9, 211, 215, 216
aftermath, 78, 86, 123, 125, 127, 129, 131, 133, 135, 151, 163, 164, 172, 177, 179, 191, 196, 215
agencies, 35, 73–75, 77, 78, 81, 86, 90, 95, 99, 101
aggrieved, 115, 130, 134, 190, 195, 198, 199
agreement, 74, 120, 127, 165, 166, 168, 172, 207

agriculture, 143, 147, 148, 150–53, 205
America, 2, 9, 22, 34, 37, 39, 49–51, 186, 190
American, 2, 3, 6–8, 36, 40, 78, 114, 208
amnesty, 52, 118, 126, 129, 192
ancestors, 113, 135, 136, 145, 177, 182, 184, 185, 187–89, 191, 192, 194, 213, 215, 216
ancestral, 33, 113, 119, 132, 134–36, 211, 213
anthropology, 10, 24, 49–52, 63–65, 114, 115
apology, 164, 180, 182, 184, 185, 187, 190, 191, 198
appeasing, 20, 37, 117, 134
artifacts, 37, 187, 188, 195, 210
authoritarian, 37, 49, 52, 77, 82, 91, 95, 96, 101
authoritarianism, 38, 51, 71, 73
authorities, 43, 83, 91, 101, 102, 116, 146, 172, 185, 194, 211, 216

Bechuanaland, 178, 210, 211
black, 11, 13, 107, 141, 148, 151, 152, 158, 205, 209, 212, 214, 215
Botswana, 178, 185, 189, 210, 211, 214
boundaries, 12, 41, 76, 77, 94, 142–44, 148, 150, 152, 153, 155, 156, 158
boundary, 150, 154–56

219

brigade, 13, 80, 109, 117, 120, 130
brutality, 171, 178, 194
burial, 113, 114, 116, 193
bystanders, 19, 24, 28

capitalism, 4, 56, 58, 62
capitalist, 9, 22, 34, 63–65, 82, 91, 94–96, 101
Catholic, 11, 75, 125
ceremony, 113, 135, 188, 192, 213, 214
Chimurenga, 80, 81, 92, 146
churches, 101, 103, 104, 171, 214
citizenry, 86, 163, 179
citizens, 2, 4, 13, 29, 60, 63, 82, 124, 127–29, 146, 155, 166, 171
civilians, 13, 80, 109, 112, 125, 128, 130, 171
closure, 3, 6, 10, 11, 13, 38, 43, 124, 126, 181, 184, 188, 189, 191, 195, 196, 199, 201, 216
collective, 18, 33, 36, 57–60, 63, 74, 84, 124, 143, 149, 154, 157, 158, 164, 181, 185–88, 191, 193, 194, 213, 215, 216
colonial, 5–7, 9, 12, 13, 25, 35, 40, 50–54, 56, 58, 61–65, 79, 81, 83, 97, 107, 108, 131, 178–82, 184, 185, 187–89, 195, 197, 199, 205, 206, 208, 214–16
colonialism, 2, 3, 5–8, 33, 35, 36, 40–42, 52, 53, 61, 64, 107, 158
colonialists, 51, 53, 58, 61, 63
coloniality, 2, 5, 23, 33, 39, 180, 196
commissions, 3, 4, 10–11, 17, 19, 21–25, 28, 33, 34, 38, 40, 43, 50, 72, 73, 75, 78, 81, 110, 111, 118, 125–29, 136, 145, 166, 181, 189, 207, 208
committed, 1, 2, 6, 21, 27, 52, 53, 73, 123, 126, 128, 133, 169, 179–82, 184, 192, 195, 201, 207, 212, 216
committees, 12, 120, 125, 143, 147, 148, 152–53, 155–57, 168, 177, 179, 180, 183, 184, 186, 194, 196, 199
communal, 11, 41, 89, 145–48, 150, 151, 153, 154, 158, 198, 208

communalism, 209, 216
communities, 1, 2, 4, 6–12, 18–29, 33–35, 37–43, 62, 74, 77, 86, 88, 90, 107, 110, 112–19, 124–27, 130–37, 141–49, 152–58, 164, 165, 168–73, 177, 182–86, 188, 190–93, 195–202, 210–14, 216
conflicts, 1, 8, 9, 12, 18, 20, 21, 23–27, 29, 35, 39, 43, 60, 63, 73–78, 80–82, 91, 93, 95–97, 103, 112, 123, 125–27, 142–58, 164–66, 168–71, 173, 182, 183, 187, 191, 195, 197–202, 207
Congo, 24, 59, 77, 91, 198, 205
constitutional, 34, 53, 57, 61, 109, 128, 165, 168, 169, 172
countries, 2, 5, 9, 11, 13, 17, 20, 23–24, 26, 29, 35, 37, 41, 50, 51, 55–57, 59, 62–64, 71, 72, 76, 78, 80–86, 88, 90, 93, 96–100, 102, 104, 107, 110, 124, 126, 129, 131, 143, 145, 154, 158, 165–68, 171, 172, 180, 196, 198, 207, 210, 212, 213, 216
coup, 57, 58, 108, 120, 129
courts, 2, 5, 17–19, 21, 26–28, 35, 38, 40, 56, 74, 77, 80, 82, 92, 93, 98, 125, 153–55, 157, 180, 182, 186, 190, 199, 201
criminalization, 86, 96, 97
criminalizing, 96, 97
cultural, 5, 7, 12, 13, 24, 33, 35, 41–43, 50–52, 55, 56, 59, 62, 76, 79, 113, 142, 147, 152, 187–89, 192, 194, 195, 208–10, 216
cultures, 6, 12, 23, 25, 30, 33, 36, 37, 42, 51, 53, 55, 59, 64, 73, 76, 79, 82, 102, 134, 154, 157, 180, 187, 198, 200, 208, 210, 213, 215
customary, 6–8, 17–19, 24–26, 37, 38, 40, 55, 112, 145, 153, 154, 158, 187, 190, 212
customs, 6–7, 11–13, 25, 26, 40–41, 132, 135–37, 145, 207, 213

Index

decolonization, 9, 49, 60, 61, 64, 65, 72, 146
democracies, 1, 2, 17, 21, 23, 29, 30, 35, 53, 55–60, 62, 76, 78, 79, 95, 99, 145
democratic, 4, 9, 21, 24, 26, 29, 34, 49, 50, 52, 54–57, 59, 71, 74, 75, 91, 100, 109, 127, 172, 190, 198
democratization, 9, 29, 39, 49, 51–55, 57–61, 63, 65
demolitions, 79, 83, 85–87, 96, 97, 102
descendants, 12, 53, 177, 181, 182, 187, 189, 191, 193, 196, 212, 214, 216
developmental, 4, 19, 29, 34, 62, 90, 180, 183, 185, 195, 196
developments, 1, 2, 5, 8, 17, 22, 23, 25, 29, 33, 35, 42, 50, 56, 60–63, 72, 74, 76, 79, 80, 89, 99, 102, 103, 110, 113, 144, 146, 157, 158, 163–67, 169–73, 188, 208, 212
dialogue, 102, 133, 168–71, 185, 187
dictatorships, 1, 34, 38, 51, 78
disputes, 7, 26, 143, 146, 153–56, 199
districts, 10, 123, 125, 130, 133, 134, 136, 142–44, 147, 148, 151–53, 155–58, 163, 164, 169
disturbances, 71, 80, 109, 126
donor, 9, 19, 29, 35, 39, 73

economic, 5, 23, 29, 30, 33, 35, 37, 41, 50, 51, 53, 56, 62, 63, 79, 81, 82, 84, 88–91, 93, 96, 98, 99, 101–3, 142, 158, 164–66, 169, 189, 192, 195, 209
economically, 20, 23, 93, 96, 169
economies, 2, 9, 23, 30, 50, 58, 61, 91
environment, 7, 40, 42–43, 60, 124, 135, 144, 148, 153, 164, 168, 170, 185
ethnic, 124, 125, 131, 142, 152, 214
ethno-regional, 12, 141, 142, 152, 158
ethno-regionalism, 143, 144, 152, 153
Euro, 2, 3, 6–8, 27, 36, 51
exhumations, 114–20
exhumed, 114, 117–18

experts, 19, 22, 24, 28, 33, 36, 37, 73
fact, 3, 11, 19–21, 29, 36, 50, 53, 54, 57, 60, 74, 78, 84, 87, 88, 95, 98, 99, 109, 111, 117, 178, 183, 197, 198, 201, 207–9
fact-finding, 18, 73, 75
families, 3, 6, 10–12, 28, 38, 73, 91, 94, 96, 110, 113–20, 124, 130, 132–36, 141, 142, 151, 153–55, 157, 158, 169, 170, 172–73, 188, 194, 209, 213
farm, 11, 12, 110, 141–44, 147–58
farmers, 54, 109, 148–53, 155–58, 212
farming, 147, 149, 150, 152–54, 157, 158
foreign, 2, 9, 33, 57, 59, 73, 81, 85, 101, 199, 210
forgiveness, 135, 154, 164, 181–83, 190, 191
formal, 23, 25, 26, 29, 34, 37, 38, 40, 43, 81, 83, 101, 103, 107, 111, 112, 146, 148, 150–59, 166, 167, 172, 173, 184, 208
frameworks, 18, 35, 36, 38, 52, 76, 78, 84, 127, 181, 200, 208

genocides, 1, 3, 9–13, 17, 27, 37, 55, 56, 77, 123–31, 133, 136, 137, 177–92, 194–202, 205, 206, 209–12, 214–16
Germans, 12, 13, 177–92, 194–97, 199, 201, 202, 205, 206, 209–16
Germany, 12, 27, 34, 178–80, 182, 183, 185, 187, 189, 190, 192–97, 199–202, 210, 214, 216
Ghana, 4, 24, 35
globalization, 1, 5, 33, 63
governance, 38, 92, 95, 98, 144, 166, 169, 170
governments, 2, 9, 11–13, 22, 23, 35, 38, 49, 50, 52, 56–58, 71, 72, 75, 80–93, 95–104, 107, 108, 110, 111, 124–31, 133, 137, 141, 148, 153, 154, 156–58, 164–67, 169–71, 173,

179–83, 185–87, 189, 190, 192–97, 199–202, 207, 211, 213, 216
grassroots, 13, 23, 117, 141–45, 147, 149, 151, 153, 155, 157–59, 169
graves, 3, 10, 103, 113–17, 188, 213
Gukurahundi, 3, 10, 11, 13, 71, 75, 80, 81, 92, 108, 109, 112, 118, 120, 123–33, 135–37, 166

healing, 3, 5, 9–11, 13, 20, 21, 23, 35, 38, 42, 79, 107, 109, 111–15, 117, 119, 125, 127, 128, 136, 146, 167, 171, 182, 187, 188, 190, 193–95, 207, 216
herero, 3, 12, 13, 37, 40, 177–79, 184–86, 188, 189, 192–94, 196, 199–201, 205, 206, 211, 213–16
Herero-Nama, 12, 181, 195, 201
Hereros, 12, 177–79, 181–83, 186–95, 197, 199–202, 206, 209–16
historical, 1, 5, 6, 9, 20, 23–25, 33, 34, 36, 39, 50, 52, 54, 55, 60–62, 64, 76–78, 84, 96, 98, 108, 114, 179–82, 184–91, 196, 197, 200, 201, 212, 213, 215
households, 83, 88–90, 143, 148–50, 152–54, 209, 213
humanity, 3, 12, 27, 53, 55, 56, 77, 124, 134, 146, 163, 177, 181, 182, 184, 187, 191, 192, 195, 197–99, 201, 216

identity, 5, 6, 33, 36, 60, 97, 115, 118, 120, 188, 194, 202, 207, 210, 216
ideologies, 4, 9, 34, 52, 53, 58–63, 65, 81, 98
illegal, 20, 53, 57, 58, 82, 86, 97, 98, 211
immoral, 53, 54, 57, 171
imperial, 3, 12, 97, 178, 182, 192, 194, 199
imperialism, 3, 5, 33, 97
imperialist, 59, 97, 215
implementation, 9, 22, 39, 72, 78, 81, 85, 103, 125, 169

impunity, 38, 53, 77, 79, 108, 128, 191, 207
independence, 4, 5, 9, 23, 35, 61, 79–81, 107, 109, 111, 112, 125, 126, 129, 165, 166, 179, 189, 190, 193, 211
independent, 5, 13, 35, 41, 74, 79, 80, 83, 111, 125
indigenes, 12, 52–54, 58, 59, 61, 63, 64
indigenous, 3, 5–9, 12, 13, 17, 18, 20, 23–26, 29, 33–43, 51, 110, 112, 137, 145, 146, 181, 183–85, 187, 190, 191, 195–202, 205, 207, 208, 211, 212, 215, 216
informal, 11, 25, 26, 40, 82, 83, 86, 89–91, 97, 101, 102, 146, 150–52, 170, 173, 198
injustices, 9, 28, 49–56, 61–65, 80, 110, 123, 124, 127–29, 133, 135, 153, 154, 159, 179–81, 184, 189, 195, 200, 201
inquiry, 10, 11, 25, 34, 40, 42, 126, 136, 145, 206
institutional, 18, 19, 24, 36–38, 40, 53, 145, 207
institutions, 2, 5–7, 18–25, 28–29, 34–36, 39–41, 60, 64, 74–76, 78, 79, 82, 91, 95, 104, 110, 124, 126, 129, 137, 143, 145, 153–58, 164–65, 167, 169, 171, 181, 199, 207, 209, 210

judicial, 72, 73, 145, 154, 159, 181, 183, 207
jurisdiction, 27, 42, 114, 155
jurisprudence, 42, 190

killed, 110, 131, 178, 188, 206, 214
killings, 80, 119, 123, 182, 195
knowledge, 42, 72, 76, 78, 79, 94, 126, 156–58, 198

Lancaster, 110, 165, 166
lands, 5, 6, 11–13, 33, 34, 36–38, 54, 56, 61, 62, 71–73, 80, 82, 85, 86, 91, 92, 100, 101, 109, 110, 117, 135,

141–44, 146–58, 165, 178, 179, 182, 189–92, 194, 195, 197, 205, 206, 209–14
leaders, 11, 52, 56–60, 64, 81, 113, 116, 132, 145, 147, 148, 151, 154–57, 164, 171, 172, 183–85, 189, 190, 192, 196, 197, 202
leadership, 58, 110, 113, 114, 116–19, 129, 143, 150, 153–56, 167, 197
leading, 74, 81–83, 92, 108, 115, 126, 129, 149, 151–53, 155
legacies, 13, 50, 61, 64, 65, 75, 76, 205, 206, 209, 216
legal, 18, 19, 25, 27, 34, 38, 41, 49–54, 58, 61, 63–65, 74, 79, 81, 82, 84, 90, 93, 145, 151, 154, 157, 172, 181, 186, 199, 200, 207, 208, 212
legalistic, 4, 35, 91
legality, 85, 98
legally, 54, 155, 212
legitimate, 3, 22, 23, 53, 54, 57
liberation, 13, 79–81, 108, 111, 151, 165, 216
life, 5–8, 10, 11, 20, 33, 41, 42, 51, 52, 55, 60, 63, 71, 82, 91, 92, 114, 124, 132, 133, 149, 157, 158, 187, 198, 210, 215, 216
livelihoods, 11, 82, 83, 90, 101, 110, 169
lives, 10, 13, 18, 42, 73, 95, 107, 124, 133, 135, 136, 178, 189, 191, 200, 209, 215
livestock, 135, 136, 152, 172, 178, 179, 190, 191, 215
living, 7, 10, 11, 25, 26, 61, 90, 102, 113, 117–19, 124, 129, 132–34, 136, 145, 152, 209, 210, 216
local, 4, 5, 7, 8, 10, 13, 18–27, 35, 37–43, 77, 80, 81, 85, 87, 89, 93, 101, 102, 109, 114, 117, 118, 123, 124, 133–35, 137, 142, 143, 145–47, 153, 154, 156–59, 164, 193, 205, 208

marginalization, 33, 43, 192, 196
marginalized, 64, 167, 169

massacres, 72, 107, 112, 182, 187
mechanisms, 1–9, 11–13, 17–27, 29, 33–43, 49, 54, 63–65, 78–81, 89, 93, 95, 96, 101, 102, 104, 107, 111, 118, 124, 126–27, 141–47, 149, 151, 153–55, 157–59, 163, 181–85, 187, 189, 190, 194, 195, 197–202, 207, 208
memorialization, 18, 188
memorials, 34, 40, 78, 187, 192–94, 214
memories, 18, 36, 60, 81, 97, 102, 114–15, 117–19, 179, 180, 182, 186, 187–89, 191–94, 213, 214
militarized, 98, 108
military, 13, 34, 52, 57, 58, 108, 110, 120, 128–30, 133, 178, 179, 206, 214
moral, 17, 50, 51, 53, 62, 92, 124, 173, 187, 209
morality, 53, 185, 186, 216

Nama-Hereros, 3, 12, 13, 40, 177, 178, 183–86, 188–90, 196, 197, 199, 201, 202, 205, 206, 211, 216
Namas, 12, 177–79, 181–89, 192, 193, 197, 199–202, 210–12
Namibia, 9, 13, 26, 37, 41, 43, 63, 177, 179–81, 184, 185, 190–93, 195–97, 199, 201, 205, 209–12, 214–16
Namibian, 13, 179–83, 185, 186, 190, 194, 196, 197, 199, 200, 205, 209–11, 216
negotiations, 7, 40, 165, 180, 183, 185, 187, 196, 197, 199, 202, 211
neoliberal, 2, 9, 50, 53, 56
nongovernmental, 2, 9, 10, 22, 112, 192
non-state, 3, 8, 9, 12, 17–20, 24, 29, 33, 35, 37–43, 101, 102, 104, 112, 118, 123, 130, 179, 181, 184–86, 190, 195, 197, 200, 201, 211
non-statist, 181, 183, 191, 200, 201
nonviolence, 153, 156, 158

offenders, 123, 129, 135, 146, 198
offendership, 19, 28
organizations, 8, 9–12, 19, 22, 27, 28, 34, 39, 41, 50, 73, 77, 85, 86, 101,

103, 104, 111, 113, 125, 151, 154, 157, 158, 164, 167–69, 171, 173, 177, 179, 190, 192, 197, 208
Ovaherero, 12, 177–79, 181, 184–86, 189–94, 196, 197, 199, 210–12, 214, 216
ownership, 12, 13, 22, 53, 54, 61, 143, 144, 148–53, 155, 178, 202, 207

parliament, 111, 128, 165, 169, 190, 192
peacebuilding, 2, 9, 20, 35, 71, 74, 77, 79–81, 103, 142, 144, 153, 163–73
perpetrated, 12, 13, 49, 177, 181, 194, 215
perpetrators, 1, 3–4, 8, 19, 22, 24, 25, 27, 28, 54, 73, 74, 77, 80, 81, 86, 93, 95, 98, 100, 103, 118, 123, 126, 128, 135, 181, 190–91, 193, 195–97, 199–201
perpetratorship, 24, 28, 41
police, 83, 86, 87, 91, 98, 112, 128, 143, 151, 153, 171, 210, 211
policies, 2, 56, 57, 59, 62, 63, 82, 84, 86, 96, 99, 101, 102, 112, 126, 143, 144
politicized, 5, 6, 33, 36, 126, 167
population, 2, 13, 23, 76, 89, 93, 97, 102, 125, 126, 131, 142, 148, 163, 168, 170, 173, 209, 210, 212
post-conflict, 2, 17, 19–24, 26–29, 37–39, 43, 77, 145, 185, 193, 194, 200
principles, 5, 28, 35, 43, 50, 53, 56, 59, 63, 95, 178, 180, 181, 183, 187, 197
prosecutions, 4, 7, 25, 35, 53, 55, 72, 86, 118, 126, 129, 186, 194, 207
punishment, 10, 56, 123, 186, 190

rape, 110, 170, 171, 191, 192, 194
realms, 7, 50, 132, 134, 136
reburial, 114–17, 119
reconcile, 38, 146, 166, 187, 190, 191, 193, 196
reconciliation, 4–6, 9, 17–21, 23, 24, 28, 35, 36, 38, 40, 42, 43, 50, 60, 73, 78, 81, 100, 103, 111, 118, 119, 123–27, 131, 133, 145–47, 153, 155, 158, 164, 167, 181–84, 190, 193, 194, 199, 207, 216
reconstruction, 84, 96, 102, 167, 169
redress, 23, 49, 65, 71, 72, 78–80, 85, 92, 123, 124, 126, 136, 137, 145, 146, 163
reparations, 12, 13, 18, 28, 34, 36, 42, 72, 73, 92, 93, 100, 101, 104, 109, 110, 112, 118, 119, 145, 177, 179, 180, 182–86, 190, 195, 196, 199, 201, 202, 205, 207, 211, 212, 216
resolution, 6, 23, 36, 63, 93, 116, 142, 145, 150, 153–55, 157, 158, 170, 171, 183, 187, 191, 198–200, 207
restorative, 82, 123, 145, 146, 182, 184–87, 190, 191, 196, 198, 199, 201
retributive, 4, 35, 52, 62, 63, 81, 123, 145, 146, 182, 184–86
rituals, 10, 41, 113, 117–19, 136, 137, 145, 153, 158, 186, 188, 192, 194, 215, 216
Rwanda, 23, 26, 27, 30, 38, 74, 78, 199, 200, 207
Rwandan, 17, 19, 28, 182, 184, 198–200

spirits, 5, 19, 36, 93, 103, 113–15, 117–19, 124, 132–36, 143, 145, 157, 190
spiritual, 34, 59, 136, 198, 213
squatters, 86, 100, 147, 148, 151
statist, 29, 43, 124, 125, 136, 181, 183, 184, 189, 190, 193, 199–202
survivors, 1, 3, 4, 8, 13, 19, 22, 24, 25, 27, 28, 74, 131, 132, 215

traditional, 3, 5–9, 12, 17–20, 24–26, 29, 33, 35–43, 58, 113, 114, 116–19, 135, 142–48, 150, 151, 153–59, 164, 172, 181–92, 194–202, 207, 208, 210, 212, 216
tradition-based, 133, 134, 136
traditions, 6–8, 11–13, 18, 19, 25–26, 36, 59, 75, 81, 107, 114, 134, 135, 146, 155, 198, 212, 213
transformation, 29, 34, 131

transformational, 17, 37, 141
transformative, 1–5, 7, 9, 11, 13, 18, 20, 79, 142, 144, 182
transitology, 1, 3, 5, 7, 9, 11, 13, 49–55, 57, 59–63, 65
trauma, 24, 115, 182, 184, 186, 189, 192, 213, 215, 216
tribunals, 4, 19, 26, 28, 35, 73, 74, 78, 80, 82, 200
truth, 1, 3, 4, 6, 17–19, 21–26, 28, 36, 38, 40, 50, 72–74, 78, 79, 107, 109, 111, 112, 118, 119, 126, 145, 181, 189, 207, 208, 216

Uganda, 26, 30, 43, 77, 207

victimhood, 41, 111
victimized, 188, 191, 196, 197, 201
victimizer, 191, 201, 202
victims, 1, 3, 4, 8, 10, 12, 13, 19, 20, 27, 28, 36, 50, 53, 54, 62–64, 72–75, 78, 81, 82, 85, 87–89, 92, 93, 95, 100–103, 107, 111–13, 123, 124, 126, 127, 129, 145, 146, 169, 173, 177, 181, 183, 186–92, 194, 196, 197, 200, 205, 212, 214, 216

violations, 6, 11, 27, 41, 53, 71–75, 77, 79–83, 85, 89, 90, 93–97, 99–101, 103, 145, 166, 167
violence, 3, 24, 28, 53, 64, 65, 71, 72, 74, 79, 81, 82, 91, 92, 107, 110–13, 123, 126, 128, 129, 132, 146, 152, 155, 163–70, 172, 173, 177, 179, 181, 184–86, 188, 189, 191–95, 200, 202, 208

weaponization, 2, 25
weaponized, 29, 37, 39

ZANLA, 79, 80, 108, 131
ZANU, 72, 81, 82, 86, 92, 96, 102, 108–12, 126, 127, 129, 166
ZANU-PF, 28, 58, 108, 127–29, 131
Zimbabwe, 3, 6, 9–13, 20, 22, 24–27, 35–37, 40, 43, 54, 57, 58, 63, 71, 72, 75, 78–86, 88–99, 103, 104, 107–9, 111–15, 117–20, 123, 125–32, 134, 137, 141–44, 146–48, 153, 158, 163–73, 211
Zimbabwean, 13, 81, 84, 86, 90, 92, 95, 98, 99, 119, 130, 134, 165, 167, 168, 170, 198
ZIPRA, 13, 79, 108, 130, 131

About the Contributors

Everisto Benyera is an associate professor of African Politics and Acting Head of the Department of Political Sciences the University of South Africa in Pretoria, South Africa (Unisa). He holds a PhD in African Politics from Unisa and an MSc in International Relations from the University of Zimbabwe. Everisto's areas of research interest include decolonial studies and transitional justice especially customary and indigenous peacebuilding, healing and reconciliation mechanisms. He is the editor of *Politeia*: The Journal of political Sciences and Public Administration which is a peer-reviewed scholarly journal listed under the South African Department of Higher and Tertiary Education. His ORDID ID is: http://orcid.org/0000-0002-2706-9097

Clement Chipenda is a doctoral research fellow at the South African Research Chair Initiative—Chair in Social Policy, College of Graduate Studies at the University of South Africa (UNISA). He holds a Master of Science in Development Studies and Bachelor of Science Honours in Sociology, attained at the National University of Science and Technology (NUST) and University of Zimbabwe (UZ), respectively. Having worked for the government of Zimbabwe and several NGOs, he has accumulated wide hands-on community practice and experience in research and publication in social policy, human rights, and development. He is widely published in journals and books in pursuit of empirically informed development practice.

Shari Eppel is Director of Ukuthula Trust. She lives and works in Bulawayo, Zimbabwe, focusing on community reconciliation and empowerment processes. In the 1990s, she was the sole researcher and primary author of "Breaking the Silence, Building True Peace: a report on the disturbances in Matabeleland and the Midlands, 1902–1988", written on behalf of the

Catholic Commission for Justice and Peace and the Legal Resources Foundation of Zimbabwe. This documented the Gukurahundi massacres that took place soon after independence in Zimbabwe. Originally a psychologist by training, as director of Solidarity Peace Trust, she has authored or coauthored more than 30 human rights reports since 2000, on torture, government demolitions, humanitarian disasters, and the impact of diasporization on rural families in Matabeleland. In the 1990s, as director of Amani Trust, Matabeleland, she spear-headed exhumations and reburials in rural Matabeleland for purposes of "healing the dead." Since graduating in May 2014 with an MSc Anthropology, Forensic and Biological Sciences, she has been training a forensic anthropology team for Zimbabwe, so that mass and single graves resulting from politically motivated killings can be professionally exhumed, and the murdered dead can be appropriately identified and reburied by their families. Ukuthula Trust works currently on community empowerment and conflict resolution in rural Matabeleland north and south. Since early 2018, they are also working collaboratively with the National Peace and Reconciliation Commission to promote professional reburials as part of reparations, in Matabeleland in particular. Eppel is currently completing a doctorate in anthropology through the University of Cape Town.

Chenai Matshaka is a PhD candidate at the University of Pretoria in South Africa. She holds a BSc Honours in Political Science from the University of Zimbabwe, a BSocSci in Justice and Transformation from the University of Cape Town, and an MA in Political Science from the University of Pretoria. She has worked in the human rights field in Zimbabwe and South Africa briefly focusing on organized violence, torture, political violence, as well as migrant and refugee rights. She has worked at various centres, including the Centre for Mediation in Africa, the Centre for Human Rights and the Centre for the Study of Governance Innovation. Her research interests include issue to do with transitional justice, memory and conflict, political violence, and peace building.

Tafirenyika Madziyauswa is a PhD in English Studies candidate at the University of the Witwatersrand in Johannesburg, South Africa. He was born in Bulawayo in Zimbabwe in 1972 where he did part of his primary schooling. He attended Nashville and Chaplin High schools for Ordinary and Advanced level education, respectively. He is a qualified teacher with a Diploma in Education—Secondary, gained from the now defunct Gweru Teachers' College. He also holds a Bachelor of Arts Honours Degree in English and Communication and a Master of Arts in African Diasporean Literature, both from Midlands State University in Gweru, Zimbabwe. He has extensive teaching experience having taught English, Literature in English and History at a number of schools in Zimbabwe. Tafirenyika briefly taught Communication Skills (2006-2007) as a pilot project at Midlands State University where he was a teaching assistant. He also taught English and English for Speakers of Other Languages at International Training College in Namibia from 2014 to March 2016. His research interests include autobiography, Caribbean and Afro-American literature, African literature especially Zimbabwean, South African, Kenyan and Nigerian literature, children literature, identity and gender studies, aging and older people in literature, language planning and policy and he is also interested in political studies and anthropology. Currently, he is researching on the representation of aging and older people in Zimbabwean literature as part of his PhD in English.

Torque Mude is lecturer in the Department of Politics and Public Management at Midlands State University in Zimbabwe. He holds a doctorate in literature and philosophy in International Politics from University of South Africa. In the thesis, I examined the potency of the direct effect of international law in human rights enforcement in the domestic courts of Zimbabwe and South Africa. His areas of research interest are international politics, peace and security, and international law. He teaches international law, international politics, peace and security studies at both undergraduate and postgraduate levels.

Ruth Murambadoro is a researcher and project coordinator at the Centre for Sexualities, Aids and Gender (CSA&G) University of Pretoria, South Africa. She holds a DPhil in Political Sciences, an MA in Political Sciences, BA (Hons) in International Relations, and BPolSci Political Studies all from the University of Pretoria, South Africa. Ruth also holds several postgraduate certificates in conflict management, political psychology, post-conflict transitions, African thought leadership and international justice from the International Peace and Security Institute (IPSI), the Central European University (CEU), and the Thabo Mbeki Leadership Institute (TMALI). She serves in the board of the African Studies Association (ASA) and is a research associate at the Centre for the Study of Governance Innovation (GovInn). She has published her work with the Council for the Development of Social Science Research in Africa (CODESRIA), the African Journal for Conflict Resolution (AJCR), the Strategic Review of Southern Africa (SRSA), and Kujenga Amani, just to mention a few. She is currently working on various research projects in Zimbabwe that cover issues on maternal and neonatal health, gender justice, transitional justice, governance, social justice, spirituality, and tradition-based justice systems.

Artwell Nhemachena holds a PhD in Social Anthropology, MSc in Sociology and Social Anthropology, and BSc Honours Degree in Sociology. In addition to having a good mix of social science and law courses in his undergraduate studies, he also has a Certificate in Law. He has lectured in Zimbabwe before pursuing his PhD studies in South Africa. His current areas of research interest are Knowledge Studies; Development Studies; Environment; Resilience; Food Security and Food Sovereignty; Industrial Sociology; Sociology and Social Anthropology of Conflict and Peace; Transformation; Sociology and Social Anthropology of Science and Technology Studies, Democracy and Governance; Relational Ontologies; Decoloniality and Anthropological/Sociological Jurisprudence. He has published in the areas of social theory, research methods, democracy and governance; conflict and peace; relational ontologies; industrial sociology; development; anthropological and sociological jurisprudence, environment, mining, biotechnology, and knowledge studies; transformation and decoloniality.

Tom Tom is a doctoral research fellow at the South African Research Chair Initiative—Chair in Social Policy, College of Graduate Studies at the University of South Africa (UNISA). He is also a senior lecturer in the Department of Development Studies, Faculty of Applied Social Sciences at the Zimbabwe Open University (ZOU). He holds a Bachelor of Science Honours in Sociology and Master of Science in Sociology and Social Anthropology, both attained at the University of Zimbabwe. His research, publication, and teaching focus on sociology, social policy, development, and gender. He has also done several consultancies in these critical areas. His works have been published in various journals and books. The thrust of his work is to enhance the wellbeing of societies.

Umali Saidi is a lecturer in the Communication Skills Centre, Midlands State University. He holds a BA(Hons) in English & Communication Studies, an MA in Applied Linguistics, and a doctoral degree in Philosophy in Linguistics. He teaches Communication Skills modules to Arts, Social Sciences, Sciences, Mining & Engineering, Law and Medicine students. Umali Saidi has a passion in Applied Linguistics, specifically, Semiotics, Communication, Discourse Analysis, Onomastics, Cultural Studies and related fields. He has published in these study fields and he is also very active in the supervision of postgraduate and undergraduate research in the same research areas. Further, he is a reviewer of research articles with prominent academic journals in the country, region, and beyond. He has also been teaching Linguistics and Communication Studies for the past ten years. This chapter is an outcome of his research and teaching of Applied Linguistics, Cultural

Studies and Communication to undergraduate and postgraduate students at Midlands State University as well as his active role as an editor and reviewer of journals.

Patience Thauzeni is a masters' students in Organizational Psychology with UNICAF University. She is also in the final phase of the Zimbabwe Human Rights Capacity Development Program, focusing on the equal status and human rights of women, with the Raoul Wallenberg Institute of Human Rights and Humanitarian Law, Lund Sweden in partnership with Center for Applied Legal Research. Patience is a frequent facilitator at community dialogues in rural and urban communities in efforts to bring young women closer to decision makers. She has a Bachelor of Arts Honours Degree in International Studies from Midlands State University in Zimbabwe. Patience's areas of research interests are peacebuilding, gender studies, and international studies.

Tapiwa Victor Warikandwa holds a Doctor of Laws in International Trade Law. He is a senior lecturer in the Faculty of Law at the University of Namibia. He specializes in International Trade Law, Labour Law, Indigenisation Laws, Mining Law and Constitutional Law amongst other disciplines. Prior to coming to Namibia, Dr. Warikandwa worked as a legal officer and later legal advisor in the Ministry of Public Service Labour and Social Welfare in Zimbabwe. Key amongst his duties was legal drafting. Dr Warikandwa worked with the law reviser of the Ministry of Justice in Zimbabwe in reviewing laws administered by the Ministry of Public Service Labour and Social Welfare. Dr Warikandwa also completed an ordinary and advanced training in Labour Law Making at the International Labour Organization's International Training Centre in Turin Italy. On numerous occasions, Dr. Warikandwa was actively involved in the activities of the Cabinet Committee on Legislation on behalf of the Ministry of Public Service Labour and Social Welfare. Dr. Warikandwa has since written books on labour law and women's rights in South Africa and Namibia amongst others, as well as publishing articles in accredited peer-reviewed journals such as Law, Development and Democracy, Speculum Juris, Potchefstroom Electronic Law Journal, Comparative International Law Journal for Southern Africa and the African Journal of International and Comparative Law, amongst others. He was also a postdoctoral Fellow and has also worked as a senior lecturer at the University of Fort Hare in South Africa. Dr Warikandwa studied for his Bachelor of Laws, master's degree, and doctoral degree at the University of Fort Hare in South Africa. He currently is the Advisory Editor of the Namibian Law Journal and the Managing Editor of the SADC Law Journal.

www.ingramcontent.com/pod-product-compliance
Lightning Source LLC
Chambersburg PA
CBHW050903300426
44111CB00010B/1358